GREENHOUSE THEOLOGY

Greenhouse Theology

Biblical Perspectives on
Caring for Creation

RON ELSDON

MONARCH
Tunbridge Wells

First published 1992

ISBN 1 85424 153 2

British Library Cataloguing-in Publication Data
A catalogue record for this book is available from
the British Library.

Production and Printing in England
for MONARCH PUBLICATIONS
Owl Lodge, Langton Road, Speldhurst, Kent TN3 0NP by
Nuprint Ltd, Station Road, Harpenden, Herts AL5 4SE.

Contents

Introduction

FOR A LONG TIME Christians did not read books on the environment, nor did other Christians write them. Then Green issues hit the headlines. TV companies started making programmes about the Greenhouse Effect and the Amazonian rain forests. People began to express anxiety about the direction the world was moving in: would there be anything left in fifty years' time? Organisations such as Greenpeace and Friends of the Earth, once full of cranks (or so it was thought), became respectable.

Now Christians do write books on the environment, and some Christians read them. Indeed, there is the luxury of choice, as the references at the end of each of these twelve chapters will show. But given the choice, why write another—why this one in particular?

I have written this book in this way because I believe it fills an important gap. Some of the other Christian books on the subject do not take the Bible sufficiently seriously. Others owe too much to Green philosophy or New Age thinking, which are allowed to stand alongside God's revelation of himself and his purposeful activity as recorded in Scripture, as though of equal status.

Other books are far more praiseworthy in their treatment of the Bible, recognising its authority over how we view the world God has made. Yet even here the use of the Bible may sometimes leave something to be desired. It is easy to base too much on a few key texts from Genesis, leaving the reader with the impression that the rest of Scripture does not have a great deal to say on issues of environmental care, especially the New Testament. It is then relatively easy for Christians to stand on the near side of the cross, historically speaking, and conclude that Christianity is far removed from such mundane matters.

Over the past few years I have given countless talks and slide shows to Christian and secular groups about the Bible's understanding of the physical world in which we live. Inevitably the questions followed (except for one university Christian Union audience of 100 students, who could find nothing to ask me: had they all had a hard day?). The questions came from all sorts of people with all sorts of reactions—hostile, sympathetic, apathetic, worried, complacent; theological students, parish clergy, Mothers' Union members, men at Saturday breakfasts. Many of the questions were searching, especially when those who asked them had a feeling I was leading them astray from the real business of the Christian— evangelism and mission.

I am deeply grateful to all the people who asked the questions. Many of them will have long since forgotten everything I said to them; they made a greater impression on me than I on them. They forced me to think more deeply: if the God of the Bible really is concerned about our care of his creation, that theme should be there throughout, from Genesis to Revelation. More than that, it should be possible to trace this concern as a continuous thread running right through the history of the Creator's dealings with his world. Even further, it should be possible to uncover a fundamental link with the gospel itself.

I believe I have been able to find and trace this thread. I can even give it a name: the goodness of creation. I therefore dare to believe that in this book I can show the many different ways the thread can be seen throughout the Bible: I can demonstrate how extraordinarily rich is the scriptural testimony to the goodness of creation, and its continuing—even eternal—place in the loving and inexpressibly wise purposes of the Creator. I am convinced that responsible care for creation is an integral part of God's will for human life—a conviction which does not rely on the Old Testament alone, and certainly not on a few key verses in Genesis. I am also convinced in a new way that the goodness of creation is so important in the purposes of God that it can legitimately be seen as an integral part of the gospel, and certainly not peripheral to it.

I am not so pessimistic as to believe that there is nothing a few concerned Christians can do about such enormous problems as global pollution and disappearing rain forests. The story of Christians changing the world has always been about small minorities with tiny resources conquering in the power of the Holy Spirit. One tiny group of early Christians, entering a stronghold of paganism in the Roman Empire, were branded as 'these men who have turned the world upside down....' (Acts 17:6, RSV). Why should it not be the same today?

I have several hopes for this book: first, that people will not only buy it, but also read it carefully. That, as a result, some of them will join actively in the task of cleaning up a spoiled world and thereby help ensure that it displays something of the glory for which its Creator intended it. That disciples of Jesus Christ, who was there at the beginning (Prov 8:22–31; Col 1:15–17), will have confidence in their master's word to speak just as powerfully to the present age as to any other in the past (Heb 4:12,13). That they will be so confident of this powerful word that they will want more than ever to share its fullness with people living in darkness, whether complacent or anxious about their lack of illumination. That many new disciples will join the ranks as a result.

However many shortcomings the following pages contain (and they are entirely my fault), I am deeply grateful to a number of people without whose patience there would have been many more. They include all the questioners—hostile and sympathetic—whom I have already mentioned. More specifically, there are friends and colleagues who have encouraged me to complete what I started. They include Peter and Miranda Harris of the A Rocha Centre (see Chapter 9), John Ball, Sue Knight and other colleagues in BCMS Crosslinks, and Tony Collins of Monarch Publications, who has allowed me a great deal of freedom to write what I wanted to write. To others too numerous to mention here, go my grateful thanks.

To my wife Janice, and teenage sons Peter and Andrew go the deepest thanks of all. In the midst of a busy life they may have begrudged me so much time in front of the word processor, but they never said so. Without their support it would never have been finished at all.

Now read on.

Chapter One

WAY IN

W<small>HY WRITE</small> a Christian book on the environment? After all, many Christians either don't see Green issues as their concern or else think them completely irrelevant. This book was written because of people—people such as David, Caroline and Miriam.

TALES OF THREE PEOPLE

David (not his real name) teaches environmental geography at a university in northern England. A number of years ago he went through a deep personal crisis. His first marriage had broken up, and he had remarried only to find the new relationship also starting to come apart. One day he poured out his woes to a colleague who replied, more wisely than he knew, 'It's enough to make you want to turn to religion, isn't it?' It was at that point that David started to explore the Christian faith, partly in the light of his own problems; but he was unwilling to take it on board unless it was also relevant to the world of his work. Happily, he was able to find some Christian writing on environmental issues, and the result was that he became a Christian. When I first met him a number of years ago he was actively involved in the life of his local church, and his marriage was beginning to come together again.

Caroline (her real name, this time) has a different story. She describes how the creative side of her personality was repressed by a series of difficult family relationships including the divorce of her parents, and by a heavily analytical course in Human Sciences at Oxford University. While there her interest in conservation issues grew; she also became a Christian at this time. It seemed entirely natural to her that her faith should mould her concern for the natural world, and she feels called to some kind of Christian service which involves this dimension. In 1989 a visit to Kenya gave her a new experience of God's presence in creation, and this has been one of the turning points of her life. It helped to heal the pains that were born out of those hurtful family relationships.

Miriam (again, her real name) used to be a student of mine. She was, and still is, very concerned about humanity's treatment of creation. She was brought up in a religious atmosphere, and believes that the churches are as culpable as anyone else in our failure to care for the earth. So convinced is she of this that it remains for her a barrier to personal faith in Christ.

This is not to suggest that every reader should now rush out and join Friends of the Earth or the Green Party. The discipleship to which Jesus Christ calls his people is as many-sided as a gemstone. There are certain non-negotiable elements involved in following him, and these he made unmistakably and uncomfortably clear to all who took the risk of listening to him. There are, however, many ways of responding to the challenges involved—many different areas of life upon which the light has to shine. The area of environmental issues is just one of them, as David, Caroline and Miriam found.

The question is: how many Davids, Carolines and Miriams are out there? I do not know, but I am persuaded that they are not alone in the way that the God who loves both to create and to redeem has led two of those three to relate their faith to these urgent issues of the late twentieth century. One of the great Spirit-inspired discoveries (or is it a rediscovery?) of recent times has been the awareness of the church as the Body of Christ. Christians have always believed in this, of course, because it is in the Bible; what was often missing was the church's ability to express its beliefs and lifestyle corporately. At the heart of Christianity lies the personal relationship between a believer and the Lord, and that is also the foundation on which the authentic Christian community is built. Even though many people will not be actively involved in environmental issues in the way that David and Caroline have come to be, they need to be supporting the activists through prayer and encouragement. That depends in turn on Christians being persuaded on biblical grounds that Green issues are vitally important. I trust this book will help, in some small way, to make these things happen.

Many Christians are not convinced—or, at least, not yet. There is apathy in many areas of the church, while others remain sceptical about Green issues for a whole variety of reasons that need to be sympathetically identified. The remainder of this chapter attempts to do just this.

GREEN RELUCTANCE

Uninformed Churches

There have always been small numbers of individual Christians involved in the environmental debate. Churches, however, have dragged their feet. This was recognised twenty years ago, when the 1972 United Nations Conference at Stockholm on the Human Environment was addressed by Dr Elfan Rees, of the WCC Churches' Commission for Churches in International Affairs:

> I admit, Mr President, that the churches were slower than you were in realising the terrible implications of this problem. You have awakened us, but in so doing you have lit a fire you cannot extinguish. We will follow you as long as you advance, we will spur you if you halt, and we will take a vociferous lead if you turn back.[1]

Stirring words indeed! The problem was, what did 'us' and

'we' refer to? The ideal answer would be that Dr Rees was speaking on behalf of the whole of Christendom, but it might be more accurate to say that he was speaking on behalf of the WCC Commission. Although a few churches had appointed groups to study the mounting evidence for large-scale environmental problems, it was to be a good number of years before most denominations or national churches began to get to grips with the need for a Christian response.

There is no simple explanation for this, as we shall see. Evangelical Christians in particular tend to be very suspicious of ecumenical bodies and their public statements, but there are other more substantive reasons. Apart from the fact that few people in the 1970s realised there were impending environmental problems, the real difficulties were bureaucracy and communication, which work just as spectacularly badly in churches as elsewhere. So the people in the pews never heard what Dr Rees said at Stockholm.

Things have not changed greatly since then. Countless church assemblies and para-church organisations have debated environmental problems and issued well-meaning statements, but what happens at such rarified events is not often of great interest to ordinary churchgoers, even if (as seldom happens) they do hear what took place there. The process of communication has failed elsewhere also.

The WCC has devoted a large amount of effort to its programme *Justice, Peace and the Integrity of Creation*, culminating in a congress in Seoul in the spring of 1990. Similarly, the Conference of European Churches organised its own major inter-church consultation on *Peace with Justice for the Whole Creation*. From this event flowed the 1989 Basel Declaration, and with it a determination that its contents should be made known as widely as possible in the churches of Europe. A great deal of work is being done to bring this about. Assuming, then, that the communication problem can be overcome this time, the other major obstacle is the mind-set which is still sceptical of the need for Christians to be concerned about environmental issues.

Red Herrings?

Anyone who gives talks to church groups on the environment knows that someone is bound to ask: 'But isn't all this peripheral or irrelevant to the gospel?' There need to be demonstrably good reasons for Christians to take Green issues on board. One of the major tasks of this book is to demonstrate these reasons and to show that there is something central to the gospel here. So it is worth looking at some of the reasons for Christian reluctance to respond to environmental issues.

Evangelical Christians especially need to be convinced that there are biblical grounds for involvement in environmental issues. Some may well be reluctant on the grounds that 'Green Christians' find ammunition for their cause in some unlikely ways that strain the credibility of the biblical interpretation. Three examples will suffice.

1   In a recent book, Tim Cooper of Christian Ecology Link attempts to argue a case against meat-eating with the following argument about Old Testament animal sacrifices:

> ...the sacrificial system had fallen into disrepute and was beginning to wane even before the coming of Christ, and from then onwards animal sacrifice represented a form of unnecessary bloodshed...Old Testament prophets had pointed to an end of the need for animal sacrifices....[2]

Almost every assertion made here can be argued with. Of particular concern for some is his interpretation, in a chapter on animal cruelty, of the texts from Isaiah 1:11–17, Micah 6:6–8 and Hosea 6:6 which, he argues, 'pointed to an end of the need for animal sacrifices'.[3] Only at face value can this interpretation be put on them; when the wider context is considered, statements such as

> For I desire steadfast love and not sacrifice,
> the knowledge of God, rather than burnt offerings

can only mean that the sacrificial system on its own will not do; it must be accompanied by love, mercy and fair dealing on the part of its devotees. In the Epistle to the Hebrews the sacrificial system was abolished, not because it was cruel to animals, but because its purpose was completely superseded by the death of Christ.

2   The November 1989 edition of Christian Ecology Link's magazine Green Christians contains a study on the word 'Cross' which rightly states that 'The cross touches all of creation—it lies at the heart of Christianity.' It then cites the words 'May I never boast except in the cross of our Lord Jesus Christ, through which the world has been crucified to me, and I to the world' (Gal 6:14) and concludes: 'It follows then that it is foundational to a distinctly Christian environmental ethic.' This conclusion seems to assume that 'world' refers to creation itself, but the context clearly points to a different use of the word here.

3   Mention has already been made of the WCC. The 1991 conference at Canberra, which again dealt with the theme of *Justice, Peace and the Integrity of Creation*, raised much criticism from evangelical Christians. The new Archbishop of Canterbury said of the meeting in retrospect:

> We have no divine mandate to create fresh theologies
> unrelated to the faith delivered to the saints. Some of
> the things I have read and heard make me wonder if I
> am hearing the authentic tones of biblical and historic
> Christianity or the tones of a spirituality which have but
> an uneasy connection with Christian truth.[4]

Particular criticism was levelled against Korean theologian Chung Hyun-Kyung whose plenary address was variously described as 'animistic, syncretistic, pagan and apostate'. In more general terms, many view the WCC's view of salvation as virtually synonymous with justice, peace and the integrity of creation, to the extent that there is no room left for (and presumably no need for) evangelism.

In various ways, then, some Christian writers on Green issues have fallen into the temptation of overstating their case. Here, as so often, it is inadvisable to throw out the baby with the bath water. There are plenty of Christian publications on all subjects imaginable which have wittingly or otherwise bent the Scriptures to say what they could not reasonably be meant to say. The answer is 'better Bible study!', and such lapses as these should not weaken the case for a serious Christian response to environmental issues.

Encounter With Other Faiths

In the realm of environmental issues, some Christians are deeply aware of the danger of a compromising encounter with other faiths. This stems especially from the meeting of world spiritual leaders called by HRH Prince Philip, Duke of Edinburgh, in his capacity as President of WWF (World Wide Fund for Nature) International at Assisi in 1986. In Britain controversy was focussed on the 1989 Canterbury Festival of Faith and the Environment, an event surrounded by protest organised by ABWON (Action for Biblical Witness to Our Nation).

Whatever convictions people might have about the uniqueness of Christ and the words 'I am the way, the truth and the life; no one comes to the Father except through me' (Jn 14:6) it is simply impossible to avoid contact with people of other faiths (or none), given the global swell of concern about our planet's future. Even if inter-faith worship is unacceptable to many Christians, it is far from obvious that co-operation on issues of mutual concern should be shunned, or that compromise need be involved. The alternative is to give ground to people of every other persuasion on an issue which (we argue) ought to be of concern to every Christian. On another level, such contacts give an opportunity for sharing the gospel that might never otherwise exist!

Many Christians are highly suspicious of the possible infiltration of New Age ideas into the church, and believe this can happen especially through shared concern for the environment, because ecology is a major theme in New Age thinking. There is little doubt that such infiltration is going on, and some church members are receptive to New Age ideas.

Gordon Strachan, a Church of Scotland clergyman, has written a book based on a course of extra-mural lectures at the University of Edinburgh.[5] In it, the work of Christ is interpreted in New Age categories from the start; the first chapter includes a section on 'Crystal Consciousness', incorporating into his theology ideas on the 'powerful psychic and spiritual properties of crystals', and the importance of gems and their link with astrology, religion and healing (p 17f). Chapter 7 ('Aquarius: the Spirit Pourer') deals with the rise of the modern Pentecostal movement and asks:

> How can we understand this when many other churches are in decline? Could it be that, as the Piscean age wanes and the Aquarian age begins, so Christ is manifesting himself in his new role as Aquarius the Spirit Pourer who 'baptizes in the Holy Spirit'? Not that he wasn't always this from the first Pentecost, but it is only now 'in the fullness of time' that this particular aspect of his person and work can be received.[6]

The final chapter of the book is entitled 'Christ: the Aquarian Logos'.

Given that one of the main tenets of New Age thinking is environmental well-being, it is unavoidable that concerned Christians will find here an overlap of interest. But it would be wrong to see every reference to environmental issues within Christianity as evidence of infiltration of New Age ideas as, for example, Constance Cumbey has done. Even such a mainstream evangelical writer such as Ron Sider is not spared; part of her analysis of his book *Rich Christians in an Age of Hunger* reads as follows:

> The first thing noticeable about Sider's book to one

versed in New Age lore is his use of a vocabulary
prevalent among New Agers. Words such as Spaceship
Earth, vanguard, holistic, New Age, and global village,
are a common part of his vocabulary.[7]

This is presumably why Martin Palmer, director of ICOREC
(International Consultancy for Religion, Education and Culture) while applauding recent progress in environmental
awareness in churches around the world, has also written:

> Yet in recent months I have also seen some Christians
> protest against the Churches' being involved with
> conservation. I have heard ecology described as Satanic
> and environmental concern as being a heresy and a
> forerunner of the anti-Christ. This has disturbed and
> saddened me deeply—especially as much of this
> anxiety and even fear has been directed at me
> personally.[8]

Yet if, as this book aims to show, biblical Christianity
demands responsible care for creation, obedience is not an
option and we shall have to find ways of combining this
obedience with methods of confronting the false teaching we
shall encounter.

The Irrelevance of Creationism

As we shall see later, the opening chapters of Genesis are vital
to our understanding of the world we live in, and our responsibility for it. Even if it can be 'proved from Scripture' that the
world was created in seven consecutive days some 6,000 years
ago, does this exhaust the message of Genesis 1—3? That is
the strong impression given by the creationists; in some
church circles, people's views on the matter become a test of
orthodoxy.

Creationism refuses to face two key questions which arise in
the interpretation of the opening chapters of the Bible. First,
what did Genesis 1—3 say to people before the age of science,

and especially to the people of Israel who received it first? Secondly, how do these chapters fit into the flow of Old Testament history?

Detailed answers to these questions must wait until the next chapter, but in outline they go as follows: Genesis 1—11 forms a prologue to Israel's entry into the promised land which God gave as a covenant gift. Continued fruitfulness of the land depended upon continued obedience to God. The Genesis narrative sets man's life in terms of a relationship with the Creator on the one hand, and with the world he made on the other. Thus one Old Testament theologian has written:

> By making possession of the land dependent upon faithfulness to the covenant, God includes Man's relation to Nature within the sphere of responsible human behaviour, and impresses upon him his distinctive position in the world of creatures. His sin means that the land is defiled, and the same land will vomit forth the nation which has become untrue to its moral responsibility.[9]

This particular way in to understanding the early chapters of Genesis does not come down on one particular side of the evolution versus creation debate: it pronounces it irrelevant instead. At the same time, it makes a true understanding of these same words absolutely vital to a Christian assessment of environmental issues, and insists that the issue cannot be ducked.

The Challenge to Christian 'Other-Worldliness'

Evangelical Christians are still accused of a kind of holy other-worldliness which leads to withdrawal from involvement in the affairs of this world. Although this is not as true as it once was, there are still some who tend to think this way. John Stott has identified five reasons for this withdrawal into pietism:[10]

1   It is a reaction against theological liberalism in the early

part of the twentieth century, when Christians were preoccupied with the defence of historical biblical Christianity. 'When evangelicals were busy seeking to vindicate the fundamentals of the faith, they felt they had no time for social concerns.'[11]

2   It is a reaction against the so-called 'social gospel', involving the politicisation of the Kingdom of God and a Christian vision of Utopia on this earth.[12]

3   It reflects the widespread disillusionment and despair which followed the First World War and its attendant exposure of the depths of human evil. 'Earlier social programmes had failed. Man and his society appeared to be irreformable. Attempts at reform were useless.'[13]

4   It reflects the spread of pre-millenialism, through the teaching of J.N. Darby and its popularisation in the Schofield Bible. It

> portrays the present evil world as beyond improvement or redemption, and predicts instead that it will deteriorate steadily until the coming of Jesus, who will then set up his millenial reign on earth. If the world is getting worse, and if only Jesus at his coming will put it right, the argument runs, there seems no point in trying to reform it meanwhile.[14]

This kind of approach can easily find references to environmental disasters in the Bible as sure signs of the last times. Taken to its logical conclusion, there is a powerful argument here for doing nothing. Caring for creation only becomes a way of resisting the purposes of God!

5   It reflects the identification of Christianity with middle-class society, 'who tended to dilute it by identifying it with their own culture'. This leads to a portrait of religious-minded people who are preoccupied with saving their own souls, hav-

ing an other-worldly orientation, and indifferent at best toward social systems that perpetuate social inequality and injustice.[15]

In fact, the creation-denying spirituality which John Stott explains in this way has deeper historical roots. It has surfaced many times in the history of the church, and can be traced back to the infiltration of gnostic ideas into the early church.[16]

Admittedly, too much can be made of this. The 39 Articles of Anglicanism have almost nothing to say on the subject of creation and the natural world, and one writer has referred to the 'appalling neglect of creation by the 39 Articles'.[17] In this particular case the criticism has little foundation because the 39 Articles were not meant to be a complete statement of faith, but rather expressed Anglican theology on the points of disagreement with the Roman Catholic Church at the time of the Reformation; the doctrine of creation was not one of the points of controversy.

Also to be dismissed here is the criticism that some of the New Testament is creation-denying, particularly the Fourth Gospel and the Epistle to the Hebrews. Santmire's major work on creation describes John's Gospel in the following terms:

> It is almost as if the dimensions of human history and the universal world of nature did not enter John's mind, except in terms of the negative connotations associated with his image of the 'world'.[18]

Various references to the Fourth Gospel and Hebrews in subsequent chapters will show that, however different their emphases may be from those of other parts of the New Testament, they do in their own way affirm the importance of the created world. Santmire's position has been refuted in detail elsewhere.[19]

The Need For 'Hands-On' Theology

The Bible is the world's best-selling book; even though all its buyers may not be regular readers, there are huge numbers of people who know its contents very well and who rightly would claim to 'love the book'. The very idea of theology, on the other hand, is a sure turn-off. Whatever the reasons for this (presumably including the idea that theologians talk to each other and write books to each other in language that no one else can understand) it means that people miss out on the essential task of relating the Bible to the issues of the modern world, which is an essential part of the business of the 'queen of sciences'.

To explain further: the world of the Bible is very different from that of the twentieth century. Our world is different in terms of politics, history, philosophies, lifestyles, cultures and customs. The issues that concern people most deeply are not the same as those of Palestine at the time of Christ. In particular, there is no evidence of a Green movement in those days! So the Bible does not necessarily say anything directly to such issues, such that we could make a list of relevant verses, or 'proof texts'.

But that does not mean that the Bible has nothing whatsoever to say on the subject of environmental issues. The chapters which follow demonstrate exactly the opposite. The challenge is to do some theology—by digging below the surface of the biblical text, so that we can apply the two thousand year-old message to a present-day issue. (Theologians, of course, have a long word for this task—hermeneutics.) So for a Christian to start grappling with environmental issues means doing some theology—and there are plenty of other important subjects that require the same approach.

If our lack of enthusiasm for theology were not enough, there is another problem to be faced here. It has to do with the easily argued idea that theology cannot match the stupendous strides of progress that scientific discovery has allowed us to take. Bernard Ramm sees the roots of this comparison in the events of the nineteenth-century battles between science and faith, and states the problem like this:

> What could theologians offer as a parallel to this? A
> theologian's product is a book, but so few of our

population read the books of the theologians. Further,
the reasoned argument of a book cannot compete
popularly with the practical gadgets of science.[20]

Think of the impact upon our lives of moon landings,
computers, heart transplants and satellite TV, and the idea
sounds convincing. Yet the very fact that there is an impending environmental crisis which could radically affect the
quality of life on the whole of planet Earth suggests that
something has gone wrong in the world of science (Chapter 6).
Perhaps there is a need for some theology after all.

Thoughtful people are coming to see that the responsible
use of science demands moral decisions based on a correct
world view. The Christian faith provides this. In 1988 I taught
some theology to a class of fifty lay people in Dublin. Some of
them confessed to trepidation: how could they cope? Together
we explored how theology was related to environmental issues.
They made two discoveries: firstly, it was something they
could cope with after all, and secondly, it was too important to
leave to the theologians! This is 'hands-on' theology, because
it is about issues that concern people.

So far we have looked at specifically religious reasons why
Christians fight shy of environmental issues. In fact, there are
others reasons which have to do with attitudes in society:
attitudes against which we are always fighting, and by which
we are influenced more than we care to admit.

Slavery to Secular Humanism

There is a view which states that Christianity is irrelevant to
the concerns of the modern world, except on the level of
charity. Some Westminster MPs were openly hostile to the
Faith in the City report commissioned by the Archbishop of
Canterbury. 'None of the church's business!' they complained,
'Stick to saving souls!' Similarly hostile was an article in the
Guardian newspaper in April 1990 which attacked Jonathon
Porritt for bringing a religious world view to his work with
Friends of the Earth. 'As a scientist I believe that the way out

of the mess is through more and better science,' the author wrote. The article was entitled *The Hijack of Reason*, highly appropriate because it shows clearly the positive and negative assertions of secular humanism: firstly, God is irrelevant (at best) and secondly, we can solve our own problems, given enough time, money, effort and science.

This leads to a view of science which is nothing less than idolatrous, a theme to which we shall return in Chapter 6. Christians should be opposing this world view loudly, but many have actually gone along with it. Its attraction is that it encourages us to be happy with the quest for what Francis Schaeffer once called personal peace and affluence.[21] If the world has problems, others will surely solve them; they need not concern us or make demands upon us. Thus Klaus Bockmuehl wrote:

> The growth in material things occupied us as well and we were concerned with ourselves. The church of Jesus Christ was no longer a centre of integrity and discipline, which gave men illumination. The reason for this lies very deep; not only in practice, but also in thought we sought unknowingly to copy our surroundings. Our theology resembled an intellectual cargo cult; whatever the tide of time spilt on the beach was eagerly taken up and venerated.[22]

People do want to do 'their bit for the environment', of course. More affluent people are using bottle banks, ozone-friendly aerosols, lead-free petrol, paper recycling, buying organically-grown food, and making their own compost heaps, than ever before. This all sounds good, and on one level it is. But it often betrays a wrong attitude, which comes from a conviction that the world's environmental problems can be solved by a slight shift in the habits of the well-off. As we shall see in Chapter 11, there is a sociological explanation for this, which may often be no more than a middle-class fad.

If the Greenhouse Effect turns out to be as serious as some scientists predict it will be in fifty years' time, or if the link between global poverty and environmental disaster is as close as it seems to be (Chapter 11), then what we are now doing will turn out to be like rearranging the deckchairs on the *Titanic*. If the world's problems are as deep as is often feared, the changes to our lifestyles will be far-reaching and painful, no longer matters of consumer choice but forced upon us as a matter of urgent necessity—of survival.

Then, if not before, secular humanism, and its elevation of science and technology to the status of the gods, will be seen to be sadly lacking.

The Problem of Inadequate Motivation

It may be heartening to see that others are concerned about environmental issues, but when the question of motivation arises, Christians need to be cautious. A report from the Church of England General Synod Board for Social Responsibility suggests two reasons.[23] Firstly, there is a human-centred concern for aesthetic satisfaction: people wish to enjoy the beauty of the world. Secondly, there is a belief that nature too has rights.

All this seems very bland, seen against the backdrop of oil spills and the Greenhouse Effect. If it were right, why is there no similar widespread concern for human rights? The report seems to have overlooked a stronger reason—that people are afraid of the consequences of what is happening to the world. Pollution problems have repeatedly surfaced over at least two millenia, but are now on such a vast scale that the well-being of the whole planet is under threat. But if people are driven by fear of the future, environmental concern will wane whenever the major threats are seen to recede, or as soon as some larger threat to human well-being appears. On the other hand, Christian convictions on these issues ought to prove more long-lasting.

Paralysis of Fear and Pessimism

A speaker on a religious 'five-minute spot' on radio once told the story of a man whose illness was caused by an inability to cope with the torrents of bad news the media send our way. Even if the man was unique (which is doubtful!), there seems little doubt that many of us are weighed down by the cares of a world seemingly out of control. I know more than one Christian whose conversation starter goes something like: 'Isn't it all terrible? The world is bound to end soon.'! The words of a well-known hymn take on a new significance:

> Change and decay in all around I see,
> O thou who changest not, abide with me.

Fresh revelations about the Greenhouse Effect or pollution of the local beach do not spur people to action. How can individuals possibly do anything about a global problem, especially when they feel so far removed from where the real decisions are made? Nor is the Greenhouse Effect the only global problem the TV programmes remind us about. It seems that a new one is discovered each week. Even on a local scale the same apathy rises to the surface. The more likely reaction is one of paralysis based on overload—yet another problem that demonstrates how little influence people feel they have over their own lives, let alone anyone else's.

This leads to a curious paradox—in spite of all the optimistic propaganda about how some more scientific breakthroughs can confidently be expected to solve major problems, people do not believe this as readily as a few years ago. There is a dark side to the popular conception of scientific progress; we are all more aware of the problems of nuclear power, vivisection, genetic engineering, automation-led unemployment, impersonal medicine, and so on. So Hugh Montefiore writes:

> It is commonly said that man cannot control the
> industrial juggernaut he has created, and we have daily
> evidences of how powerful forces that were once under

human control seem now to have acquired a
momentum of their own and to be dragging us along
whether we like it or not. How could it be otherwise, if
man no longer has any clear belief about who he is, or
any vision of the direction in which he wants society to
develop?[24]

One of the interesting side-effects of this pessimism is that
in some societies people are returning to the churches. Take
the 'baby boomers' of the United States, for example. This is
the generation born shortly after the end of the Second World
War, when American servicemen returned home—called
'baby boomers' because of the sharp rise in the birth rate in
the following years! These people are now parents of teenage
children, deeply worried about what kind of polluted and
crime-ridden world their offspring are about to inherit.

So, looking for some sort of moral guidance, comfort and
reassurance that everything will turn out right, they turn to
the churches. Note that it is not the gospel itself they are
responding to. This does provide a marvellous evangelistic
opportunity for churches able to take it, and challenges these
churches also to think out how to relate the Bible's teaching on
care of creation to the gospel itself (Chapter 9).

These feelings of powerlessness are one reason why people
find it so difficult to resist the weight of consumerism.

Today we are likely to suffer all seven assaults upon our
consciousness all at once, by TV commercial, by
posters, by coupons through the letter box, by national
newspaper advertisements, by lead-line display in
several local shops, by local newspaper ads with cut-out
coupons for cash-off enticements to quicker sales, and
by actually seeing the product on a neighbour's kitchen
table. Somewhere along the line we have lost the ability
to say 'why?' any more. Why must my sights be raised
constantly beyond that which would be sufficient for me
and mine? Why must I continue to be edged along into

expecting more and more of life quantifiably measured in goods and services?[25]

THE GOODNESS OF CREATION

If this is an accurate analysis of the way people think about environmental issues, it is important for Christians to distance themselves from such ways of thinking. What is urgently needed is a profound conviction that the Bible has important things to say about our care of the world God has made.

Because, as was mentioned earlier, we live in a different world from that of the biblical text itself, some theology will be involved. Gathering texts will not be adequate, as if one verse might provide a golden key for solving the problem of the Greenhouse Effect. Would that it were so simple! What is needed is a way of looking at everything scripture asserts about creation, from the opening words of Genesis to the closing verse of Revelation. The solution is not difficult to find; there is a unifying theme which can be traced, and which forms a satisfying theological context for the wide variety of biblical texts.

That theme is the goodness of creation. Obviously, Genesis 1 comes to mind immediately, and that will be the starting point for the next chapter. But when the theme is examined closely, it turns out to be a unifying thread that connects a large number of Old and New Testament references to creation. It does more than this, however. It also brings to the surface a number of urgent ethical issues to do with enviromental care. But first: what does the goodness of creation mean?

REFERENCES

1. Commission of the Churches in International Affairs of the World Council of Churches, *The Churches in International Affairs: Reports 1970-1973* (WCC: Geneva, 1974), p 144.

2. Tim Cooper, *Green Christianity* (Hodder & Stoughton: London, 1990), p 219.

3. *ibid* p 219.

4. Quoted in *Church of England Newspaper*, no 5044, 1st March 1991, p 8.

5. Gordon Strachan, *Christ and the Cosmos* (Labaram Publications: Edinburgh, 1985).

6. *ibid* p 110.

7. Constance Cumbey, *The Hidden Dangers of the Rainbow: the New Age Movement and Our Coming Age of Barbarism* (Huntingdon House: Shreveport, 1983), p 156f.

8. Quoted in Church of England Newspaper, 17th November 1989, p 9.

9. Walter Eichdrodt, *Theology of the Old Testament* vol 2 (SCM: London, 1967), p 119.

10. John R.W. Stott, *Issues Facing Christians Today* (Marshall Pickering: London, 1986).

11. *ibid* p 6.

12. *ibid* p 7.

13. *ibid* p 8.

14. *ibid* p 8.

15. *ibid* p 8.

16. Christopher Derrick, *The Delicate Creation* (Tom Stacey: London, 1972).

17. Lawrence Osborn, *Meeting God in Creation* (Grove Books: Nottingham, 1990), p 24.

18. Paul Santmire, *The Travail of Nature* (Fortress Press: Philadelphia, 1985), p 213.

19. Lawrence Osborn, *Stewards of Creation: Environmentalism in the Light of Biblical Teaching* (Latimer House: Oxford, 1990), p 37.

20. Bernard Ramm, *The Christian View of Science and Scripture* (Paternoster: Exeter, 1964), p 17.

21. Francis Schaeffer, *The New Superspirituality* (Hodder and Stoughton: London, 1973), p 10.

22. Klaus Bockmühl, *Conservation and Lifestyle* translated by B.N. Kaye (Grove Books: Nottingham, 1977), p 23-24.

23. Church of England General Synod Board for Social Responsibility, *Our Responsibility for the Living Environment* (Church House: London, 1986).

24. Hugh Montefiore, *Man and Nature* (Collins: London 1975), p 72-73.

25. John Poulton, *People Under Pressure* (Lutterworth Press 1973), p 103.

Chapter Two

THE GOODNESS OF CREATION

INTERPRETING GENESIS 1

A T THE END of the last chapter we introduced the idea of the goodness of creation. Like a recurring theme in a symphony, this forms the motif for the whole book, and so several chapters are needed to explore it fully. The task is important, however, because it should then be the basis of Christian environmental concern. The theme of the goodness of creation is to be found not just in a few scattered verses of the Bible, but can be traced right through the history of the way God deals with his people.

But first, a word of caution. Some books about the Bible claim that their authors have discovered the unifying thread that fits everything together and makes it intelligible (often in a 'new way'). It might be a serious work of theology, or something as fanciful as Erich von Däniken's 'God-was-an-astronaut' theory, but the point is that such claims usually prove over-ambitious.

The claim of this book is altogether less extravagant: it is that the goodness of creation, long recognised as a major theme in the opening chapter of Genesis, can be traced right through the Bible from beginning to end. This does not mean that other themes, such as sin and salvation, are any the less important. But as we trace this concept of the goodness of creation, it quickly appears that it is not an independent theme; it is closely related to the others.

Of course, commentators have been correct to see the goodness of creation as an important theme in Genesis 1:1—2:4, as much so as any other theme which concerns the creationists. There are several pointers to this:

1   There are few direct references to Genesis 1 in the rest of the Old Testament, and some theologians conclude that creation is not really important; salvation, they say, is the main concern. Many Christians either believe this or at least assume it. First impressions can be misleading, however, and it soons becomes apparent that the creation of a good world is the backdrop against which the drama of Old Testament history takes place.

This is not because creation stands alongside salvation as a major theme, as if there were no real meeting point between them. They turn out to be so closely related, in both Old and New Testaments, that they cannot be completely separated; the one cannot be fully understood without reference to the other. Nor is this only for academics in ivory towers; the doctrine of creation, as developed in the Old Testament, is all about humanity's relationship with the rest of the created order. This is why it must be a starting point for Christians to think about how they should respond to modern environmental issues.

2   Genesis 1—11, called by some theologians a 'primeval history', forms a prologue to the rest of the Pentateuch (and, indeed, to the whole of the Old Testament). In this respect it is similar to the role of John 1:1–14. It presents the creation and fall, the flood and subsequent covenant with Noah and the whole of creation, and the scattering of the human race throughout the earth. These first eleven chapters make gloomy reading, showing how tragically the human race has fallen from the glory its Creator intended. Then the spotlight is focussed on one man—Abram—called out by God (12:1–3) for a special purpose. He was to be the founder of a nation

whose history is the subject of the rest of the Old Testament. But the divine purpose embraces more than a single nation (Deut 7:7,8); through Abram all the inhabitants of earth would subsequently be blessed (Gen 12:2,3).

The self-identity and purpose of Israel has therefore to be seen in the context of God's dealings with all peoples, and his loving determination to set them free from the plight of sin and alienation. Israel was called to be a light to the nations (Is 42:6,7; 49:6) as she lived in a covenant relationship with the God who creates and redeems.

The calling of Israel to this purpose involved the gift of a land to live in. Possession of this land involved its responsible care, and it needed to be a relationship radically different from that held by the Canaanites (Chapter 5). This land was a covenant gift: that is, caring for it was part of a solemn undertaking in which Israel undertook to live obediently in response to God's grace. God initiated the covenant; Israel was then faced with a choice: live obediently and be prosperous, or live disobediently and face ruin on every level, including a polluted and infertile land (eg Deut 28). This is not theoretical theology; it is about how to live successfully.

One of the ways in which Genesis 1—11 forms a prologue to the life of Israel in the promised land is its treatment of humanity's relationship with the land. Old Testament theologian Walther Eichrodt sees this clearly when he sums up the relationship between Genesis 1—11 and the rest of the Old Testament history in the following words:

> By making possession of the land dependent upon faithfulness to the covenant God includes Man's relation to Nature within the sphere of responsible human behaviour, and impresses upon him his distinctive position in the world of creatures. His sin means that the land is defiled, and the same land will vomit forth the nation which has become untrue to its moral responsibility.[1]

3   Genesis 1 repeatedly states that creation is good (vv

4,10,12,18,21,25) and there is the striking final statement, 'God saw all that he had made, and it was 'very good' (v 31). The evolution versus creation debate has sadly ensured, however, that the interpretation of the word 'day' occupies centre-stage with everything else subsidiary. The theological significance of the days will reappear later, but if the goodness of creation is mentioned on nearly every 'day', then this theme must be of at least equal importance, and deserves more attention than it usually receives.

4   As we shall see shortly, many of the pointers in Genesis 1 to the exact meaning of the goodness of creation can also be found in Psalm 104, although the language is different. This is more than coincidence; one Old Testament commentator states: 'The structure of the psalm is modelled fairly closely on that of Genesis 1, taking the stages of creation as starting-points for praise.' He then goes on to demonstrate in detail how Genesis 1 and Psalm 104 are similarly constructed.[2]

5   The creation narrative also emphasises the goodness of creation in altogether more subtle ways. Theologians have often noted how, at face value, this chapter sounds very similar to other ancient Near East creation stories (any good commentary on Genesis will give the details). One of the most striking features, however, is that while the stories look similar in details, they present totally different world views. For example, other ancient Near East world views saw the created order as hostile and malevolent, and the way Genesis 1 was written seems to indicate that part of its original intention was polemical: that is, to counter alien world views by emphasising the goodness of creation. For example, the creation of the 'two great lights' (sun and moon; vv 15–17) robs them of the power other religions gave them to govern the destinies of people. Compare the words of Psalm 121:5,6:

The Lord watches over you—
the Lord is your shade at your right hand;

the sun shall not harm you by day,
nor the moon by night.

Thus Walter Eichrodt writes:

> Where Yahweh was acknowledged as Creator, it was
> inconceivable that the creation should be based upon
> impulsive caprice, or the unpredictable and aimless
> sport of kindred or hostile or divine powers; the
> sovereignty of God experienced in the present moment
> meant that it could only have been transcendent
> rationality and moral force which determined the
> character of the created order.[3]

Another example is the way that Genesis 1:2 talks of primordial chaos in a totally different way to the ancient Near East cults: it is no longer the 'actively aggressive matrix of the gods' but merely the raw material out of which the universe is fashioned by its Creator.[4]

This is all of more than academic interest; similar false attitudes to creation are alive and well today, in an unbroken succession with the gnostic heresies which threatened to inundate the early church. Gnosticism was a philosophical system which saw each member of humanity as an essentially good and immortal divine spark or soul trapped in a mortal body which was part of an essentially evil creation; salvation then consisted of acquiring the knowledge (gnosis) which would allow the soul to be liberated and thus be released for a heavenly journey to its true home.

Modern manifestations of gnosticism include the current fascination with horoscopes, in which people cede control of their destinies to the planets and stars, and to a whole range of occult practices based on the same kind of world view. The New Age movement has a fundamental contradiction at its core: although it proclaims means of healing and wholeness, and a concern for a clean environment, its underlying philosophy (indebted as it is to Hindu thought, amongst other sources) is built upon a view in which created reality is an illusion and therefore valueless.

THE MEANING OF GOODNESS

Given that the goodness of creation is a central theme in the Old Testament (and, as we shall see later, in the New Testament also), the next task is to explore the meaning of the word 'goodness'. In Genesis 1 the statement is repeatedly made, but its exact meaning is not immediately obvious; but Genesis 1 itself, and other Old Testament passages, do show that there are at least five different aspects to its meaning.

The Good Creation Bears Witness To Its Creator

The created order bears the stamp of its Creator. This idea is not explicit in Genesis 1, but is confirmed elsewhere, particularly in the Psalms:

> The heavens declare the glory of God; the skies proclaim the work of His hands (Ps 19:1).

> I lift up my eyes to the hills—where does my help come from? My help comes from the Lord, the Maker of heaven and earth (Ps 121:1,2).

Social surveys continue to show how many people, young and old alike, stubbornly insist on believing in God (or, at least, that there is a God) even though only a minority are churchgoers. Why is this? There are many reasons, but one is almost certainly a vague awareness that there is a Creator. Reductionist 'explanations' of the existence of things, and of our reflection upon our own existence, fail to satisfy. Existence only makes sense if a Creator is responsible for it all and is still there somewhere.

This is true even though urbanisation has largely removed millions of people from direct contact with the world of raw creation; thus some city children have no idea where milk comes from. In their experience they can only link it with a bottle, a carton or, at best, a milkman. In countries where most people live in rural communities, such as in Africa, there is no such problem: whatever religion people follow, at its heart is usually the idea of a Creator God.

Another reason for this awareness of a Creator God comes through the awesome spectacle of natural forces. Thunder and lightning, earthquakes and volcanic eruptions, storms and driving rain still inspire awe in their beholders, even though part of their mind might be on the need for an insurance claim! This mirrors the experience of the psalmist:

> May the glory of the Lord endure for ever;
> may the Lord rejoice in his works—
> he who looks at the earth and it trembles,
> who touches the mountains and they smoke (Ps 104:31,32).

> The voice of the Lord is over the waters;
> the God of glory thunders,
> the Lord thunders over the mighty waters.
> The voice of the Lord is powerful;
> the voice of the Lord is majestic...
> The voice of the Lord strikes
> with flashes of lightning.
> The voice of the Lord shakes the desert...
> The voice of the Lord twists the oaks
> and strips the forests bare (Ps 29:3–9; cf 77:16–20).

Elsewhere the Psalms depict creation as praising God:

> The meadows are covered with flocks
> and the valleys are mantled with corn;
> they shout for joy and sing (Ps 65:13).

> Shout for joy to God, all the earth!
> Sing the glory of his name;
> make his praise glorious!
> Say to God, 'How awesome are your deeds!

> So great is your power
> that your enemies cringe before you (Ps 66:1–3)

Other texts show how creation bears witness to particular aspects of God's character—his goodness, strength, constancy and his concern to sustain life:

> But ask the animals, and they will teach you,
> or the birds of the air, and they will tell you;
> or speak to the earth, and it will teach you,
> or let the fish of the sea inform you.
> Which of these does not know
> that the hand of the Lord has done this? (Job 12:7–9).

> And the heavens proclaim his righteousness,
> for God himself is judge (Ps 50:6; cf. 148:1–14).

These ideas are also picked up in the New Testament, particularly by Paul. He used his understanding of creation as a point of contact with the world of Hellenistic philosophy (see also Chapter 9):

> Yet he has not left himself without testimony: he has shown kindness by giving you rain from heaven and crops in their seasons; he provides you with plenty of food and fills your hearts with joy (Acts 14:17).

> From one man he made every nation of men, that they should inhabit the whole earth; and he determined the times set for them and the exact places where they should live. God did this so that men would seek him and perhaps reach out for him and find him, though he is not far from each one of us (Acts 17:27).

At the beginning of his letter to the Romans, Paul takes up the same theme:

> For since the beginning of the world God's invisible qualities—his eternal power and divine nature—have been

clearly seen, being understood from what has been made, so that men are without excuse (1:20).

This statement has sometimes been taken as the starting point of an elaborate 'natural theology' like that of the Greek philosophers. They believed that by reflecting on creation people could know more of the Creator. Paul's point here is totally different, however. He argued that this is impossible in practice, because men have rejected this revelation so that their minds are darkened and God is hidden from them—a tragic but vitally important theme to which we shall return.

Because some scriptures describe creation praising God, some theologians have deduced that it somehow possesses a consciousness all of its own; thus G.E. Wright states, '...there was no sense of nature's being inanimate in either heaven or earth; instead the various elements all possessed some kind of psychic life.'[5]

This is unduly speculative, but to understand the language of these scriptures simply as metaphorical is to err on the side of caution, possibly influenced by the modern idea that creation's only purpose is to supply human need (see below). If the Creator has created everything good, why should it not be able to witness to him?

A common objection to this kind of world view is that it is 'pre-scientific', implying that scientific explanation renders it obsolete. Often quoted are the words of the French scientist Laplace when he presented Napoleon with his treatise on astronomy. The Emperor said to him, 'M Laplace, they tell me you have written this large book on the system of the universe, and have never even mentioned the Creator.' Laplace replied: 'Sire, I had no need of any such hypothesis.' It is important to explore this tension further, because the goodness of creation is not an abstract proposition: it is foundational to a truly Christian response to urgent environmental problems.

The question therefore arises: given these modern scientific explanations of the world (and indeed, the universe!), do they scuttle ideas of a Creator whose handiwork points back to his character? The answer to this question is emphatically in the negative, for two reasons.

Firstly, while science tells us how things work, it falls short of answering other equally important questions regarding purpose and origin. This has been persuasively argued by Michael Polanyi. An analogy from the world of literature identifies the nub of the matter. Imagine you are thoroughly enjoying a Shakespeare play (or whatever takes your fancy). On one level the sounds you hear, which your ears register and your brain interprets, can be understood in terms of the physics of sound waves—a complete scientific explanation. But a moment's thought shows how inadequate this is on the level of human experience. The Shakespeare play—the nuances of its performance, your enjoyment of it, the author's purpose in writing it, and the abiding place of Shakespeare in literary tradition, go far beyond the scientific 'explanation'. For a complete understanding of what is going on, higher levels of explanation are needed.[6]

Secondly, scientific explanations of how things work fail to cope with the way that people 'meet God in creation'. We have already seen how this is expressed in the Psalms, but do people really have this kind of experience today? The answer is 'Yes, they do!'. Some of the hymns we sing assume that this is so, whether it be a golden oldie such as 'O worship the King all-glorious above', or a more modern offering from the pen of Michael Saward:

Powerful in majesty, throned in the heavens—
Sun, moon and stars by your word are upheld;
Time and eternity bow within your presence,
Lord of the nations: we praise and adore.

Apart from the resources of worship (see also Chapter 12), there is also a rich seam of creation-centred spirituality in secular literature, stretching back many centuries. Equally important here is the fact that the theme is still abundantly represented in modern art and poetry. Take, for example, the poetry of Gerard Manley Hopkins. Lawrence Osborn writes of it:

> If you ignore the critics and listen instead to the poems you will discover someone who was carried away with the sheer music of words. His poems also display a passionate love for the natural world and an acute awareness that, as he enjoyed nature, he was also enjoying the presence of God...Such examples...may feed our expectation of a meeting of God in creation. Another requirement is some contact with the natural world. Wherever you live that is possible. You may meet God on a Welsh hill (with Hopkins or R.S. Thomas) or in the New Forest, but you do not need to live in a national park or a place of great natural beauty for this to be a practical possibility. All that is required is a walk in your local park or a nearby piece of waste ground, time to pay attention to the life that can be found there, and the expectation that God will meet you.[7]

Significantly, Osborn's own experience is that this awareness brings with it another, less welcome, kind of awareness: that of the negative impact humanity has made upon the goodness of creation. But that subject must wait for a little while.

There is another important consideration to be mentioned here. What has been said so far in this section has implied that our knowledge of God as Creator is something common to many religions. To some extent this is true, but there are also aspects of the goodness of creation which are quite distinctive to Christianity. This is because the God we worship has revealed himself as God-in-Trinity.

It is impossible to deduce the doctrine of the Trinity from Genesis 1, of course. What is involved is a reading-back (an exercise in 'eisegesis') of Trinitarianism into the Genesis text, in order to deal fully with the question of what sort of creation reflects the nature of the God who creates. There are, however, hints of a divine plurality in the statement 'Let us make man in our image, after our likeness....' (Gen 1:26). This could simply be a formal royal plural ('we have become a grand-mother') or an inclusion of angels as co-agents in creation, but the latter explanation is not consistent with Isaiah 40:14. F.D. Kidner, however, refers to it as the 'plural of fullness', which is glimpsed elsewhere in the use of a singular verb with the plural noun *elohim*.[8]

There are four clear reasons why this consideration of the divine plurality is important.

1   A unitarian view of God inevitably leads to a view in which he is dependent upon creation. Put crudely, God needed to create because he was lonely and wanted someone to talk to! Yet the Bible clearly shows how God's decision to create was freely taken; a Trinitarian understanding of God, and of the relationships of love (to follow Augustine) that exist within the Godhead, safeguard our understanding of this divine freedom. To quote the theologian Roger Nicole:

> ...the doctrine of the Trinity helps us to apprehend in God something of his own inner life, and to see in him the intimate attachment of the Father to the Son, of the Son to the Father, of both of them to the Holy Spirit, and of the Holy Spirit to both of them. This may help us to grasp how God is self-sufficient and how creation, involving as it does all three persons of the Trinity, was not, however, necessary for God's own existence or happiness.[9]

2   Both Old and New Testament scriptures testify to the involvement of Father, Son and Spirit in the work of creation (eg Ps 104:30; Col 1:15–20). Thus:

> The Father is the ultimate origin of all things. He creates through his Word or Wisdom, who thus shapes creation. The Spirit indwells that creation as the source of all energy and life; he delights in or is grieved by what goes on in

creation. This Trinitarian approach safeguards both the transcendence and the immanence of God.[10]

This is of vital importance. Many of the ways in which people abuse creation are linked with too great an emphasis on either immanence or transcendence. If God is entirely immanent in his handiwork, it becomes sacred, and cannot be utilised; God is restricted by the creation in which he is immanent, and is not free to act in grace, to 'play with creation joyfully'.[11] If he is so 'other' that he cannot have any direct dealing with the world of creation, then we are free to do with it (or to it) whatever we wish. In fact, both the full range of scriptural teaching on creation, and the issues of modern environmental mismanagement, require a Trinitarian, and thus balanced, approach.

3   We can understand the concept of God-in-Trinity as being about relationships: from the interior relationships within the Godhead flow those that exist between God and humanity, and within and between the human and non-human levels of creation. We can understand these relationships in terms of diversity and interdependence, and this is another aspect of what the Bible describes as the goodness of creation.

4   The self-revelation of God as God-in-Trinity is a revelation of diversity in unity. If God himself is like this, it is not surprising that creation reflects this inner nature.

As long as the earth remains, there can never be a single plant among the hundreds of thousands that exist that does not belong to its own species within this whole. Just because it belongs to its kind, each individual is directed to the ordered whole, God's Creation.[12]

The Good Creation Reveals Diversity and Interdependence

The first statements of the diversity of creation are in Genesis 1:

> And God said, 'Let the water teem with living creatures, and let birds fly above the earth across the expanse of the sky... Let the land produce living creatures according to their kinds: livestock, creatures that move along the ground, and wild animals, each according to its kind' (vv 20,24).

Estimates of the meaning of this text vary. Using purely literary criteria, Claus Westermann can talk of the style of this chapter as possessing 'peculiar and effective monotony'.[13] Psalm 104, however, treats the theme with an unmistakable note of wonder:

> How many are your works, O Lord!
> In wisdom you have made them all;
> the earth is full of your creatures.
> There is the sea, vast and spacious,
> teeming with creatures beyond number
> living things both large and small (vv 24,25).

The same theme is emphasised in a different way in the story of Noah and the ark, where domestic and wild animals and birds are preserved (Gen 6:13—8:1), and in the repeated questions the Creator asks in Job 39.

It is only with the rise of modern science, and efforts at rigorous classification of species from the seventeenth century onwards, that we have come to realise just how amazingly wide this diversity is.[14] Even a spadeful of ordinary garden soil teems with a huge range of minute life forms. Recent concern over the future of tropical rain forests has focussed attention on the incredible biological diversity within them. Some 1.7 million species have been identified, but up to 30 million species of plants, animals and insects may yet remain to be fully described. A single tree in the Amazon rain forest has been found to host forty-three different species of ant, approximately the same as the entire ant fauna of the United Kingdom.

This diversity is extremely important. It is not about lists, as if we could think of the earth's surface as a gigantic museum composed of exhibits in separate cages. It is to do with interdependence, and here again our understanding of creation flows from the Trinitarian understanding of God which is uniquely Christian: God is three in one; he is diversity in unity. The Old Testament sees the dependence of creation in two ways: firstly, everything is dependent upon the sustaining power of its Creator for its continuing existence (eg Gen 6:17; 7:15,22; Ps 104:27–30; 136:15; 145:15f; 147:9; Eccles 3:19,21; cf Heb 1:3). Secondly, there is interdependence within creation. For example, the bird and animal kingdoms rely on creation for food (which God, of course, provides: eg Gen 1:29,30; Ps 104:14–17,21,27,28). Again, this is an area where scientific inquiry and biblical revelation converge. The millions of species referred to earlier do not live in glorious isolation; there are webs of interdependence of intricate complexity, investigated through the science of ecology.

The Good Creation Is A Beautiful Creation

'Never lose an opportunity to see anything beautiful', said Charles Kingsley, 'Beauty is God's handwriting.' It has been suggested that the Hebrew word which is translated as 'good' encompasses the idea of beauty. This is not explicit in Genesis 1 but there is a broad hint of the idea in Ezekiel's lament for the King of Tyre (Ez 28:11–19):

> You were the model of perfection, full of wisdom and perfect in beauty. You were in Eden, the garden of God; every precious stone adorned you: ruby, topaz and emerald, chrysolite, onyx and jasper, sapphire, turquoise and beryl. Your settings and mountings were made of gold. On the day that you were created they were prepared (vv 12b,13).

In Chapter 4 we shall return to the main emphasis of this

passage: the glory from which the king has fallen. But here, in the language of the garden of Eden, beauty is involved in his creation (see also v 17). An even stronger hint comes in Ezekiel 31:1–9 where Egypt is described as having had a beauty greater than any tree 'in the garden of God'. There are only a few other references in the Old Testament to beauty in creation. Genesis 2:9 states: 'And the Lord God made all kinds of trees grow out of the ground—every tree that is pleasant to the sight and good for food...' and Ecclesiastes 3:11 affirms: 'He has made everything beautiful in its time.'

A popular view of science (though not held by all scientists!) is that the investigation of things is for utilitarian purposes: once we understand them, how can we use them? But scientists sometimes take the same kinds of holidays as other mortals, and can enjoy a beautiful view with them. I am a geologist, and some of my field work has been done in County Donegal in the Irish Republic. If you assume my attention was solely on the rock structures I was investigating, you would be wrong. Donegal is endowed with a majestic and rugged beauty, and I was often aware of it as intensely as the main purpose of my being there.

In fact, science itself uncovers beauty. Good scientists will, at least occasionally, get excited about something they have discovered; there is a kind of beauty in what has become known, and an experience of delight as real as viewing any spectacular landscape. Even the apparently dry and mathematical discipline of physics is not immune:

> The regimes of concern to fundamental physics, which are the regimes of the very large (cosmology) and the very small (elementary particle physics)... seem to display a remarkably beautiful structure. The evolution of the universe according to the laws of general relativity, and the patterns described by particle physics are sources of considerable intellectual delight to those privileged to study them.[15]

For readers whose memories of school physics are more to

do with pain, perplexity or plain boredom, all this may come as a great surprise. It would take too long, for example, to explain the concept of supersymmetry which modern physicists use to probe the fundamental structure of our space-time universe, but it is revealing that one expert on the subject has written:

> But the fact that these things work, that these seemingly bizarre rules give ways of computing things in quantum gravity, giving sensible results and finite answers and leading in many different directions to all kinds of beautiful areas in mathematics, is a very deep mystery—probably one of the deepest which has ever been encountered in physics. It is unlikely that a proper understanding of this mystery will be found either soon or simply. But it will be worth the wait.[16]

Physicists also believe that as they probe ever deeper into the great mysteries at the heart of the universe, things do not get more complicated: they actually become simpler. Again, this is a matter of beauty and excitement:

> To my mind, there must be, at the bottom of it all, not an equation, but an utterly simple idea. And to me that idea, when we finally discover it, will be so compelling, so inevitable, that we will say to one another, 'Oh, how beautiful. How could it have been otherwise?'[17]

This use of mystical, almost religious, language by scientists (and there are many other examples) leads to a third significant property of beauty in the created universe: that it is apprehended on many different levels. The whole of reality is cut through and through by beauty. We started off with beautiful scenery, then beautiful physics, then mathematics. Then there are the arts—music and ballet, literature and drama, sculpture and painting. The fact that some of these appeal only to minorities does not alter the argument, which affirms that beauty is a very important feature of the goodness of creation.

The Good Creation Brings Joy To Its Creator

Christians often assume that the creation of humanity is the pinnacle of God's creative acts (see Chapter 3). It sometimes comes as a surprise, then, to find that this is not the climax of the creation narrative. Here, the pinnacle is reached only on the seventh day:

> By the seventh day God had finished the work he had been doing; so on the seventh day he rested from all his work. And God blessed the seventh day and made it holy, because on it he rested from all the work of creating that he had done (Gen 2:2,3).

The idea of God resting cannot be understood in purely literal terms, as if he were tired and needed physical refreshment. Here, rest is to do with the completeness of creation, which has now been pronounced 'very good' (1:31). Physical rest was certainly involved in the Sabbath observance of the people of Israel, but by the time of Jesus the core meaning had been lost under a mass of convoluted Pharisaic laws. These then formed the background to many of Jesus' controversies with the religious leaders of the day. Sabbath legalism is still alive and well in some circles!

But among all the other themes which combine to give the Old Testament Sabbath its full richness of meaning, there is the idea of celebration, which is made explicit in one of the Old Testament laws:

> For six days work is to be done, but the seventh day is a Sabbath of rest, holy to the Lord. Whoever does any work on the Sabbath day must be put to death. The Israelites are to observe the Sabbath, celebrating it for the generations to come as a lasting covenant. It will be a sign between me and the Israelites for ever, for in six days the Lord made the

heavens and the earth, and on the seventh day he abstained from work and rested (Exod 31:15–17).

Comparison of the Sabbath laws and the text of Genesis 2:2f suggests that human Sabbath observance mirrors a divine activity, and the common feature appears to be this note of celebration: if the Creator celebrates the completeness of his work on the seventh day, then so should his people!

Our Sabbath rest is the opportunity God gives us to share his delight...The six plus one alternation of work and rest is not the rhythm of work plus recovery so as to be able to go back to work. It is a rhythm of engagement with the world in work, and then thankful enjoyment of the world in worship. By 'worship' we do not mean simply—or even primarily—'church activity'. 'Worship' is our offering back to God, for him to enjoy, our enjoyment of his world...What is our creation for? That we may be creatures of the seventh day! That we may...share the delight of his rest...that we may be caught up in praise with the sun and moon and stars, the trees and flowers and birds; with all creatures great and small, of fish and of beasts. All these look to God for their life and their sustenance; all these in their silent ways sing the song of their Creator.[18]

REFERENCES

1. Walther Eichrodt, *Theology of the Old Testament* vol 2 (SCM: London, 1967), p 119.

2. Derek Kidner, *Psalms 73—150* (IVP: Leicester, 1975), p 368.

3. *ibid* p 98.

4. Lawrence Osborn, *Stewards of Creation: Environmentalism in the light of biblical teaching* (Latimer House: Oxford, 1990), p 28.

5. G. Ernest Wright, 'The Lawsuit of God' in B.W. Anderson and W. Harrelson, *Israel's Prophetic Heritage* (New York, 1962), pp 26-67.

6. Michael Polanyi, *Knowing and Being* (Routledge and Kegan Paul: London,1969). See also: David Atkinson, *The Message of Genesis 1—11*

(IVP: Leicester 1990), p 57-59 and John C. Polkinghorne, 'A Scientist's View of Religion', *Science and Christian Belief*, vol 2 (October 1990): pp 83-94.

7. Lawrence Osborn, *Meeting God in Creation* (Grove Books: Leicester, 1990), p 17.

8. *ibid* p 51f.

9. Roger Nicole, 'The Meaning of the Trinity' in Peter Toon and James D. Spiceland, *One God in Trinity* (Samuel Bagster: London, 1980), p 7.

10. Unpublished paper by Peter Mott.

11. James Houston, *I Believe in the Creator* (Hodder and Stoughton: London, 1979).

12. Claus Westermann, *Creation* (SPCK: London, 1971), p 45f.

13. *ibid* p 42.

14. Keith Thomas, *Man and the Natural World: Changing Attitudes in England 1500-1800* (Allen Lane: London, 1983), pp 51-70.

15. John Polkinghorne, *Science and Creation* (SPCK: London, 1988), p 34.

16. Quoted in Michael Atiyah, 'What is supersymmetry?', *Nature* vol 324 (4th December 1986): p 419.

17. American physicist John Archibald Wheeler, quoted in Timothy Ferris, *Coming of Age in the Milky Way* (Bodley Head: London, 1988), p 346.

18. David Atkinson, *The Message of Genesis 1–11* (IVP: Leicester 1990), p 49.

Chapter Three

MADE IN GOD'S IMAGE

IN THE PREVIOUS chapter we examined four aspects of the goodness of creation as expressed in the Old Testament: its witness to the Creator, its unity in diversity, its beauty, and the Creator's joyful celebration of his handiwork, shared by his people in the weekly observance of the Sabbath. There is a fifth aspect, so important that it needs a separate chapter, and has deliberately been left until last so as to keep a sense of proportion.

The four aspects already discussed have little to do with the place of humanity within the created order; creation is good independently of our presence here and our ability to perceive it. In the Book of Job, and elsewhere in the Old Testament, this is forcefully asserted:

> Who cuts a channel for the torrents of rain, and a path for the thunderstorm, to water a land where no man lives, a desert with no one in it; to satisfy a desolate wasteland and make it sprout with grass? (Job 38:25–27).

Similarly, in Job 39:13–18 God deals with the ostrich in a way that cannot possibly concern humanity. The climax of the Book of Job is about the fact that Job cannot understand the ways of the Creator. To be sure, the main question being explored here is that of undeserved suffering, but within this context the Creator puts to him a whole series of questions about the world around him which he confesses himself unable to answer; it is when he reaches this point that things begin to improve!

THE GOOD CREATION FULFILS HUMAN NEED

But when we come to this fifth aspect of the goodness of creation, humanity is directly involved, because the creation has the capacity to fulfil our needs. In Genesis 1 and Psalm 65 the emphasis is on food:

> Then God said, 'I give you every seed-bearing plant on the face of the whole earth and every tree that has fruit with seed in it. They will be yours for food (Gen 1:29).

> You care for the land and water it; you enrich it abundantly. The streams of God are filled with water to provide the people with corn, for so you have ordained it (Ps 65:9).

This text on its own might suggest that mere survival is being described, but elsewhere the idea of enjoyment is introduced. The Creator intended the goodness of creation to be comprehensive enough to enrich human life on many different levels:

> And the Lord God made all kinds of trees grow out of the ground—trees that were pleasing to the eye and good for food (Gen 2:9).

> He has made everything beautiful in its time. He has also set eternity in the hearts of men; yet they cannot fathom what God has done from beginning to end. I know that there is nothing better for men than to be happy and do good while they live. That everyone may eat and drink, and find satisfaction in his toil—this is the gift of God (Eccles 3:11–13).

> [He makes] wine that gladdens the heart of man,
> oil to make his face shine,
> and bread that sustains his heart (Ps 104:15).

The earth is crammed full of raw materials which can enhance and enrich every dimension of human existence. Genesis 2:12 mentions gold, aromatic resin and onyx; while Cain and Abel were agriculturalists (Gen 4:2–5), Cain later built a city (Gen 4:17, though we cannot make too much of this—the Hebrew word can refer to human settlements both great and small); Tubal-Cain made tools from bronze and iron (Gen 4:22). Exodus 35—39, with its detailed instructions for the construction of the Temple, shows how this diversity can be incorporated into worship, the highest activity of which we are capable. The land Israel received as a covenant gift was a land 'flowing with milk and honey' (Ex 3:8, etc).

What was true for the people of Old Testament times is even more true for the sophisticated dwellers of many twentieth-century countries. The sheer variety available on the supermarket shelves speaks not only of human ingenuity but also of the amazing potential of creation to do everything that Psalm 104:15 speaks of! While we usually manage to take this all for granted ('choice' is the name of the game), a stroll through the local supermarket can be a bewildering experience for someone recently arrived from Africa, whether an African or a European who has been there even for a matter of weeks.

The Old Testament mentions a limited range of metals; we now know of many more, with a wide range of ingenious uses, as any chemistry textbook will testify. Cobalt, for example, increases the hardness and high-temperature strength of steel to which it is added, and such steel is then suitable for cutting tools in lathes, for jet engine components and nuclear reactors, and heating coils in electric radiators. It is also used in the production of magnets, paints and medicines; the radioactive isotope Co-56 is employed in radiotherapy.

The much-publicised clearing of rain forests such as those of Amazonia jeopardises known and potential sources of many materials which can also be used in the service of humanity. Timber is not the only resource; there are also fruits, oils, latex, fibres and drugs. Cycads provide dopamine, valuable in treatment of Parkinson's Disease; alkaloids in Madagascar periwinkles provide effective treatment for Hodgkin's Disease by preventing cell division. Steroids from yams can be used to treat rheumatoid arthritis. It is impossible to estimate how many more useful substances in the world's rain forests are waiting to be discovered.

The fact that we are able to tap the potential of creation in this way (and there are countless other examples which could have been given) should cause us to stop and reflect upon our own place in creation: because we are able to use creation and modify our environment in a way unique among earth's life forms, are we 'special' in some way, or are we simply one more of the many forms of animal life on Earth's surface? The biblical portrayal of humanity's place in creation answers 'yes' to both questions, as we shall shortly see.

IS GENESIS ANTHROPOCENTRIC?

It is sometimes stated, and more often assumed, that the biblical account of creation is anthropocentric, that is, it is 'unashamedly man-centred'.[1] This view of creation is nothing new. It is at least two centuries old:

> Ask any one of the undistinguished mass of people, for what purpose every thing exists? The general answer is, that every thing was created for our practical use and accommodation!...In short, the whole magnificent scene of things is daily and confidently asserted to be ultimately intended for the peculiar convenience of mankind. Thus do the bulk of human species vauntingly elevate themselves above the innumerable existences that surround them.[2]

Toulmin's somewhat sarcastic appraisal of human self-awareness is shared by many today. People like Miriam (Chapter 1), sensitive to and troubled by our mistreatment of the created world, believe that Judeo-Christian teaching is largely to blame. The best-known of a number of statements of this position comes from the lips of historian Professor Lynn White, in a now-famous address to the American Association for the Advancement of Science:

> We are superior to nature, contemptuous of it, willing to use it for our slightest whim...We shall continue to have a worsening ecological crisis until we reject the Christian axiom that nature has no reason for existence but to serve man...Both our present science and our present technology are so tinctured with orthodox Christian arrogance towards nature that no solution for our ecologic crisis can be expected from them alone. Since the roots of our troubles are so largely religious, the remedy must also be essentially religious, whether we call it that or not.[3]

It would be hasty to dismiss such criticisms out of hand, even though non-Judeo-Christian civilisations have had their fair share of environmental disasters during the course of history. At the heart of these criticisms is unhappiness about the ways that the texts from Genesis 1 and Psalm 8 have been used in the past to elevate the status and power of humanity far beyond anything that the context of these texts can justify. Keith Thomas cites examples from earlier centuries in which this approach was carried to remarkable lengths, by stressing in a one-sided way how different humanity is from the rest of creation. Thus, according to one early Stuart doctor:

> Man is of a far different structure in his guts from ravenous creatures as dogs, wolves, etc, who, minding only their belly, have their guts descending almost straight down from their ventricle or stomach to the fundament: whereas in this noble microcosm man, there are in these intestinal parts many anfractuous

circumvolutions, windings and turnings, whereby,
longer retention of his food being procured, he might so
much the better attend upon sublime speculations, and
profitable employments in Church and
Commonwealth.[4]

Humanity's Solidarity With The Rest of Creation

The Genesis account of creation subtly warns against over-
inflated ideas of humanity's place in the created order. It
stresses how much we are part of that created order. In the
previous chapter there was a hint of this in that it is the
Sabbath which is the culmination of creation, not humanity.
Much more explicit, however, is the parallelism of the language used to describe how humans and animals reproduce
their lines:

> God blessed them and said, 'Be fruitful and increase in
> number and fill the water in the seas, and let the birds
> increase on the earth (1:22).

> God blessed them and said to them, 'Be fruitful and
> increase in number; fill the earth and subdue it' (1:28a).

The same literary device is used to show how men and
beasts are provided with the same kinds of food:

> Then God said, 'I give you every seed-bearing plant on the
> face of the whole earth and every tree that has fruit with
> seed in it. They will be yours for food' (1:29).

> And to all the beasts of the earth and all the birds of the air
> and all the creatures that move on the ground—everything
> that has the breath of life in it—I give every green plant for
> food' (1:30).

Other hints in Genesis drive the point home. In Chapter 1,
man and beasts were created on the same day. Genesis 2
makes the same point in its description of humanity as being

'formed...from the dust of the ground' (v 7), and through a closely similar description of the origin of birds and beasts (v 19). In later books of the Old Testament this statement is linked with ideas of sinfulness, corruption and mortality (hence the hymn line 'Frail children of dust, and feeble as frail...'), but there is no such hint here. Rather, the use of the verb 'formed' emphasises the skill[5] or artistry[6] of the Creator in this work (cf. Ps 94:9; 139:14–16; Is 44:9f; Je 18:2); again, literary devices are used to emphasise the point: the Hebrew words for 'man' and 'earth' are very similar—*adam* and *adama*. For good measure, 2:19 describes the creation of the beasts of the field and the birds of the air in the same way, and the covenant which follows the flood encompasses not only Noah's descendants but also 'all living creatures of every kind' (Gen 9:15).

The implications of this carefully stated estimate of the human race in Genesis 1, 2 must wait a little while. To deal with it on its own would be like handling a one-sided coin; here we must understand the Bible's witness to human solidarity with the rest of creation in the light of another assertion—that we are also distinct from the rest of creation.

Humanity Is Distinct From The Rest of Creation

To affirm that we are unique in the world of creation, in some sense, is not necessarily an exercise in human arrogance. It is to take seriously, and to attempt to fathom, some of the most striking words of Genesis 1 and Psalm 8:

> Then God said, 'Let us make man in our image, after our likeness, and let them rule over the fish of the sea and the birds of the air, over the livestock, over all the earth, and over all the creatures that move along the ground.'...God blessed them and said to them, 'Be fruitful and increase in number; fill the earth and subdue it. Rule over the fish of the sea and the birds of the air and over every living creature that moves on the ground' (Gen 1:26,28).

When I consider your heavens, the work of your fingers; the moon and the stars, which you have set in place, what is man that you are mindful of him, the son of man that you care for him?

You made him a little lower than the heavenly beings and crowned him with glory and honour. You made him ruler over the works of your hands; you put everything under his feet: all flocks and herds, and the beasts of the field, the birds of the air, and the fish of the sea, all that swim the paths of the seas.

O Lord our God, how majestic is your name in all the earth! (Ps 8:3–9).

The Creator decided to fashion human beings in his 'image' and 'likeness'. In this we are unique. No other act of divine creation is preceded by words like those of Genesis 1:26. The Old Testament scholar Gerhard von Rad states, 'God participates more intimately and intensively in this than in the earlier works of creation.'[7] Elsewhere it is always less personal, such as 'Let there be... let the earth bring forth'. The following verse also emphasises human uniqueness in its introduction of the special verb *bara* for 'create'. The verb is used here three times for emphasis, and is usually used elsewhere in the Old Testament of divine dealings with humanity.

With the infallible benefit of hindsight we can laugh at the ludicrous attempts of people like the Stuart doctor, in his essay on the structure of the human gut, to demonstrate how different we are to the rest of the animal kingdom. But the danger is in throwing out the baby with the bathwater. Scripture asserts that we are unique among all that God created; we are made in his image. But exactly what does this mean?

Attempts have been made to understand 'image' etymologically, that is, in terms of the root meaning of the word (Hebrew *selem*). It can refer to a statue which accurately copies an original (and thus, by extension, an idol). This leads to the ingenious idea that the divine image refers to our upright stance, most animals being four-footed. Other less fanciful interpretations state that, since statues in some sense 'represent' the original, humanity represents the Creator upon the earth.

Etymological arguments can be dangerous, however, if they take no account of the context, and many discussions of the meaning of *selem* suffer from this omission.[8] We will return to the context very soon, because it is obvious that it exerts a strong control over the meaning of 'image'. 'Likeness' (Hebrew *demut*) is a more abstract word for appearance or analogy and on its own gives little indication as to the precise way we are to understand it.[9]

Other attempts to understand these words start with the assumption that 'image' and 'likeness' are not the same thing. So, for example, some theologians have taken the former to refer to man's indelible constitution as a rational and morally responsible being, and the latter to that spiritual accord with the will of God that was lost at the Fall (see Chapter 4). There are three reasons for rejecting this interpretation.

1   As F.D. Kidner has pointed out, the distinction between these two categories does exist, but it does not coincide with the terms 'image' and 'likeness' as the Bible understands them.[10] Thus, the Fall does not change the fact that people are made in God's image (Gen 9:6) and likeness (Jas 3:9); at the same time humanity needs to be renewed 'in the image of its Creator' (Col 3:10; cf Eph 4:24).

2   It ignores the Hebrew understanding of humanity. Men and women in their totality are made in the divine image, which is not to be located in some particular aspect of their makeup. So it seems more likely that the sequence 'image...likeness' is a reflection of Hebrew parallelism rather than a subtle distinction between two different aspects of human life.

3   It ignores the juxtaposition of the statement which follows, which is about human dominion over the rest of creation:

'And let them rule over the fish of the sea and the birds of
the air, over the livestock, over all the earth, and over all the
creatures that move along the ground.'...God blessed them
and said to them, 'Be fruitful and increase in number; fill
the earth and subdue it. Rule over the fish of the sea and the
birds of the air and over every living creature that moves on
the ground' (Gen 1:26,28).

We have already hinted (quite deliberately) that the context of a word is crucial in understanding its meaning. Therefore part of the meaning of 'image' is to do with its link in
Genesis 1:26 with human dominion over creation. Modern
concern over environmental mismanagement makes this an
attractive way to understand the divine image, but this leaves
it open to the accusation that it has more to do with twentieth-
century fears than accurate biblical interpretation.

However, this interpretation has an impressive pedigree. It
can be found in pre-rabbinic exegesis of Genesis 1:26, and in
Ecclesiasticus 17:3–5 and 4 Esdras 8:44. It is also consistent
with the function of Genesis 1—11 as the 'ethical prologue' to
the rest of the Old Testament, as discussed in Chapter 2. This
is not to imply that the divine image is exactly the same as our
position of dominion over the rest of creation; that would be to
mistake the purpose of the text. But it is clear that our ability
to exercise dominion over creation follows from the divine
image.[11]

But even establishing the link between image and dominion
does not clear up the problem of exactly what this image is and
where it is to be found. We have seen that it would be misleading to understand the divine image as some component within
human life. Many theologians see the image in terms of relationship; that is, God creates human beings in his own image
so that they can enjoy a personal relationship with him. Old
Testament theologian Claus Westermann states, 'What God
has decided to create must stand in a relationship to him. The
creation of man in God's image is directed to something
happening between God and man.'[12]

This is a satisfying explanation because it again reflects the inner nature of God-in-Trinity, between whose Persons there exist 'loving creativity and personal communion.'[13] This understanding of image is reflected in the way Genesis 2 describes the creation of the man; as we have already seen, he is fashioned from the dust of the ground, but it is only when God breathes his breath into him that he becomes a living being (v 7). This breathing is a warmly personal act: 'God gives himself to what he has created.'[14]

This relational model of the divine image in human beings also solves another problem where other models fail. There is an apparent tension between two sets of biblical texts, both of which have already been referred to. In the one, the image continues after the Fall; in the other, the image needs to be renewed. Either these sets of texts are contradictory, or else we have to seek a precise understanding of the divine image that can hold them together; only the relational model is able to do this.[15]

All this is of enormous relevance to the theme of the goodness of creation. Humanity was created in the image of God: two dimensions to this important theological statement are, firstly, that this image is about the possibility of an ongoing relationship between people and their Creator and, secondly, that the image leads to the possibility of dominion over the rest of the created order.

What sort of dominion is implied? We have already referred to writers who have laid environmental mismanagement at the foot of 'Judeo-Christian arrogance' towards creation. This may have been true in the past, but the more pressing issue is whether this attitude is present in the Bible itself, especially Genesis 1. In the next section we shall examine more closely another text which has been used to justify this claim, but the repeated assertion that creation is 'very good' should cause warning bells to ring: why would Genesis 1 lay such emphasis on this if the same chapter also means to imply that humanity can do whatever it likes with the world of creation?

More specifically, if the scriptures show that the goodness of creation is to do with its role of reflecting the Creator's glory, how could the same scriptures encourage us to do to it what would mar this role? If creation's goodness is to do with diversity and interdependence within it, how can we find justification in the Bible for practices which eliminate species by the million and threaten the existence of all the others? In Psalm 8, the other main text which sets humanity above the rest of creation, the tone of those verses is one of reverent awe and wonder, and the apprehension of the human role is one of privilege.

The Task of Dominion

The divine word about the creation of humanity in Genesis 1:26 is followed by a direct command: 'Be fruitful...increase...fill...subdue *(kabas)*... rule *(rada)*' (v 28). These words must be carefully examined, because some of them are alleged to have violent overtones, and they become important in the issue of what sort of dominion we are called upon to exercise. Some Christian authors attempt to resolve the problem by suggesting that this is appropriate language to describe the activity of peoples at the dawn of creation, bringing the ground under control for the first time. Thus Tim Cooper writes:

> Several thousands of years ago forceful language was appropriate to sanction primitive people to use their power to force nature to meet their needs. Even in the current age the state of the land in the poorest regions makes food difficult to grow and often the land needs treatment before it can be fertile; in these circumstances the strong language of Genesis seems fitting. In the struggle for mere survival, human force against the elements is often necessary. The problems arise when the force used is unwarranted or undisciplined and applied with little foresight.[16]

Commendable as is this attempt to do justice to Scripture, it suffers from several drawbacks. It fails to recognise that many 'primitive' peoples coax fertility from the ground by living in sensitive harmony with it rather than by 'force'; it also fails to recognise that many infertile areas of the earth are those whose soil has been systematically mismanaged.

Nor does it take sufficient account of linguistic considerations. Again, as with the word 'image', etymology and context are important. The word *kabas* probably comes from the Akkadian word *kabasu* ('tread down') or an Arabic equivalent, but it does not necessarily mean this in the Old Testament. Some of its uses certainly have violent overtones; in Esther 7:8 it is used of rape and in Micah 7:19 it is used of God who treads underfoot the sins of his people and hurls their iniquities into the depths of the sea. But elsewhere it refers simply to the act of ruling (eg Num 32:22,29; Josh 18:1; 1 Chron 22:18). The same applies to the second verb *rada*; most of its uses, again, mean simply to rule (eg Lev 25:43,46,53, where 'ruthlessly' is a separate adverb narrowing the meaning of the verb; 1 Kings 4:24; Neh 9:28; Ps 49:14; 110:2; Is 14:2; Jer 5:31; Ezek 29:15). Etymological considerations are thus inconclusive here.

There are two arguments which demonstrate that the concept of dominion described in Genesis 1 refers specifically to a non-violent kind of dominion. Firstly, as we have seen, the context is the goodness of creation. It is impossible to reconcile an aggressive, domineering kind of activity with this; the goodness of creation is something to be protected and maintained. A similar concept of dominion is outlined in the words, 'The Lord God took the man and put him in the Garden of Eden to work it and take care of it' (Gen 2:15).

Here two activities are held in tension—development and conservation. Each on its own can deflect humanity from its true role. Development without conservation can easily lead to exploitation and the kind of aggressive domination that Professor Lynn White and others protested against. Conservation without development is little better. It frustrates the goodness of creation because it prevents us unlocking all its potential to satisfy human need. We often forget that we take for granted in our present lifestyles all that has been uncovered by previous generations: where would we be without cars, planes and trains; without computers, hi-fi and telephones? Whatever we may have to say later about the negative spin-offs of 'progress', few would dream of returning to the lifestyle of two hundred years ago!

Secondly, the arguments about aggressive domination rely upon a concept of kingship which bears little relation to that of early Israel. James Barr has demonstrated that the ideal monarch portrayed in the Old Testament (and elsewhere) is the shepherd king, not only exercising authority over his subjects but also totally responsible for their welfare. This is supremely portrayed in Psalm 72, whose opening words are:

> Endow the king with your justice, O God, the royal son with your righteousness. He will judge your people in righteousness, your afflicted ones with justice. The mountains will bring prosperity to the people, the hills the fruit of righteousness (vv 1,2).

Thus Old Testament scholar Claus Westermann writes:

> As Lord of his realm, the king is responsible not only for the realm; he is the one who bears and mediates blessings for the realm entrusted to him. Man would fail in his royal office of dominion over the earth were he to exploit the world's resources to the detriment of the land, plant life, animals, rivers and seas.[17]

Here the main application to humanity in general is that of responsibility. Few people wear crowns or live in palaces: we are not royal in that sense, but we share with the kings of the Old Testament the burden of responsibility for the care and well-being of creation. Obviously some bear greater responsibility than others. At the cutting edge of the management of the world's resources are scientists and engineers, agriculturalists and technologists, politicians and economists, all of whom wield immense power over the world of creation. The fallacy would lie in assuming that they bear all the responsibility and the rest of the human race none. Responsibility is generally shared through the political and social life of

nations, even though this is more accurately true of some
nations than others. But most governments react to the expectations of their peoples, and their values are, by and large,
those of the societies which reared them. This raises the vital
issue of the value-laden nature of science, and the unrealistic
expectations that we sometimes have of the role of science
(Chapter 6).

The Genesis 1 and 2 texts we have been looking at also raise
another important responsibility issue here—the biblical portrayal of Paradise, or the Garden of Eden. A common idea is
that Genesis 1 portrays a world where men and women never
had to do anything except laze around and sun themselves; a
world in which everything for human well-being somehow
automatically appeared just at the right moment without any
human effort or intervention. This is a world without responsibility, and a totally unreal world at that—more of a night-
mare than a dream. The Old Testament scholar Gerhard von
Rad paints a far more realistic picture of the Garden of Eden
in his comments on Genesis 2:15: 'He is to work it and preserve
it from all damage, a destiny that contrasts decidedly with the
commonly accepted fantastic ideas of "Paradise" ',[18] and he
goes on to remind us that the word 'Paradise' has mythical
overtones and does not even occur in the Old Testament!

The relationship between humanity and creation presented
here is therefore a dynamic one, involving tasks of development and protection from harm. The human task—the task of
dominion—of developing the resources inherent in the created world is therefore a matter central to human life and
purpose. It is also presented as a task which was bound to be
successful, for it flowed from an open relationship between
humans and the Creator God who made them and remained
in fellowship with them. It would be wrong to infer from this,
however, that the task of dominion was to be 'effortless', to go
back to the fallacy of Paradise. It is more accurate to see it as a
task demanding much thought, effort and ingenuity (the 'toil'
and 'sweat' of which Genesis 3 speaks is work of a different
significance, as the next chapter will show). After all, Genesis
2:7 shows how the creation of the man demanded self-giving

on God's part, and the divine task of redemption, later described as 'by my outstretched arm', shows it to be far more than the flick of a celestial magician's fingers (eg Ex 6:6; 15:16; Deut 4:34; 5:15; 7:19; 9:29; 11:2; 26:8).

The intellectual dimension to the task of dominion is particularly clear in the naming of the animals:

> Now the Lord God had formed out of the ground all the beasts of the field and all the birds of the air. He brought them to the man to see what he would name them; and whatever the man called each living creature, that was its name. So the man gave names to all the livestock, the birds of the air and all the beasts of the field (2:19,20a).

On one level this was to do with dominion, because in the ancient Near East name-giving was an exercise in sovereignty. Here, therefore, the man takes authority over the rest of the created order. Yet it was more than this. Giving something a name is an exercise in making sense of what is named. To quote a familiar example: we call Saturday and Sunday the 'weekend', because the word tells us what we mean when we think of those days.

Something similar happens today, for example, when a new scientific phenomenon is discovered, perhaps in the field of astronomy (quasar; black hole) or particle physics (quark; gluon), or when a geologist first describes a new rock type (komatiite; boninite). Thus David Atkinson, commenting on this section of Genesis 2, states: 'Man the scientist is not too far away.'[19] In Douglas Adams' book *The Restaurant at the End of the Universe* a race of singularly useless people colonised the Earth millions of years ago. They called it 'Fintlewoodlewix'; the whole point of the ridiculous name is that it has nothing at all to do with the said-named planet![20]

It would be wrong to think of this as an abstract theological idea. In the previous chapter we suggested that Genesis 1—11 is an ethical prologue to the rest of the Old Testament, so that these chapters have to be understood as a backdrop to the history of the people of Israel in the land which God gave them as a covenant gift. The primary application of these verses is therefore in a specific geographical situation, and a delicate one at that (see Chapter 5). There was, as we shall see, a great deal of scope for getting things wrong, and it is not possible to infer from the biblical text that, even with perfect fellowship between God and humanity, no mistakes would be made. What can be said is that fewer mistakes would happen under these ideal circumstances, and that mistakes would be relatively easily corrected.

When Genesis 2:15 is more specific and describes the human task as to do with prevention of damage, what kind of damage could possibly be in mind? Again, common misapprehensions of Paradise have to be rejected. Many natural processes have potential to cause damage, and all the scientific evidence suggests that earthquakes, volcanic eruptions, storms and avalanches have occurred since the earliest geological times. Geological processes like these had been operating for millions of years before humanity appeared on the scene. Certainly there are numerous references to such events in the Old Testament, and whatever may have changed after the Fall (Chapter 4), the Old Testament never asserts that they can be attributed to this event. Whatever else Genesis 2:15 has in mind here, it is reasonable to infer that its meaning includes the human task of protecting the land from the ravages of natural forces. The picture of life in the Garden is of a task demanding much effort and ingenuity on the part of its first occupants.

So far, much of what has been said would be readily agreed by many people concerned for environmental issues, whether convinced Christians or not. And some Christian treatments of human responsibility for creation effectively end at this point. When asked about why things have gone so badly wrong, the answer might well be that, now we have seen our mistakes, we can proceed to put them right. The emphasis is on education, and on the intrinsic reasonableness of human beings to respond to a situation which needs correcting.

As we shall see in the next chapter, the causes of modern environmental problems go far deeper; the kind of approach just outlined turns out to be hopelessly superficial. Since the possibility of human responsiblity for creation is based on a wholesome relationship with the Creator, the fact that things have gone so badly wrong ought to warn Christians that the root cause lies in a disturbed relationship with the Creator. This is, in fact, the way the problem is explained in Genesis 3, to which we now turn.

REFERENCES

1. Peter Moore, 'The Exploitation of Forests', *Science and Christian Belief*, vol 2 (October 1990): p 137.

2. G.H. Toulmin, *The Antiquity and Duration of the World* (1780) quoted in Keith Thomas, *Man and the Natural World: Changing attitudes in England 1500-1800* (Allen Lane: London, 1983), p 17.

3. Lynn White, 'The Historical Roots of Our Ecologic Crisis', *Science*, vol 155 (1967): pp 1203-1207. See also F.F. Darling, *Wilderness and Plenty* (BBC: London, 1970), p 35; P.R. Ehrlich, *The Population Bomb* (Pan/Ballantine: London, 1972), p 151; A. Toynbee, 'The Religious Background to the Present Environmental Crisis', *International Journal of Environmental Studies*, vol 3 (1972): pp 141-146; M. Nicholson, *The Environmental Revolution* (Pelican: London, 1971), p 305; T. Passmore, *Man's Responsibility for Nature* (Duckworth: London 1974), p 10ff.

4. Keith Thomas, *op cit*, especially Chapter 1.

5. F.D Kidner, *Genesis* (IVP: Leicester, 1967), p 60.

6. David Atkinson, *The Message of Genesis 1—11* (IVP: Leicester, 1990), p 56.

7. Gerhard von Rad, *Genesis* (SCM: London, 1972), p 57.

8. P. Cotterell and M. Turner, *Linguistics and Biblical Interpretation* (SPCK: London, 1989), especially Chapters 4 and 5.

9. G. von Rad, *op cit* p 58.

10. *ibid* p 51.

11. E. Jacob, *Theology of the Old Testament* (Hodder and Stoughton: London, 1967), p 169-172.

12. Claus Westermann, *Creation* (SPCK: London, 1971), p 56.

13. D. Atkinson, *op cit* p 38.

14. D. Bonhoeffer, *Creation and Fall* pp 33,35.

15. E. Lucas, unpublished paper.

16. Tim Cooper, *Green Christianity* (Spire: London 1990), p 51; see also Wesley Granberg Michaelson, *A Worldly Spirituality* (Harper and Row: New York, 1984), p 63.

17. C. Westermann, *op cit* p 15.

18. G. von Rad, *op cit* p 78.

19. D. Atkinson, *ibid* p 69.

20. Douglas Adams, *The Restaurant at the End of the Universe* (Pan Books: London, 1980), p 171.

Chapter Four

HOW ARE THE FALLEN MIGHTY

THE CONSEQUENCES OF THE FALL

As Lord of his realm, the king is responsible not only for
the realm; he is the one who bears and mediates
blessings for the realm entrusted to him. Man would fail
in his royal office of dominion over the earth were he to
exploit the world's resources to the detriment of the
land, plant life, animals, rivers and seas. Only now,
when there is a direct threat to the fertility of the land,
the purity of the air, and to the state of the water, has
there been awakened the long-delayed horror at the
lethal consequences of the sweeping progress of the age
of technology. Only now are some beginning to learn
through the mistakes which show that something has
gone wrong in the process.[1]

THE CREATION of humanity involved both glorious
privilege and solemn responsibility. This is the clear
teaching of Genesis 1 and 2, as we have seen in the
previous two chapters. The privileges are those of being
lovingly and skilfully made in the image of God, and being
able to enjoy the almost limitless goodness of all that the
Creator had made; the only limitation lies in our capacity to
comprehend the privilege! The responsibility is closely linked
to it—being charged with the care of creation, as its stewards

and as representatives on earth of the Creator himself. Nor is this a matter of mere caretaking. It was to be demanding and enthralling, because it involved not just conservation but a gradual unlocking of the awesome potential of creation through what we now think of as science and technology.

But if Genesis 1 and 2 are painted in dazzling white, the following chapters are in the deepest black. From the heights of privilege and responsibility man falls into a pit of failure and alienation from which he cannot escape on his own (even if he wanted to). Through falling for the attractive non-future the serpent offers her, first Eve and then Adam find alienation to be the tragic and inescapable reality which flows from the assertion of their independence and automomy.

The biblical concept of sin includes a wide variety of terms and concepts. That of disobedience is as important as any, and its effects are universal (cf Rom 5:12–21). Rowland Moss points out that the appalling breadth of the consequences of the human fall have to be seen against the backcloth of human nature:

> Man's disobedience is thus not simply the breaking of a
> divinely given rule—a forensic act—but even more
> fundamentally a denial of his true creaturely nature, a
> contradiction of the very essence of the created order. It
> is disobedience, it is rebellion, but it is also refusal to
> accept the true constituted nature of the universe of
> which man is a part.[2]

Thus in the New Testament Paul describes human rebellion in terms which have been seen by biblical scholars as deriving directly from the language and concepts of Genesis 3:

> The wrath of God is being revealed from heaven against all
> the godlessness and wickedness of men who suppress the
> truth by their wickedness, since what may be known about
> God is plain to them because God has made it plain to
> them...although they knew God, they neither glorified him
> as God nor gave thanks to him, but their thinking became

futile and their foolish hearts were darkened. Although they claimed to be wise, they became fools and exchanged the glory of the immortal God for images made to look like mortal man and birds and animals and reptiles...since they did not think it worth while to retain the knowledge of God, he gave them over to a depraved mind...(Rom 1:18ff).

The idea of the Fall of man has been of far-reaching significance in Christian interpretation, as the reference to Paul suggests. But Old Testament scholar Claus Westermann makes a very different claim. He states that the Fall is 'nowhere cited or presumed in the Old Testament; its significance is limited to the primeval events'.[3]

The charge is the same as that often cited against Genesis 1: that is, there are few if any direct references to these verses in the rest of the Old Testament. We have already had cause to disagree with this, because of the function of Genesis 1—11 as a prologue to Israel's history in the promised land. The same is true of Genesis 3 because it is part of that prologue. It is also true because, as we shall see in this chapter, the consequences of the Fall loom large in the tragic side of the nation's history, culminating in almost total failure. But before that, we must return to the Genesis 3 narrative.

The alienation the man and woman come to experience in the Garden operates on every level, because they were meant to experience positive relationships on those same levels through being made in the image of God-in-Trinity. (This brings us to the term depravity, which means not that humanity cannot possibly do anything good—a common assumption but demonstrably untrue—but rather that sin affects every level of his being). Alienation from God is seen in the way the man and woman hide from God (vv 8–10), and in Adam's feeble attempts to excuse his behaviour, while blaming God at the same time: 'The woman you put here with me—she gave me some fruit from the tree and I ate it' (v 12). Cain will later express despair at being hidden from God's presence (4:12), and that sentence turns out to be universal (Prov 15:29; Isa

59:1,2; Hab 1:14; cf Jn 9:31; Rom 5:10; Eph 2:12; 4:18; Col 1:21, etc).

The shame that Adam and Eve experience at finding themselves naked and needing to hide from the Lord (vv 7–11) is a way of describing the internal psychological alienation in which sin's effect is to disrupt the human personality (cf Rom 7:15–20). Inter-personal alienation erupts as Adam blames Eve (as well as God) for his fall into disobedience (3:12), as God sentences them to a relationship of domination and subservience (3:16b) and as Cain murders his brother out of jealousy (4:4–8). Further signs of internal alienation are shown in the refusal of each man to accept responsibility for his own actions (3:12; 4:9). All this has been well described many times before.

What is important for the subject of this book, but often less well explored, is the alienation which also arises between humanity and the world of nature. If man's relationships with God, with other human beings, and within himself, are split asunder, it is inevitable that creation is also affected. The divine image in man and the care of creation are inextricably bound up together. How could the one be corrupted and the other remain unaffected?

The results of human sin upon the world of nature are brilliantly woven into the Genesis 3 narrative. In the lead-up to the first act of rebellion, the created order features in two important ways: first there is the role of the serpent, and secondly there is the moral test itself which the serpent challenges.

The Role of The Serpent

What exactly is the significance of the serpent, who appears as the agent of temptation in 3:1? Is this snake the devil in disguise? Later biblical imagery would certainly suggest so (Rev 12:1; 20:2); the curse of Genesis 3:15 is consistent with this, and the satanic ministry of deception (Jn 8:44; 2 Cor 11:14f) is the serpent's speciality (thus compare the words of

3:1 with 2:16f). However valid this may be, the Genesis 3 narrative places no weight on this particular interpretation.

Instead, the emphasis is on the serpent as a creature (that is, something created). In the context of the creation narrative itself, this is stressed in three ways: first, the fact that the creature has a name means that it was one of the creatures given a name by Adam in 2:19. Secondly, it is described as 'more crafty than any of the wild animals that the Lord God had made' (3:1) and thirdly, the curse pronounced on the serpent in v 15 is one which reflects its essential nature as a creature, a curse reiterated later by Isaiah:

> The wolf and the lamb will feed together, and the lion will eat straw like the ox, but dust will be the serpent's food (Is 65:25).

The Moral Test

God is often accused of being a spoilsport, surrounding human life with all sorts of restrictions, presumably for his own amusement. Genesis 2 and 3 present a different view. There is only one restriction; they are not allowed to eat from the tree of the knowledge of good and evil (2:17). This then becomes a moral test, an invitation to free and trusting obedience. It is significant that this test is to do with their relation to the created order (2:17; 3:6). Obedience to God is thus portrayed not as irksome and restrictive (as the serpent portrays it, of course) but as joyful and expansive. Nevertheless, obedience to God, and the responsible care of the good creation which is part of it, remains a decision which is to be freely made and which can therefore be rejected.

The attractiveness of the alternative future presented by the serpent, described in terms of eating from a forbidden tree, lies in what the woman and then the man see as freedom from responsibility toward God. 'To be like God, knowing good from evil' (3:5) is not a glorious hope but a state of rebellion, because it implies being independent of God and no longer answerable to him:

> The way of rebellion puts immediate pleasure in front of possible consequences, and sets our own perception of what is good for us against what God has told us about ourselves and his world. Sin is the name given to that separation from God which begins with the abandonment of trust in God's goodness and God's love.[4]

This is why the prospect of the forbidden tree becomes so attractive; it offers, in the pithy phrases of Genesis 3:6, the possibility of material ('good for food'), aesthetic ('pleasing to the eye') and intellectual ('to be desired to make one wise') enrichment. These were always available, but now the man and woman seek them by crossing boundaries lovingly erected by the Creator, rather than in dependence upon him.

THE CURSE ON THE CREATED ORDER

> Cursed is the ground because of you; through painful toil you will eat of it all the days of your life. It will produce thorns and thistles for you, and you will eat the plants of the field. By the sweat of your brow you will eat your food until you return to the ground, since from it you were taken; for dust you are, and to dust you will return (vv 17b–19).

In biblical studies these words have often received less attention than they require. Genesis 1 and 2 describe human life in terms of a rich web of relationships, involving supremely the personal Creator in whose image all are made, and deriving from that, with other people and with the whole created order. If the Fall leads to alienation from God, it leads inexorably to alienation in all other relationships. Human life cannot be properly understood without reference to the earth on which we live. Therefore these words of curse are taken as descriptive rather than prescriptive: that is, they describe the inevitable effect of human sin, rather than God making a decision to institute a new order of things.

The words of Genesis 3:17b–19 are sombre indeed, and, as we shall see later, they show how human sin is particularly clearly displayed for all to see. Sin comes from within (Mk 7:14–23) so that its source is often hidden, especially from those who do not want to see it, but its effects upon the world of creation can hardly be avoided; environmental degradation is one of the major issues facing the world at the end of the twentieth century. So Gerhard von Rad writes:

> The curse...goes more deeply to the lowest foundation of all human existence...the earth. And here too is a cleft, a mutual recalcitrance that now breaks into creation as a profound disorder: man was taken from the earth and so was directed to it; she was the material basis of his existence; a solidarity of creation existed between man and the ground. But a break occurred in this affectionate relationship, an alienation that expresses itself in a silent, dogged struggle between man and the soil. Now it is as though a spell lay on the earth which makes her deny man the easy product of subsistence.[5]

This theme reappears elsewhere in Genesis 1—11. It is often assumed that God's words to Cain after the murder of Abel ('Your brother's blood cries out to me from the ground...When you work the ground it will no longer yield its crops for you. You will be a restless wanderer on the earth' 4:10,12) are purely symbolic, but this may not be so. Given the new state of alienation between people and their land, there may be a greater degree of literalism intended here than has been assumed.

The tragic shift in the relationship between humanity and nature is also expressed in God's first words to Noah after the flood had abated. These words echo those of Genesis 1, but it is the new phrases which are particularly important here:

> Then God blessed Noah and his sons, saying to them, 'Be fruitful and increase in number and fill the earth. The fear

of you and the dread of you will fall upon all the beasts of the earth and all the birds of the air, upon every creature that moves along the ground, and upon all the fish of the sea; they are given into your hands' (Gen 9:1f).

The key words, which contrast Genesis 1 with Genesis 9 are 'fear...dread... delivered'. This is alienation as seen from the non-human side of creation. Any view of Genesis 9 which does not take this into account is missing the point of the deliberate contrast with the commands of Genesis 1, as for example in the following words:

> The biblical view of nature is unashamedly man-centred, for God told Noah that 'everything that lives and moves will be food for you. Just as I gave you the green plants, I now give you everything'. It is acceptable, therefore, that we should seek uses and application in the advancement of human welfare for all living creatures.[6]

The sombre estimate of creation's fear of the human race that the Bible portrays supports the idea that it is itself somehow 'fallen'.[7] From this it is possible to argue that violent methods of control are legitimated, but it is these which have contributed towards modern environmental problems.

Jesuit theologian Robert Faricy has taken this as a starting point for a kind of Protestant theology which, he believes, sanctions insensitive environmental practices.[8] But this is to confuse two different theological concepts: firstly, what is—our dominion over nature is such as to instill fear into it; and secondly, what is legitimate—we are justified in acting in this way. To argue in this way is parallel to taking Jesus' words 'You will always have the poor with you' as justifying the existence and perpetuation of poverty. Genesis 9 is a divine statement about human inability to control the environment properly, even though the responsibility of dominion has not been removed; it does not suggest that violence is to be encouraged.

The Genesis 3 text describes the effects of the fall upon the earth in two slightly different, though closely related ways. Firstly, there will be difficulties in food production ('through painful toil you will eat of it all the days of your life... by the sweat of your brow you will eat your food'). For the modern reader, possibly scanning these words after a visit to a well-stocked supermarket, such an idea may seem strange. But because of intractable failures to distribute food stocks and share wealth and agricultural expertise properly, millions of people in the world are malnourished; nor is the state of agriculture as rosy as the supermarket seems to suggest. Rowland Moss writes:

> The earth yields its fruit only reluctantly and unreliably because of the disturbed relationship of man to nature. The history of agricultural research and development is one of problems being solved, and in their solution, new problems being created. New solutions produce new problems and so on. It is true that crop yields have generally increased as agricultural technology has developed, but not in phase with the demands made by a growing population and a more sophisticated society and only at a rapidly accelerating cost in energy inputs. But each development has posed new problems. This is a situation which seems to be paralleled in the history of medicine, and in particular at the present time in the 'antibiotics race' whereby new drugs have continually to be developed in order to keep one step ahead of the resistance developed by the organisms they are designed to control.[9]

Secondly, the balance of nature is profoundly disturbed ('it will produce thorns and thistles for you'). This statement has two possible meanings. One is that the man and woman did something specifically wrong that resulted in the growth of thorns and thistles, but a more likely interpretation is that, as a result of the Fall, something goes seriously wrong with the order of things, and that shows itself in ecological misfortunes.

In this case the thorns and thistles are not newly created at this point, but take on a new significance instead (Prov 24:31; Is 34:13; Hos 10:8).

Here is the futility which inevitably arises when people attempt to live autonomously, as if the Fall were a good idea. The Wisdom literature of the Old Testament provides ample commentary on this way of life. Fallen humanity sees wisdom as 'know-how', the knowledge which leads to power, to manipulation. True wisdom is totally different; it is based on 'the fear of the Lord' (Prov 1:7 etc) and is therefore to do with seeing things whole, recognising authority, dependence and limits. This wisdom, later to be seen personified in the person of Christ, was present at the creation of the universe (Prov 8:22–31). On the other hand, Ecclesiastes is a devastating commentary on the futility that arises from human attempts to continue asserting independence from God. All this is pointedly restated in the New Testament, notably by Paul (Rom 1:18–32; 5:10; Eph 4:17f; Col 1:21).

Thus the Fall of humanity is seen not just in personal terms; it is an event whose repercussions are truly cosmic. Further consequences of the Fall follow in rapid succession in the succeeding chapters of Genesis : there is the murder of Abel by Cain (4:8), the arrogance of Lamech (4:23,24), the coming together of the sons of God and the daughters of men (6:1–4), the continually evil thoughts of mankind (6:5), general corruption and violence (6:5,6,11,12), the sin against the nakedness of Noah by his son Ham (9:20–27) and the arrogance and fear that lead to the building of the tower of Babel (11:1–9).

THE GRACE OF GOD HAS
THE FINAL WORD

To leave the story of the Fall at this point, with alienation and corruption as the last words, would lead to a pessimism which is actually unwarranted, even when we might want to argue that we now live under a covenant of grace. That same grace pervades even the story of the Fall and the universal violence which leads to the Flood.

Thus, the serpent is told in Genesis 3:15, 'he will crush your head, and you will strike his heel', often taken as a 'proto-evangelical' statement of the ultimate victory over sin and death which Christ would one day win on the cross (Col 2:15). Then there are other hints—statements of an almost throwa-way nature that beg for further explanation: the expulsion from the Garden took place only after God had provided the man and woman with clothing (3:21–3); even the act of expul-sion can be seen as a gracious act of protection:

> The perplexing unfinished sentence in 3:22 conveys the sense that God is not only banishing man from the Garden as a judgement, but also for his own good. Is it a way of saying that God does not want man to eat of the tree of eternity in his present broken state—indeed that there are fearful and eternal consequences, known to God, unknown to us, should he do so?[10]

Similarly, Cain's punishment for the murder of Abel was tempered by a divine mark to ensure that he be protected from reciprocated violence (4:15). Chapter 9 outlines the first of the divine merciful covenants. Significantly, it is given not only to Noah and his descendants but also the whole of creation:

> Then God said to Noah and to his sons with him: 'I now establish my covenant with you and with your descendants after you and with every living creature that was with you...every living creature on earth. I establish my cov-enant with you: Never again will all life be cut off by the waters of a flood; never again will there be a flood to destroy the earth.' And God said, 'This is the sign of the covenant I am making between me and you and every living creature that is with you, a covenant for all generations to come: I have set my rainbow in the clouds, and it will be the sign of the covenant between me and the earth. Whenever I bring clouds over the earth and the rainbow appears in the

clouds, I will remember my covenant between me and you
and all living creatures of every kind. Never again will the
waters become a flood to destroy all life. Whenever the
rainbow appears in the clouds, I will see it and remember
the everlasting covenant between God and all living creatures of every kind on the earth' (vv 8–16).

The form in which the covenant is expressed underlines the
expression of God's grace which we have already noted. Later
Old Testament covenants (like the suzerainty treaties of the
second millenium whose structure they seem to follow) were to
demand a response from the inferior member of the agree-
ment. The covenant of Genesis 9, however, is unilateral. God
takes the initiative, but no response is required here. This
covenant is simply a statement of what the Creator will do to
preserve his good creation from a repeat of the Flood. Thus in
v 12 the rainbow is a sign, like the Sabbath of Exodus 31:13–
16, but this time to remind God of the covenant that he has
instigated. This work of protection may also reflect God's
determination to take back to himself a task he had entrusted
to humanity but who are now, on the wrong side of the Fall,
unable to fulfil it.

Because Genesis 1—11 is an 'ethical prologue' to the rest of
the Old Testament, the covenant of Genesis 9 gives form and
purpose to Israel's entry into the Promised Land. Although
the grim events of Genesis 3—11 leave no room for complacency, the words of this covenant reassure Israel that their
God can be relied upon when he promises a 'land flowing with
milk and honey' (Exod 3:6), and when they find that tending
this land with its delicate ecosystems demands obedience, skill
and effort. Other nations found reassurance in religious rituals
which Israel was forbidden; we shall see in the next chapter
how this becomes an important factor in the clash with
Canaanite idolatry. Thus one Old Testament scholar writes:

> Underlying the history of nature and the history of
> mankind is an unconditional...divine Yes to all life,
> that cannot be shattered either by any catastrophe in

the course of this history—and...by the mistakes, corruption or rebellion of man. God's promise remains rock certain as long as the earth exists.[11]

IS SIN TO BLAME?

Land and resources have become the greatest single cause of strife and warfare between men. Some resources are hoarded by a few and denied to others. Some are squandered, polluted or abused. Possession of resources, instead of being used as an opportunity for mutual sharing, as of an unmerited gift, has become a matter of conquest and seizure, a tool of oppression, greed and power.[12]

Having surveyed the implications of the Fall for humanity's relationship with creation, it is time to pause and consider the application of this event to modern issues. Recent years have seen the Chernobyl nuclear 'accident', worries over the Greenhouse Effect, huge oil slicks in the sea during the Gulf War and after oil tanker disasters, more links uncovered by medical researchers between pollution and illness. So the question arises: is 'sin' to blame?

This explanation of environmental problems sounds simplistic. First, it sounds deceptively simple when the problems are complex; secondly, it is difficult to imagine that my little misdemeanours could possibly have any bearing on such huge questions; thirdly, it seems to bring together two mutually exclusive worlds—those of faith and science. So—could 'sin' possibly be to blame? According to Genesis 3 and the rest of the Scriptures (as we shall see), 'sin' is indeed to blame, but the statement must be carefully qualified in order to meet all three of these objections.

On one level, the explanation is certainly simple, but perhaps misleadingly so. The problem is that the word 'sin' is often misunderstood. It comes to refer to little acts of naughtiness which can be easily rationalised with not a great deal of effort. But in the Bible, 'sin' is a wide concept which covers a range of scriptural terms which between them uncover a deep-seated and fatal condition affecting every level of human existence. It is a kind of theological shorthand.

Our deeds are the outworking of our thoughts and wills, and sinful acts, to which all of us are prone (Rom 3:10–26), simply reflect corruption on a fundamental level (Mk 7:6–23). Genesis 3 shows how all these ways of thinking about sin arise from a sundering of all the relationships on which humanity has to depend for wholesome living—relationships with the Creator, with each other, with the created world, and with our own selves.

Because 'sin' is theological shorthand, the statement 'sin is to blame' only appears to be simple. In fact, it is a profound and many-sided statement. The reality of this is seen when we attempt to look for answers either to the problem of sin or that of making the environment clean and safe. Ask a church discussion group how to solve the Greenhouse Effect, or a local pollution problem, for example, and the solutions soon turn out to be complex and difficult, if not downright intractable!

But how could my little misdemeanours possibly have anything to do with a polluted and corrupted world? In part, we have already answered this question by insisting on a deeper and more complex understanding of sin. But the question also betrays an individualistic understanding of sin that ignores our solidarity with the first man, Adam. This is the point of Paul's statement in Romans 5:12, 'Therefore, just as sin entered the world through one man, and death through sin, and in this way death came to all men, because all sinned...'.

Our connection with the sin of the first man is described in the expression 'original sin' which is indebted to the final phrase of Romans 5:12. More is often read into this expression than its biblical basis warrants. Indeed, it is not a biblical expression, and probably originated with St Augustine in the fifth century. The problems arise when we try to explain how sin was transmitted from Adam to succeeding generations: the Bible does not speculate on this, putting the emphasis rather on the observable universality of sin (a major theme in

Romans 1—3). Our relationship to Adam is one of solidarity, and this is the most important point for the present discussion.

Each of us is a sinful member of a universally sinful human race. Therefore it is pointless speculating on what are the precise effects on the world of creation of my individual sinfulness, as if they could be separated from those of everyone else. With each new day, every living person contributes in some way—direct or indirect—to abuse of the environment. More than this, we also share in the consequences of the abuses perpetrated, wilfully or in ignorance, by all previous generations.

Consider the Greenhouse Effect, for example. Its sudden claim to public attention and political agendas can mislead us into thinking that something new has burst upon the world. Yet the Greenhouse Effect, in which carbon dioxide is vented into the atmosphere through the burning of fossil fuels, is as old as the art of chopping down trees and gathering brushwood for lighting fires. In 1957 Roger Revelle and Hans Suess of the Scripps Institute of Oceanography warned that humanity is performing a 'great geophysical experiment' on our own planet through increasing carbon dioxide emissions into the atmosphere.[13] So it appears that we slept through thirty years of the Greenhouse Effect before reluctantly waking up.

But the Greenhouse Effect was known long before 1957. It started in earnest with the birth of the Industrial Revolution, and was first described scientifically 150 years ago. Admittedly, carbon dioxide emissions were quite small in the nineteenth century, and have increased rapidly since then, due to a complex interplay of factors such as increasing world population, increasing per capita energy consumption and deforestation (itself due to various different factors such as the demand for wood for paper, furniture and firewood, land clearing schemes for agricultural projects and geological exploration). The present scale of carbon dioxide emissions into the atmosphere is such that substantial global warming is now a distinct possibility. If this is all true, then even if we could somehow stop all carbon dioxide emissions overnight, global warming would continue for decades to come.

A word of warning is in order here, however. News media often talk about global warming as if it were a well-established fact. This is far from accurate. There is a substantial body of world scientific opinion which believes that global warming has started already, but equally reputable scientists disagree. Part of the problem is that the world's atmospheric system, and its interaction with land and sea, is incredibly complicated, and only partly understood. Hence the disagreement over the possible consequences. This is an important issue to which we shall return in Chapter 11.

But a worst-possible scenario might look something like this: further scientific research in the next few years reveals that, because of the rapid pumping of carbon dioxide and other gases into the atmosphere, together with new information about interactions between land, sea and biosphere, air temperatures are bound to rise rapidly. Sadly, the predictions turn out to be all too true. Sea levels continue to rise for the next fifty years, and desperate measures such as ruthless restrictions on the use of private transport are of no avail. Rich nations are forced to spend vast amounts of money on extensive new coastal defences in places such as California, the Gulf of Mexico, East Anglia in England, and the west coast of Holland. A measure of success is achieved, but at the cost of a huge transfer of financial resources from health, industry and education. Poorer countries, such as Bangladesh, are less fortunate. A combination of rising sea levels, storms and an exceptionally high spring tide, together with massive flood waters in the Ganges River, permanently inundate the whole coastal plain, creating 50 million refugees overnight.

The other major consequence is a profound change in the world's climatic systems. Failure of rainfall turns fertile tracts of land into desert, such as the mid-western states of the USA, and parts of Central Africa. Other fertile areas receive far less sun due to increasing cloud cover; customary crops fail. The financial consequences to the world community, and the enforced redistribution of wealth, create strains which cannot be accommodated by structures embedded in self-interest and a now-obsolete pecking order. Thirty years of bloody international conflict ensue, with some countries waging nuclear, chemical and biological war on neighbours less well endowed militarily than themselves. When the smoke dies away, the social, economic and environmental devastation are so great that it takes the world another hundred years to recover its previous level of prosperity.

Is this all too gloomy? Probably, but not inevitably, so. The scenario has been painted to show how deeply embedded sin is within the fabric of the world, not only in human life and in the structures we create, but also within the physical world whose sharing in our fallen state is described in Genesis 3 as a curse. Because sin is not just personal and 'now', but also corporate and its consequences manifested in succeeding generations, undoing its effects in the world of creation is an immensely difficult and expensive business.

Another important feature of the environmental consequences of our human fallen state is that others have to suffer the consequences of our own actions. The Greenhouse Effect, again, reveals this clearly. The Western world must claim a large share of the responsibility for global warming; our per capita energy consumption, linked to our affluence, is far higher than elsewhere, and much of this energy is generated by combustion of fossil fuels. In 1984, for example, per capita energy consumption was 280 times greater in the USA than in Benin and several other African nations. The price to be paid for this wealth is widespread poverty elsewhere in the world. Poverty leads to the highly inefficient use of energy, which itself contributes to a large-scale shortage of firewood. People—mainly women—may have to travel miles to gather sufficient wood in countries such as Ethiopia and Tanzania. The clearing of tropical rain forests is, again, fuelled by economic forces which have as much to do with Western affluence as with the rain forest nations themselves.

Yet the effects of global warming know no boundaries at all. The countries to be worst affected will be those which are relatively low-lying, irrespective of their location worldwide; those which can least find the resources to defend their coastlines will be the poorest—Bangladesh could prove to be a case in point.

The same is true of local pollution sources. Here the prime example is the 'accident' (a theme to which we shall return in a later chapter) on 26th April 1986 at the Chernobyl power station in the Ukraine. The damage in the immediate vicinity was severe. Thirty-one people, mainly firefighters, died, and the nearby town of Pripyat was evacuated and will probably remain abandoned for many years. Other effects were far more widespread. The radioactive fallout, and the contamination of soil and animals, was distributed over much of Northern Asia and Western Europe. Some countries were forced to introduce restrictions on the movement of agricultural livestock which have not yet been lifted.

Arguably the most devastating pointer to the global scale of environmental degradation effects, wherever their sources, is the number of 'environmental refugees', now estimated to be 120 million. These are people driven from their homelands by a whole range of environmental problems including drought, flood, storm, pollution and poverty. Some move to land which is increasingly difficult to work—hillsides whose soil is liable to suffer severe slope erosion, and land which is overgrazed by increasing numbers of domestic livestock, so that the environmental damage from which they are trying to escape is simply perpetuated. Many end up in refugee camps. Others join the flood of people moving into the world's cities, overloading the city services, and compounding health problems due to overcrowding and the pollution effects of large population centres with inadequate services.

THE NEED FOR VIGILANCE

It has sometimes been said that one of the most important insights that Christianity can contribute to the environmental debate is its understanding of sin. This is certainly consistent with the Genesis 3 narrative, and the way it is used throughout the rest of the Bible.

Should our view of the gravity of sin drive us to blow the whistle on any new technological enterprise that might have environmental side-effects? At first it might seem that the answer should be 'yes', but this is not necessarily the case. We are talking not about an academic proposition to be argued from the comfort of an armchair, but about situations that affect the well-being of people and communities.

Take as an example the situation of a rural community on the shore of a large lake, where there is a high level of poverty and unemployment, apart from the benefits of a seasonal tourist trade. A mining company announces that the area contains large supplies of coal not far below the ground surface, and that it proposes to dig that coal out. How should we react? One obvious reaction would be to say 'never!' The environmental hazards are obvious: a constant stream of heavy lorries on narrow roads, pollution of land and water when the excavation work gets under way, an influx of non-local labour and an unwelcome change in the nature of the local community, a loss of the scenic beauty that used to bring the tourists.

On the other hand, the mining company brings employment and prosperity that used to be beyond the reach of most of that community. It is usually the economic arguments that win the day, and it is not pleasant to live in a community bitterly divided over such an issue. In any case, at least some local Christians might want to argue that the goodness of creation is about its abundant resources, including fuel. Unless there are special factors involved that make it clear to everyone that the mining operation should not be allowed, it is likely to go ahead eventually.

It is here that the Christian has something vital and distinctive to say. A realistic view of sin means that vigilance has to be a key word. Even if the mining operation is surrounded by stringent environmental safeguards enforceable under the law of the land, things can (and probably will) go wrong somewhere. There may be a whole variety of reasons: a desire to maximise profits, complacency, a lack of respect for the local environment, carelessness, even downright malice. All this may be coupled with lack of government inspectors to enforce the environmental safeguards.

Among the least complacent members of that local community must be its Christians, whether or not they all originally welcomed the mining company into the area. Because things can go wrong, they probably will do so, eventually. But the vigilance that comes from a sombre assessment of sin could one day save that community from harm. So let the chapter conclude with the warning words of Hugh Montefiore:

> It is commmonly said that man cannot control the industrial juggernaut that he has created, and we have daily evidences of how powerful forces that were once under human control seem now to have acquired a momentum of their own and to be dragging us along whether we like it or not. How could it be otherwise, if man no longer has any clear belief about who he is or any vision of the direction in which he wants society to develop? Unfortunately man will use his powerful new weapons in industry and agriculture, to do violence to the world of nature, if he does not know what his relationship to that natural world should be.[14]

REFERENCES

1. Claus Westermann, *Creation* (SPCK: London, 1971), p 15.

2. Rowland Moss, 'The Ethical Underpinnings of Man's Management of Nature', *Faith and Thought*, vol 111 no 1 (1985): pp 23-56.

3. Claus Westermann, *op cit* p 89.

4. David Atkinson, *The Message of Genesis 1—11* (IVP: Leicester, 1990), pp 86-87.

5. Gerhard von Rad, *Genesis 1—11* (SCM: London, 1972), p 94.

6. Peter Moore, 'The Exploitation of Forests', *Science and Christian Belief*, vol 2 (October 1990): p 137.

7. Keith Innes, *Caring for the Earth: The Environment, Christians and the Church* (Grove Books: Nottingham, 1987), p 15; A.R. Peacocke, *Creation and the World of Science* (Clarendon Press: Oxford, 1979), p 286f.

8. Robert J. Faricy, 'The Person-Nature Split: Ecology, Women and Human Life', *Irish Theological Quarterly*, vol 53 (1988): pp 203-218.

9. Claus Westermann, *op cit* p 89.

10. David Atkinson, *op cit* p 98.

11. Claus Westermann, *Genesis 1—11* (Neukirchener Verlag, 1974), pp 633-4.

12. Christopher J.H. Wright, *Living as the People of God* (IVP: Leicester, 1983), p 71.

13. Roger Revelle and Hans E. Suess, 'Carbon dioxide between the atmosphere and ocean and the question of an increase in atmospheric CO_2 during past decades', *Tellus*, vol 9 (1957): pp 18-27.

14. Hugh Montefiore, *Man and Nature*, (Collins: London, 1975), pp 72-73.

Chapter Five

LAND OF MILK
AND HONEY

T HE OLD TESTAMENT is often wrongly thought of as
describing a two-way relationship between God and
his people, in which the spiritual occupies centre stage
to the complete exclusion of the physical. But the function of
Genesis 1—11 which we have already considered shows that a
proper understanding of the history of God's people rests upon
seeing a three-way relationship. The three corners of the tri-
angle are the Creator, his people, and the land he gave them as
a covenant gift.

So it is no surprise to find that much of the Old Testament
is concerned with relationship with the land: 'true humanity
does not consist in a balanced psyche or a right relationship
with God apart from the concrete context of man's relationship to, responsibility for and offering of the land God has
given him.'[1] This is vital to an understanding of some of the
divinely-given law passages, as well as other parts of the
historical books and the prophets.

The land which God gave the people of Israel was not a
barren desert. It was a very fertile area:

> For the Lord your God is bringing you into a good land, a
> land of brooks and water, of fountains and springs, flowing
> forth in valleys and hills, a land of wheat and barley, of
> vines and fig trees and pomegranates, a land of olive trees
> and honey, a land in which you will eat bread without

95

scarcity, in which you will lack nothing... (Deut 8:7–9; cf Exod 3:8 etc).

Even the faithless spies, desperately seeking an excuse not to cross swords with its terrifying inhabitants, could not bring themselves to dispute that it was a marvellously fruitful land (Num 13:17–33; Deut 1:23–25). This meant that when the people settled, and drove out their enemies, they could look forward to peace and prosperity. But even these bring temptation in their wake—the temptation to congratulate themselves on their own success and forget that the land did not, after all, belong to them unconditionally (Deut 6:10–13; 8:11–20).

THE EARTH BELONGS TO THE LORD

The Old Testament repeatedly asserts that the earth belongs to the Lord. This is a recurring theme in Israel's worship:

> The earth is the Lord's, and everything in it, the world and all who live in it; for He founded it upon the seas and established it upon the waters (Ps 24:1f; cf 50:12; 89:11; Exod 15:13,17; 19.5; Deut 32:43; 1 Chron 29:14).

But this was more than theology to be turned into songs of praise. One of the major themes of the prophets was the way that the people failed to practise in their lives the great truths that they sang about so enthusiastically. So the words of Psalm 24 also contained a fundamental principle about how the people of Israel were to manage the Promised Land of the covenant. This is seen supremely in Leviticus 25, where the principles of Sabbath and Jubilee are detailed: 'The land must not be sold permanently, because the land is mine and you are but aliens and my tenants' (v 23). The Sabbath and Jubilee principles will be considered more fully later in the chapter.

Leviticus 25, and many of the other references already mentioned, make it clear that Israel's possession of the land was a tenancy, based not on the people's own achievements—

they were 'aliens'—but on the grace of the God who, as Creator and Redeemer, determined to give them the land of Canaan as a gift as he had promised to the patriarchs.

> It is not because of your righteousness or your integrity that you are going in to take possession of their land; but on account of the wickedness of these nations, the Lord your God will drive them out before you, to accomplish what he swore to your fathers... (Deut 9:5; cf 10:14–22; 26:5–10).

This reference to the 'wickedness of the nations' is important, and we must later return to Israel's continued fascination with Canaanite idolatry and radically different view of the land (Chapter 6). Other references to the occupation of the land show that it is an outworking of God's love for his people:

> The Lord did not set his affection on you and choose you because you were more numerous than other peoples, for you were the fewest of all peoples. But it was because the Lord loved you and kept the oath he swore to your forefathers... (Deut 7:7,8).

All this should have been an antidote to the pride that comes with prosperity. The land, seen as a gift, could have been a permanent testimony to the grace of God, and a reminder to the people of how much they depended upon him for their well-being. It was to be a different story, however; more like that of the character in a George Bernard Shaw play, described as a 'self-made man who worships his creator.'

God Watches Over It

It is because God made the land of Canaan (and everything else, of course) that he continued to watch over it and care for it, thus guaranteeing its fruitfulness:

> It is a land the Lord your God cares for; for the eyes of the Lord your God are continually on it from the beginning of

> the year to its end. So if you faithfully obey the commands I am giving you today...then I will send rain on your land in its season, both autumn and spring rains, so that you may gather in your grain, new wine and oil. I will provide grass in the fields for your cattle, and you will eat and be satisfied (Deut 11:12–15).

This solved the problem of how food supplies were to be ensured during the Sabbath rest:

> You may ask, 'What will we eat in the seventh year if we do not plant or harvest our crops?' I will send you such a blessing in the sixth year that the land will yield enough for three years. While you plant in the eighth year, you will eat from the old crop and will continue to eat from it until the harvest of the ninth year comes in (Lev 25:20–22).

The language of statements such as Deuteronomy 11:12 (and of Genesis 9:8–17) recalls that of Genesis 2:15, when the Lord God put the man in the Garden to till it and take care of it, except that now it is the Creator who does the caring. Possibly the change is due to the fact that, because of the Fall, humanity was no longer able to perform this task, so God took it back to himself.

This is only one half of the picture. It does not do justice to the many texts which commanded the Israelites to a responsible stewardship. The comparison between Genesis 2:15 and Deuteronomy 11:12 is best explained as showing how human stewardship is exercised within the context of God's continued care for what is, after all, his own. A consideration of the geography of Canaan shows how important this consideration was. Other races in the Ancient Near East lived in fertile plains watered by wide, deep rivers, where irrigation was practised. Such an option was not open in Canaan, with its hilly terrain, seasonal rain, long dry periods and deep valleys. The 'brooks' of Deuteronomy 8:7 translate the Hebrew word *nahal* which refers to deep valleys gouged out by torrents in the rainy season but which are dry in the summer.[2]

Israel was not in a position to use sophisticated human technology such as irrigation. The nation was therefore continually forced back to reliance on the direct care of the Creator for the continued fruitfulness of their new land; because nothing could be taken for granted, care of the land was seen within the context of faith, as so many Old Testament texts make clear. The tragic side to this geographical context was that Israel fell into the temptation to follow other 'gods' who, they felt, could more easily produce the results they wanted (Chapter 6).

Studies of the geography of Canaan, combined with the biblical texts, show what a delicate environment it was, and how easily upset. Such hilly country was always prone to soil erosion, which is graphically portrayed in the book of Job:

> But the mountain falls and crumbles away, and the rock is removed from its place; the waters wear against the stones; the torrents wash away the soil of the earth; so thou destroyest the hope of man (Job 14:18f).

Soil erosion is always a particular danger where soil management is less than careful. Much of the land of Canaan was wooded, and burning was necessary to clear the land for terracing, planting and grazing. Assuming that prophetic oracles may use picture language from everyday life, there are various references in the Old Testament to this practice of 'slash-and-burn':

> Surely wickedness burns like a fire; it consumes briars and thorns, it sets the forest thickets ablaze, so that it rolls upward in a column of smoke (Is 9:18; cf 10:17–19; 33:12).

Isaiah 10:17–19 seems to depict a situation where forest burning was proceeding too fast:

> The Light of Israel will become a fire, their Holy One a flame; in a single day it will burn and consume his thorns and his briars. The splendour of his forests and fertile fields

> it will completely destroy, as when a sick man wastes away. And the remaining trees of his forests will be so few that a child could write them down.

Such burning is always a hazardous process, especially in a climate which is very dry between the seasonal rains. Deliberate burning could quickly go beyond control when the ground was tinder-dry, and other fires could start accidentally or by spontaneous combustion. It is not clear which kind of fires the Isaiah references depict—perhaps a combination. The effects of forest fires were particularly serious when combined with heavy seasonal rains and overgrazing.[3] Goats are notoriously destructive browsers, and by the first century AD there were laws in Judah severely restricting the rearing of sheep and goats, because of overgrazing and soil erosion. Thus one Rabbi wrote: 'Those who raise small cattle and cut down good trees...will see no sign of blessing.'[4]

The fragility of environmental well-being in Canaan was compounded by low rainfall, so that dew was important as a source of moisture. Thus dew was seen as a source of blessing:

> Ah, the smell of my son is like the smell of a field that the Lord has blessed. May God give you of heaven's dew and of earth's richness—an abundance of grain and new wine (Gen 27:27b,28; cf Deut 33:25).

This dew permitted dry-farming, aided vine harvesting and freshened dry pasture lands in times of drought. So, although there were factors, already outlined, which meant that environmental well-being could be upset through triggering soil erosion, this position can be easily over-simplified. Careful examination of Canaanite geography by D.C. Hopkins shows that there was a great diversity of local micro-environments. This meant that farmers had to be extremely careful; methods which might work in one area would not work in an adjacent one. On the other hand, this environmental diversity lowered the risk of subsistence failure, and facilitated the spreading of limited agricultural energies across the annual calendar, thus promoting self-sufficiency.[5]

So the land of Canaan, dry, hilly and wooded, demanded very careful management to ensure its continued fertility; while the diversity of microenvironments, and the importance of dew, contributed elements of stability, and mistakes could be corrected. But the ravages of war could easily upset everything:

> I will not drive them (the Canaanites) from before you in one year, lest the land become desolate and the wild beasts multiply against you. Little by little I will drive them out from before you, until you are increased and possess the land (Exod 23:29f; cf Deut 7:22).

> When you beseige a city for a long time, making war against it in order to take it, you shall not destroy its trees by wielding an axe against them; for you may eat of them, but you shall not cut them down. Are the trees of the field men that they should be beseiged by you? Only the trees which you know are not trees for food you may destroy and cut down that you may build seige works against the city that makes war with you, until it falls (Deut 20:19f; cf 2 Kings 3:25).

There are a number of contemporary records of seige warfare; invading armies used large numbers of trees, often indiscriminately, for fuel and for seige works such as towers, ladders and battering rams, and the land was laid waste. Here the command is for restraint, arguing partly from respect for creation and partly from common sense—the trees which were preserved would provide food, and would form part of the nation's new possessions when they had fully taken over Canaan.

If, at a time of limited technological capability, there had to be such laws restricting the environmental devastation that war caused, they also form a grim reminder of the destruction which can be caused by modern warfare—a factor often over-

looked in view of the loss of human life involved in hostilities.
Repeated famines in Ethiopia are often understood as simply
due to a failure of the rains, but Peter Cotterell argues that:

> the naïve analysis... which places the blame on a God
> who 'turned off the tap'... must be replaced by an
> analysis which takes into account the gross political and
> economic mismanagement of the country involved.
> Even if there is less rain than in the past (and it is not
> clear that this is the case), the mass destruction of
> ground-cover due to decades of war precisely in the
> principal famine region must be at least partially
> responsible. If there are no crops, then at least some
> account must be taken of the wholesale conscription of
> young men and women into the armies on both sides of
> the battle-front so that the farms are without labourers.
> If there is no money to pay for the needed infrastructure
> of roads, there must be some significance in the fact that
> Ethiopia has the largest standing army in black Africa,
> and spends rather more than 60% of its gross national
> product on weapons despite being, now, under
> Marxism, the poorest nation in the world.[6]

To examine more closely the environmental impact of war,
let us look at two well-documented cases: the USA in Vietnam, and the Gulf War of 1991.

THE VIETNAM WAR OF THE 1960-70's[7]

Modern technology and understanding of environmental processes now give us the ability to use 'ecocide' (that is, the
systematic destruction of environments) as a weapon of war.
Synthetic herbicides, insecticides, weather modification techniques and nuclear weapons all have this capability. Particularly well-documented here is the involvement of the USA
in the Vietnam war; most of the cities of South Vietnam were
under US control, but it was in the countryside that the North

Vietnamese insurgents could not be rooted out by conventional warfare. The Americans turned to spraying the forests with herbicides such as Picloram (so dangerous that it is not licensed for use in the USA) to kill the trees and expose the enemy. When the spraying ended in 1971, some 1.5 million hectares of land—10% of the land area of South Vietnam—had been treated with 20 million gallons of herbicides, applied at an average of thirteen times the dose recommended by the US Department of Agriculture for domestic use. Approximately one-half of the trees in the mature hardwood forests north of Saigon were destroyed.

Also, by the end of 1971, 100,000 hectares of crop land had also been sprayed, to deny food to the Vietcong and to sympathetic civilian populations, who would be driven into the cities, making them easier to control.

The effects of this destruction were very far-reaching. Forests were infested with bamboo, and soil degradation set in, especially on poisoned farmland. Large areas of mangrove forest growing along river banks, and vital to the maintenance of economically important fisheries, were destroyed. It may take the forests a hundred years to recover.

In 1967 and 1968 US bombers dropped more than 3.5 million bombs in the 500 lb to 700 lb range, each leaving upon impact a crater up to 14 metres wide and 9 metres deep. The area of craters thus produced totals 150,000 hectares (almost 1% of the total land surface), 2 billion cubic metres of soil were displaced, and further millions of hectares were contaminated with missile fragments. In many areas of Vietnam peasants have been afraid to reoccupy bombed land for fear of unexploded shells.

Another weapon with devastating environmental effects was the BLU-82B 'daisycutter' bomb. At 15,000 lb it was designed to clear an area the size of a football field for helicopter landings. It killed all plant and animal life within a radius of 65 metres, and the zone of injury extended to 400 metres. Of similar effect was the CBU-55 fire air explosive, which produced a devastating blast by spraying an aerosol cloud of fuel over an area and then detonating it. Arguably the crudest of all these weapons was the 'Rome plow', a heavily armoured 33 ton caterpillar bulldozer with a blade capable of felling any tree. In groups, these machines could clear 40 hectares of heavy forest, or 160 hectares of light forest, daily. Some 350,000 hectares of South Vietnamese forest were felled in this way, as well as considerable areas of rubber plantations, orchards and farms. The weight of the machines caused colossal soil damage, and the ecological balance of plant communities was badly upset.

Although ecocide is not formally a war crime, it contributes to the general devastation and 'wanton destruction' which are both war crimes and crimes against humanity under the Charter of the International Military Tribunal at Nuremberg. The use of herbicides is against the Geneva Protocol of 1925.

THE GULF WAR OF 1991

The deliberate attempts by Iraqi forces to poison the environment during the 1991 Gulf War led to what might prove to be the most serious oil pollution disaster of all time. It was feared that over 10 million barrels of oil had spilled into the Gulf waters from Kuwaiti oil refineries. Three separate oil spillages were involved, the first one spotted in the waters south of Kuwait soon after war started on 16 January; it had already drifted ashore in many places. More oil came from missile damage to Mina al-Ahmadi oil terminal at Kuwait, and from deliberate spillage by Iraqis at Mina al-Bakr. Tim Thomas of the RSPCA, surveying the scene, said: 'This is the worst oil disaster I have ever seen. As I walked the beaches I came across a dead bird every two or three paces. They were just blobs of oil. I saw birds diving into the black water and never coming up again. It was horrific.'[8]

It was later found that some 1 or 2 million barrels were spilled, far less than originally feared. The difficulty in predicting accurately the extent of pollution damage in the early stages of the war was due to incomplete information being supplied by the Allied forces in the area. But one of the most alarming features of the whole episode is that the Iraqi forces must have had a clear idea of what the oil spillages might achieve.

Approximately 33% of this oil evaporated within the first few days, quite rapidly due to the hot weather, but a large quantity of more viscous liquid proved more difficult to remove, now widely dispersed by the operation of tides, currents and wind. Various techniques were used that have been developed to deal with large oil spillages, although the situation was complicated in the vicinity of the war zone. Booms (made of fire-resistant absorbent tubes) are put down around a slick to restrict its movement (although the oil can sometimes lap over or flow under the boom). It can then be sucked into tankers using suction pumps ('skimmers'). In other cases, early treatment with chemicals is needed to break slicks up, otherwise the action of waves converts it into an oil-water emulsion (known as 'chocolate mousse'). Oil is relatively easy to remove when it is washed ashore on to sand, but this is much more difficult when the shores are rocky.

Oil kills marine life in various ways. The poisonous chemicals it contains dissolve in sea water, killing the plankton on which fish feed; it kills mammals and birds by poisoning them and coating them, clogging fur and feathers, and thereby destroying the mechanisms that regulate body temperature. Other birds cannot see through the oil to catch fish, and die of starvation. When heavy oil sinks to the sea floor it kills corals and plants by smothering them.

The Gulf is particularly vulnerable because the water there circulates less quickly than in other seas; a glance at an atlas shows how nearly land-locked it is. Thus Dr Brian Bayne of the Natural Environment Research Council stated: 'The Gulf is like a big sluggish pond, with the water slushing around in it. This means the oil is likely to remain on the surface of the sea for a very long time.'[9]

There are particular hazards on the western shore of the Gulf, where the water is very shallow. Large beds of sea grass were in danger of being smothered by the oil. These are important breeding grounds for fish and shrimps, and it was feared that many Saudi fishermen were in danger of losing their livelihood. The dugong (sea cow) and green turtle feed on this grass around Bahrain. Sea cows are already in danger of extinction because of over-hunting and the destruction of their habitats. Turtles were in danger from swimming in oily water, and laying eggs in sand covered by oil. Also endangered were winter-resident diving birds such as cormorants and grebes, and others such as oyster-catchers and redshanks migrating to Europe.

The extent of the damage has turned out to be less than was feared. It was later seen that most of the oil became trapped on the northern coast of Saudi Arabia in Abu Ali Bay. Happily, it missed Karan Island where green turtles breed. One TV programme (Michael Buerk's *Nature Watch*, BBC2, 8th April 1991) suggested that fears had been exaggerated by environmental organisations, who wished to generate anxiety and needed to keep up the level of support by being seen to be involved. There was also a political need to portray Saddam Hussein as an eco-terrorist.

More spectacular was the burning of Kuwaiti oil wells by the retreating Iraqi army in February 1991. Some 600 were set alight, with a loss of at least 4 million barrels of oil per day, an amount equal to England's daily oil consumption. Satellite photographs taken over the weekend of 9th March 1991 showed a plume of smoke 600 km long, blocking out sunlight over an area between 10,000 and 15,000 sq km, and causing a noticeable temperature fall in Kuwait. Paul 'Red' Adair, renowned throughout the world as the man who can extinguish any oilwell blaze, predicted at the time that it would take two years to put all the Kuwaiti fires out; happily, some amazing improvisations with unlikely equipment saw the last one doused well within the year.

The main threat from the burning wells was a photochemical smog producing ozone due to sun-induced chemical reactions in the huge soot cloud. Some scientists predicted a worldwide ecological disaster; Dr Abdullah Toukan, chief environmental adviser to King Hussein of Jordan, warned of an artificial winter because sunlight would be blocked out by the cloud. This could have led to famine and drought in Asia due to disruption of the monsoon season, on which one billion people depend for their crops. This assumed that smoke in large quantities would have reached the upper atmosphere, leading to cooling of the lower atmosphere, and the interruption of the rising air motions that lead to rain.

Meteorological Office computer models showed ozone-laden smog spreading hundreds of miles downwind from Kuwait. The main damage was predicted to occur within 200 km of Kuwait city. High rain acidity was predicted, as high as anything in Europe, especially since Kuwait oil is high in sulphur. But the models claim that carbon dioxide emissions, global warming and smoke damage to the ozone layer will turn out to be negligible.

THAT IT MAY GO WELL WITH YOU

Dotted throughout the Pentateuch there are, in addition to texts already mentioned, various injunctions to good stewardship of plant and animal life:

> When you enter the land and plant any kind of fruit tree, regard its fruit as forbidden. For three years you are to consider it forbidden; it must not be eaten. In the fourth year all its fruit will be holy, an offering of praise to the Lord. But in the fifth year you may eat its fruit. In this way your harvest will be increased. I am the Lord your God (Lev 19:23–25).

> If you come across a bird's nest beside the road, either in a tree or on the ground, and the mother is sitting on the young or on the eggs, do not take the mother with the young. You may take the young, but be sure to let the mother go, so that it may go well with you and you may have a long life (Deut 22:6,7).

> Do not muzzle an ox when it is treading out the grain (Deut 25:4; cf Prov 12:10).

There are two peculiar features to these injunctions. In the first place, there is nothing particularly 'religious' about them! Deuteronomy 25:4 is a call to kind treatment of domestic animals, and the other two are no more than common sense—careful conservation of plant and animal life is necessary, otherwise people will go hungry. Nor are such regulations unique to the Old Testament.

The second peculiar feature is the way that they form part of a larger collection of laws, involving almost every aspect of Israel's life and including what today we would categorise as both sacred and secular. As the references above show, they are dotted almost at random throughout the larger collection of laws. This is in spite of what some Old Testament scholars see as the desire for orderliness in the one who assembled the law books of the Pentateuch in their final order.

Although these features seem peculiar at first, there is actually a simple reason for their peculiarity. It is that every aspect of the nation's life, including its management of the 'land flowing with milk and honey', are subsumed under the need for faith and obedience to the God who created and redeemed them (Is 28:24–26). So one Old Testament scholar writes:

> Through the Sinai covenant God provided the bonding and moulding institutions and laws by which they were to progress from a mass of freed slaves to an ordered and functioning society. It is there, in the Torah, that we find the bulk of those features of Israel's polity that made them so distinctive: the kinship rationale of land tenure; the Jubilee and sabbatical institutions; the ban on interest; the equality of native and 'stranger' before the law; the civil rights of slaves; the diffusion of political leadership and authority among the elders; the limitation on the economic power of cultic officials. Israel at this period, though not a state in our sense of the word, did not lack social institutions with consistent goals and a coherent rationale.[10]

The Laws of Sabbath and Jubilee

As we saw in the previous section, laws to do with stewardship of the fertile land God gave Israel as a covenant gift are dotted throughout the Pentateuch, interspersed with other laws to do with subjects as diverse as worship, ritual purity and civil harmony. We have seen that this reflects a holistic view of life in the Promised Land that refuses to split apart the 'sacred' from the 'secular', so that every aspect of life reflected faith and obedience towards the giver of this good land.

Leviticus 25, however, is a major section in its own right, in which two particular land laws, and the rationale behind them, are set out in some detail: the laws of Sabbath rest (vv 1–7,18–22) and of Jubilee (vv 8–17,23,24). The former pronounces 'a year of solemn rest', in which there was to be no sowing of land or pruning of vineyards:

> When you enter the land I am going to give you, the land itself must observe a Sabbath to the Lord. For six years you sow your fields, and for six years prune your vineyards and gather their crops. But in the seventh year the land is to have a Sabbath of rest, a Sabbath to the Lord. Do not sow your fields or prune your vineyards. Do not reap what grows of itself or harvest the grapes of your untended vines. The land is to have a year of rest. Whatever the land yields during the Sabbath year will be food for you—for yourself, your manservant and maidservant, and the hired worker and temporary resident who live among you, as well as for your livestock and the wild animals in your land. Whatever the land produces may be eaten (vv 2b–7).

There are obviously ecological consequences to this legislation. The rest the land was to enjoy every seventh year would help to maintain its natural fertility: 'The conservation of natural and other resources which is prescribed by this legislation forms the basis of good agricultural and ecological practice.'[11] This is not actually stated in the text but is probably implied. But, as was mentioned earlier, there is apparently more to do here with common sense than with divine revelation, and the answer to this is that such laws put every aspect of life in Canaan within the context of faith and obedience towards the Creator who gave them this rich land. This is clearly brought out in subsequent verses:

> Follow my decrees and be careful to obey my laws, and you will live safely in the land. Then the land will yield its fruit, and you will eat your fill and live there in safety. You may ask, 'What will we eat in the seventh year if we do not plant or harvest our crops?' I will send you such a blessing in the sixth year that the land will yield enough for three years. While you plant during the eighth year, you will eat from the old crop and will continue to eat from it until the harvest of the ninth year comes in (vv 18–22).

The Law of Jubilee stipulated the same year of rest for the land (vv 11,12), but went far further. All land bought and sold within the previous fifty years had to be returned to its original owner, and the legislation decreed that the price paid was on a sliding scale, depending on the number of years before the next Jubilee; in this way the price of land depended solely on the number of crops the new owner could extract from it before handing it back! Again, it is legitimate to see ecological considerations here. First, there was still the requirement to observe Sabbath rests for the land—the laws of Sabbath and Jubilee operated together; secondly, since the value of the land depended upon the number of crops it could yield, there was every incentive to care for it properly, both on the part of original and prospective 'owners'.

But again, ecological considerations are not explicit in the text. Other reasons are given which are equally important, and, as we shall see, cannot be divorced from ecological considerations. The first is that the buyers and sellers of land are not its real owners. They are merely tenants who cannot buy and sell land on a permanent basis, because the ultimate owner is the Creator himself (vv 23f). This is the reason why Naboth refused to sell his vineyard to King Ahab: 'The Lord forbid that I should give you the inheritance of my fathers' (1 Kings 21:3).

The other vital dimension to this legislation is to do with economics. The fact that land could not be bought and sold permanently meant that, since land speculation was forbidden, the gap between rich and poor was kept relatively narrow, and exploitation by rich landowners excluded. And if, for any reason, a man became so poor that he was forced to sell his land, his relatives were obliged to step in and help him by buying back the land on his behalf without waiting for the next Jubilee year (vv 25–28).

Here we see that considerations of ecology and justice are closely related in Scripture. In the writings of the prophets the nation would be denounced for failure on both scores, as we shall see later. Since the Bible presents humanity's relationship with the land as an essential part of life, it could hardly be otherwise.

THE FAILURE TO CHOOSE RIGHT— CONSEQUENCES FOR THE LAND

When Israel entered Canaan, she was faced with a simple choice to do with her relationship to the God who had given her the land as a covenant possession: choose obedience (and its consequences) or disobedience (and its different consequences). This theme of 'two ways' is echoed repeatedly in the Old Testament, but nowhere is the choice put more starkly than in Deuteronomy 28:

> All these blessings will come upon you and accompany you if you obey the Lord your God:
>
> You will be blessed in the city and blessed in the country. The fruit of your womb will be blessed, and the crops of your land and the young of your livestock—the calves of your herds and the lambs of your flocks. Your basket and

your kneading trough will be blessed. You will be blessed
when you go out and when you come in (28:2–6).

However, if you do not obey the Lord your God and do not
carefully follow all his commands and decrees I am giving
you today, all these curses will come upon you and overtake
you: You will be cursed in the city and cursed in the
country... (28:15–19).

If all this sounds simplistic to modern ears, this is mainly
because we tend to view things in an individualistic way; it is
quite obvious that personal cause-and-effect does not always
operate (as Old Testament people knew well: see, for example,
Ps 94:3; Is 5:20; Mal 2:17). But God was giving the whole
nation this choice, and here the laws of cause and effect,
leading to blessing or to curse, are more closely followed.
There is a certain logic to this: if human life is tied up to the
Creator on the one hand and to the land on the other, then
obedience and disobedience are bound to have their consequences. How can people disobey God and the earth not
suffer as a result?

The logic goes further. The history of God's people ends in
failure, particularly in the long decline after the golden age of
David and Solomon. First there is schism in the kingdom, then
the fall of Samaria (721 BC), the sack of Jerusalem (587 BC),
and the continued poverty and obscurity of the post-exilic
country of Judah, hinted at in books such as Malachi, Haggai,
Joel, Ezra and Nehemiah. Haggai 1:6 refers to the difficulty of
raising enough crops to feed even the attenuated population,
and the same chapter reveals the root of the problem in a
continued failure to live by right priorities and loyalties.

The logic is expressed in another way. The apocalyptic
passages in some of the prophets which describe a ruined earth
seem at first to point to a future time of judgement, as similar
passages do in Revelation. But the prophets are also talking
about the consequences of Israel's present disobedience.
Again, if human life is tied up with the land, it follows that the
land shares the consequences of human sinfulness, so that

passages such as the following may describe the present (even if some exaggeration is justified by the style of the utterance and by the seriousness of the root problem) as well as the future:

> The earth dries up and withers, the world languishes and withers, the exalted of the earth languish. The earth is defiled by its people; They have disobeyed the laws, violated the statutes and broken the everlasting covenant. Therefore a curse consumes the earth; its people must bear their guilt (Is 24:4–6).

> I looked at the earth, and it was formless and empty; and at the heavens, and their light was gone. I looked at the mountains and they were quaking; all the hills were swaying. I looked, and there were no people; every bird in the sky had flown away. I looked, and the fruitful land was a desert; all its towns lay in ruins before the Lord, before his fierce anger (Jer 4:23–26; cf Isa 7:23; Amos 4:7,9,10; Zeph 1:2,3; Hag 1:10,11).

POSTSCRIPT

The story of Israel in Canaan, with such an optimistic beginning, ends in failure. The land which was the covenant gift was ruined, as the words of Isaiah 24 and Jeremiah 4 make clear. The story begins in a land flowing with milk and honey; it ends in barrenness. The people refused to obey God, and the price to be paid involved not only political ruin but also a despoiled environment. Once, Canaan was thickly wooded and very fertile. The end product of centuries of mismanagement was an infertile and treeless landscape. The Old Testament mentions all sorts of animals which could once be seen there: fallow deer (Is 35:6), lions (Prov 30:30; Judg 14:5; 1 Sam 17:34; 1 Kings 13:24; Hosea 13:7f), as well as crocodile, hippopotamus, tiger, bear and wild ox. Rock carvings in the Sinai desert testify to the presence of the ostrich. All are now long since extinct there.

Even worse, the people failed to fulfil the purpose God had given them. Their role was to be a light to the nations (Is 49:6; 60:3; Ps 67) as they enjoyed the fullness of life, both physical and spiritual, which flows from right relationships with God, with each other and with creation itself. The vision was that the surrounding nations would be so attracted to their way of life that they too would be drawn to seek the same relationship with the living God and discover the truth of his laws:

> Many peoples will come and say, 'Come, let us go up to the mountain of the Lord, to the house of the God of Jacob. He will teach us his ways, so that we may walk in his paths.' The law will go out from Zion, the word of the Lord from Jerusalem. He will judge between the nations and will settle disputes for many peoples. They will beat their swords into ploughshares and their spears into pruning hooks. Nation will not take up sword against nation, nor will they train for war any more (Is 2:3f).

But persistent disobedience meant that the outcome was exactly the opposite. Even after the return from exile, life continued to be hard. Judah became a tiny and insignificant state, overcome and governed by one occupying power after another—first Babylon, then Persia, then Greece, and finally Rome. The expectation of restored glory, seemingly clear enough in the messages of some of the prophets, came to nothing. Some of the Old Testament books reveal deepening despair born of the struggle and the increasingly distant memory of the golden age of David and Solomon. Yet even from the ashes of failure hope rises phoenix-like, because in the end God does not abandon his people. His grace has the last word, and the fundamental goodness of creation is gloriously reaffirmed, as we shall see.

REFERENCES

1. Chris Sugden and Vinay Samuel, 'A Just and Responsible Life-style—an Old Testament Perspective' in Ronald J. Sider, *Lifestyle in the Eighties: An Evangelical Commitment to Simple Lifestyle* (Paternoster Press: Exeter, 1982), p 43.

2. A.D.H. Mayes, *Deuteronomy*, (Oliphants: London, 1979), p 128.

3. M. Zohary, *Plant Life of Palestine* (Chronica Botanica: New York, 1962), p 209.

4. Quoted in David and Pat Alexander, *The Lion Handbook of the Bible* (Lion Publishing: Berkhamsted, 1973), p 15.

5. D.C. Hopkins, *The Highlands of Canaan* (JSOT Press: Sheffield, 1985).

6. Peter Cotterell, *Mission and Meaninglessness* (SPCK: London, 1991), p 276.

7. The information in this section comes from Paul R. Ehrlich, Anne H. Ehrlich and John H. Holdren, *Ecoscience: Population, Resources, Environment* (Freeman and Co: San Francisco, 1977), pp 653-656.

8. *Environment Guardian* 12th March 1991.

9. *ibid*.

10. Christopher J.H. Wright, 'The people of God in the Old Testament', *Themelios*, vol 16 no 1, (October 1990): pp 4-11.

11. R.K. Harrison, *Leviticus* (IVP: Leicester, 1980), p 223.

Chapter Six

IDOLATRIES ANCIENT AND MODERN

THE CHALLENGE OF CANAANITE IDOLATRY

A T THE END of the last chapter we left the land which once flowed with milk and honey in a sorry state, because of the persistent disobedience of the people who had received that land as a covenant gift. But before we move on to the New Testament, in which the goodness of creation is reaffirmed in a surprising and wonderful way, there is a further Old Testament theme which we should consider.

This theme is idolatry, and in the Old Testament it surfaces in the flirtation (and worse) of God's people with the gods of the Canaanites who already lived in the land. As we shall see, it has important implications for our own role as stewards of creation who are seeking ways of reversing the environmental problems which we have brought about. We are faced with the need to make choices about alternative ways of doing this responsibly and effectively. The consequences of making the wrong choices are potentially disastrous, because science and technology provide us with great power over the rest of creation. As we shall see, there is enormous temptation to choose the wrong way to proceed; the wrong way turns out to be an idolatrous way. So we need to examine the theme of idolatry in the Old Testament, as it is reflected in the relationship between the people and the land.

The first two of the Ten Commandments are about God's rightful place at the very centre of the hearts of his people (Exod 20). He declares himself to be a 'jealous' God (v 5; cf Deut 5:9; 6:15; Nah 1:2). So the people of Israel were first forbidden from putting other 'gods' in his place (v 3), and secondly, prohibited from making idols (v 4).

In these restrictions God is already warning his people about the temptations they would encounter in Canaan. The land was not empty, awaiting a people to come and occupy it. It was already peopled, and while the gift of the the Promised Land was part of God's covenant with His people, the occupation of the land was also an act of judgement upon the Canaanites who already lived there. Leviticus 18 charges the Israelites to have nothing to do with the practices of Egypt (from whence they had come) or Canaan (to which they were going). The regulations which follow then seem to reflect God's abhorrence of some of the practices of the Canaanites, particularly in the realm of sexual perversion and child sacrifice. The passage concludes:

> Do not defile yourselves in any of these ways, because this is how the nations that I am going to drive out before you became defiled. Even the land was defiled; so I punished it for its sin, and the land vomited out its inhabitants...And if you defile the land, it will vomit you out as it vomited out the nations that were before you (Lev 18:25,28).

Israel's life in Canaan could not involve peaceful coexistence with such people. The divine command to the people was quite clear. They were to destroy utterly everything and everyone before them, as a number of passages state clearly:

> When the Lord your God brings you into the land you are entering to possess and drives out before you many nations...and when the Lord your God has delivered them over to you and you have have defeated them, then you must destroy them totally. Make no treaty with them, and show them no mercy. Do not intermarry with them. Do not

give your daughters to their sons or take their daughters for your sons, for they will turn your sons away from following me to serve other gods...This is what you are to do to them: Break down their altars, smash their sacred stones, cut down their Asherah poles and burn their idols in the fire (Deut 7:1–6; cf Exod 23:23ff; Deut 20:16–18).

It is difficult for many Christians to come fully to terms with the divine command that Israel should utterly destroy the Canaanites. At least part of the explanation lies in the perverted nature of the practices which formed part of the Canaanite religion. One Old Testament scholar describes it thus:

> The amazing thing about the gods, as they were conceived in Canaan, is that they had no moral character whatsoever. In fact, their conduct was on a much lower level than that of society as a whole, if we can judge from ancient codes of law. Certainly the brutality of the mythology is far worse than anything else in the Near East at that time. Worship of these gods carried with it some of the most demoralising practices then in existence. Among them were child sacrifice, a practice long since discarded in Egypt and Babylonia, sacred prostitution, and snake-worship on a scale unknown among other peoples.[1]

Although it seems incredible at first, the Israelites were tempted to copy the Canaanites. This was partly because they did not fully obey the divine command, and spared many of the occupants of the land. And where the Canaanites survived, their religion survived also to be a snare to the new inhabitants. One of the saddest features of the Old Testament record is that the people did succumb to these temptations. All the worst features of Canaanite religion surfaced at different times, even child sacrifice (Jer 32:35; cf 2 Kings 23:10). But why should this have been? Given that there was such a yawning gap between Canaanite religion and that of the

Israelites, we might have expected that they would recoil from it in horror and revulsion. A little compromise is one thing, but to take such a horrific set of practices on board was something altogether different. Where does the explanation for this lie?

To answer this question we must consider once again the question of the land. Every religion, not just Judaism and Christianity, relates to humanity's place in the world. People expect their religions to make some sort of sense of pain and evil, including irresistible forces that lead to disasters. One popular explanation is that these are signs of the operation of angry gods who must somehow be placated. As we have already seen, the geography of Canaan lent itself to environmental disasters. On the one hand there were the long dry spells (over which, of course, the people had no control), and on the other there was the danger of massive soil erosion if they did not take great care of the forested hills. So, even though there were bound to be some years in which the crops were better than in others, the Israelites' long-term prosperity was bound up with the way they treated the land. So we saw at the end of the last chapter how disobedience led inevitably to a degraded environment and the failure of crops.

Disobedience set in soon after the occupation of the land, as the books of Joshua and Judges show. There were plenty of messengers around to remind the people of where the fault lay when things went wrong. Sometimes they listened and repented, but sometimes they did not. Because disobedience is a matter of the heart rather than lack of enlightenment, there was always the temptation to absolve themselves from their own responsibility for the degradation of their land. Adam's ability in the Garden of Eden to blame others for his own disobedience is a sin often copied.

The Canaanite View of The Land

The Israelites seem to have been quite successful at persuading themselves that they were not to blame for what was actually the result of their own disobedience. The blessings and the curses of Deuteronomy 28 were too uncomfortable to live with. A most attractive alternative presented itself. They were worshipping the wrong God! The God who had brought them out of Egypt, they argued with themselves, clearly had no authority or power in the matter of bumper crops, a reliable supply of rain, and fertile soil. So if this God could not produce the goods, they would find themselves one who could. And where better to look than to the gods of Canaan—after all, the people of the land had worshipped them long before the new arrivals, and they had done quite well for themselves.

And here we come to the heart of the Canaanite rituals. Depraved though they undoubtedly were, they had a definite purpose—to persuade the gods to bless the earth (eg 1 Kings 18:20–40). The difference between Old Testament and Canaanite religions, and the attractiveness of the latter, has been described thus:

> There appears to have been a prolonged struggle in early Israel to bring them to realise that the Lord, the victorious God of their redemptive history, was also entirely competent in the matter of land use, rain, fertility, crops and herds. The tendency to regard the Baals of the previous occupants of the land as more likely to 'produce the goods' in the economic realm seemed ineradicable, from the conquest to the exile.[2]

There is a further important point to be made here. The people of Israel had been taught that the land was a gift from God, and was to be cared for as such (Chapter 5). It was not theirs absolutely to do with as they wished. Yet this was precisely the view of the land that developed inexorably from the nature of Canaanite religion. So, succumbing to the temptation to worship the gods of Canaan also profoundly changed their view of the land in which they lived. No longer was it a gift for whose use they were answerable, but now merely an economic commodity to use as they wished. This important point is often overlooked in textbooks of Old Testament theology, but is developed in at least two important references, both of which are quoted below for emphasis:

> The Israelites were taught to understand the land as a gift for whose use they were responsible and whose distribution was ordered by moral principles. The Canaanites in their fertility religions were much more interested in the land as an asset whose fruits were to be maximised by religious ritual. Land was a marketable commodity and economic growth was the goal. The Mosaic code had no religious ritual to coax the fruits of the land: Israel had to borrow any such rites from others. For the Mosaic code, God's blessings on the land depended on covenant faithfulness to God and justice among the people of God (Deut 28). Justice and humanity in responsible use of their land came before techniques to ensure maximum profit.[3]

> [Among the Canaanites] landed property was treated as a saleable commodity and could be freely disposed of. The inclusion of Canaanite property into the Israelite state therefore meant that now two types of property ownership existed side by side. More enterprising families could now increase their estates and this tended to undermine the old principle of equality. Wealthy land owners lived in the cities and had their 'latifundia' worked by slaves or paid farm labourers. Commerce in the cities again led to increased wealth which provided the means to buy more real estate in the countryside. This tended to increase class divisions.[4]

How this became part of the tragedy of Israel's subsequent history is beyond the scope of this book, but the important point is the relationship between forms of idolatry and a wrong relationship with the land.

Isaiah's View of Idolatry

However, it is very important from our point of view to dwell on the view of idolatry taken by Isaiah. Earlier parts of the Old Testament seem to take the view that the false gods of Canaan were real gods, with some sort of power, even though puny by comparison with the God of Israel. But in Isaiah the mood is different. It turns out that these other gods are no gods at all! They are only products of the imaginations of those who invent them (eg 40:19,20; 41:6,7,22–29; 46:5–7; cf Jer 10:1–6). Isaiah records a number of oracles in poetry on this subject, but there is one striking sustained exposition of the subject in prose form. It is even more striking for the deliberate heavy sarcasm which seems to be its driving force:

> All who make idols are nothing, and the things they delight in do not profit; their witnesses neither see nor know, that they may be put to shame. Who fashions a god or casts an image, that is profitable for nothing? Behold, all his fellows shall be put to shame, and the craftsmen are but men; let them all assemble, let them stand forth, they shall be terrified, they shall be put to shame together.
>
> The ironsmith fashions it and works it over the coals; he shapes it with hammers, and forges it with his strong arm; he becomes hungry and his strength fails, he drinks no water and is faint. The carpenter stretches a line, he marks it out with a pencil; he fashions it with planes, and marks it with a compass; he shapes it into the figure of a man, with the beauty of a man, to dwell in a house. He cuts down cedars; or he chooses a holm tree or an oak and lets it grow strong among the trees of the forest; he plants a cedar and the rain nourishes it. Then it becomes fuel for a man; he takes a part of it and warms himself, he kindles a fire and bakes bread; also he makes a god and worships it, he makes it a graven image and falls down before it. Half of it he burns in the fire; over the half he eats flesh, he roasts meat and is satisfied; also he warms himself and says, 'Aha, I am warm, I have seen the fire!' And the rest of it he makes into

a god, his idol; and falls down to it and worships it; he prays to it and says, 'Deliver me, for thou art my god!'

They do not know, nor do they discern; for he has shut their eyes, so that they cannot see, and their minds, so that they cannot understand. No one considers, nor is there knowledge or discernment to say, Half of it I burned in the fire, I also baked bread on its coals, I roasted flesh and have eaten; and shall I make the residue of it an abomination? Shall I fall down before a block of wood? He feeds on ashes; a deluded mind has led him astray, and he cannot deliver himself or say, Is there not a lie in my right hand? (Is 44: 9–20).

The argument behind the prophecy is as follows. A man takes a piece of wood and cuts it in two. One half he uses to light a fire with and cook on; the other half he fashions into an idol, falls down before it and worships it, expecting it to save him from all his troubles. Put this way, it all sounds ludicrous, and that is precisely the point Isaiah is making. How can anyone rely upon something he has made to be a god to him? He cannot possibly be in his right mind! In fact, his mind is empty, because this piece of wood has no power to fulfil its maker's expectations. The rivals of the God of Israel are no-gods. They have no power to save; all they are able to do is delude the minds of those who make them.

Nor is this a purely abstract discussion. If we examine parts of the Old Testament we find the people of Israel looking to purely human institutions to do for them what God alone could have done, and would still do for them if only they would put their trust in him instead. In particular, one of their greatest follies was to put their trust in military alliances with whoever happened to be the strongest-looking power available that might protect them from other powers threatening to overrun them. This is one of the major themes underlying the book of Jeremiah (eg 2:14–19), which needs to be read against the background of how in earlier times God himself had intervened to save his people from the same sorts of enemies.

MODERN FORMS OF IDOLATRY

This consideration of the nature of the Israelites' idolatry in Canaan, and the expectations which drove them to it, is of vital importance in looking for correct ways forward in a world of serious environmental problems. Although the man depicted so cruelly in Isaiah 44 seems naive beyond words, this is only because the version of the temptation we have fallen for is far more sophisticated. The gods we are now tempted to worship are those of science and technology.

This last statement needs to be carefully explained, because it might seem like a condemnation of progress. There is no doubt that scientific and technological advances have made rapid and worthwhile changes to life on this planet. There are grounds for optimism that the correct use of them could reap many more benefits that we now foresee only dimly (or not at all). Nor could we ever envisage going back to a pre-scientific era, unless forced to do so by a global nuclear war.

The danger sets in when science and technology replace God as the ultimate ground of our hope, and their white-coated practitioners become the priests of the present age. In the specific context of environmental issues, idolatry is then the expectation that science and technology alone can solve our problems. There is no doubt that many people do actually think this way, both among the general public and among scientists themselves. Thus one microelectronics expert has said of 'Silicon Valley' in Santa Clara County, California, where many of the major developments in computing are taking place: 'Silicon Valley holds the keys of the kingdom.'[5] Other prophets of the microelectronics revolution wax eloquent on this theme. To give one example:

> Just as the industrial economy eliminated slavery, famine and pestilence, so will the post-industrial economy eliminate authoritarianism, war and strife. For the first time in history, the rate at which we solve problems will exceed the rate at which they appear.[6]

Ironically, this kind of optimism over the role of science is due, at least in part, to the way that it has hugely increased our power to control the natural world, consciousness of which goes back into the nineteenth century. Thus Bernard Ramm writes:

> [The nineteenth century] was the century of the foundation of sciences, of the development of the sciences, of the birth of many fundamental theories of science, of the creation of remarkable experiments. The scientists could point to such concrete things and to such remarkable successes. Then, too, the theoretical aspects of science found practical expressions which reached into every civilised hamlet. Steam engines, electricity, and chemistry were powerful and practical apologists for the scientific point of view. Inoculations, surgery under an anaesthetic, and brilliant new progress in surgery were medical marvels which preached irresistibly the gospel of science.
>
> What could theologians offer as a parallel to this? A theologian's product is a book, but so few of our population read the books of the theologians. Further, the reasoned argument of a book cannot compete popularly with the practical gadgets of science.[7]

Where Is Science Taking Us?

Although there is still an enormous optimism about the ability of science and technology alone to solve all our environmental problems, there is also an increasing awareness that these disciplines themselves are deeply implicated in the very problems they are meant to save us from. There could be no better illustration of this than the management of the McMurdo science base in Antarctica.

In March 1991 a Channel 4 TV programme entitled *Fragile Earth* documented environmental changes taking place in Antarctica. Part of this programme was devoted to the National Science Foundation base at McMurdo Sound, branded by one

US politician as the 'slum of Antarctica'. A shocked Congress, when they heard of the pollution at the base, voted $13 million over five years to clean it up. Contrary to the recommendations of the Antarctic Treaty, much rubbish is incinerated, polluting the local air. Before a recent tightening of environmental regulations, a huge collection of drums had built up, storing waste asbestos, oil, antifreeze, paint and miscellaneous other chemicals. Because the contents of the drums were only vaguely known, US environmental protection regulations forbade their import to a waste processing facility in California. The identification of the contents of each drum will be an expensive process.

In spite of the intentions of the Antarctic Treaty, untreated sewage is pumped into McMurdo Bay. Life-expired equipment has been dumped into the sea in the bay—tractors, storage sheds, pipelines, hoses, storage drums and tyres. Oil leaks into the bay make it one of the heaviest polluted small harbours in the world, with hydrocarbon levels five times those of the Firth of Forth in Scotland. There are significant levels of cadmium, lead, copper, zinc and silver in the sediment on the bay floor, and the best recommendation of experts is to leave it undisturbed: to recover corroding solid items from the floor would cause disturbance of the bottom sediments and disperse pollution more widely.

National Science Foundation officials on the programme noted that recent attempts to clean up the McMurdo operation came as a result of growing public awareness of environmental issues. This looks like a curious reversal of the order of things at the very least. If science really did have the ability to solve all our problems, then we might have expected it to take a lead, rather than tag along behind! Here is just one modern example of the powerlessness of human-made institutions to act as our 'gods'; of their own, they are powerless to solve anything!

The development of nuclear power is another example. In the 1960s and 1970s scientists believed that they had found the cheap, clean and inexhaustible energy source for the future, and there were persuasive prophets such as Alvin Weinberg.[8]

Every country could have its own nuclear power generating facilities. Here was the answer to the energy problems of the world.

At the beginning of the 1990s the situation has totally changed. In some major industrial countries plans for future development of nuclear power have been shelved. This is the result of nuclear accidents such as Three Mile Island, Pennsylvania (1979) and Chernobyl (1986), the revelations of human error and inappropriate training that emanated from subsequent enquiries, the knowledge of permanently poisoned ground, the problem of nuclear waste management, and the widespread fear of global instability as more and more countries gain access to nuclear weapons capability. Countries with the capability for making nuclear weapons now include Argentina, Brazil, Chile, Cuba, Egypt, Indonesia, Israel, Pakistan, South Africa, Spain, Switzerland and Turkey, many of whom have not signed international non-proliferation treaties. The 1991 Gulf War was set against the backcloth of Iraq's proximity to gaining nuclear weapons technological capability.

Exactly why is it necessary to stress that our scientific optimism is misplaced? It is because we are falling once again into the idolatry trap that Isaiah 44 warns about. This time the idol is not a piece of carved wood, and we do not literally fall down before it. We are too sophisticated for that! But the mistake is still the same. We are expecting salvation not from the living God, but from something that we have made—from a human construction. And this search can therefore only be doomed to failure.

Science As A Human Construction

The role of technology in human affairs is not a new issue. It is as old as the events of Genesis itself. Although technology involves unlocking the secrets present in God's good creation since the beginning, the ethical prologue to the Old Testament shows clearly how double-edged this process became after the Fall. Thus Cain, attempting to escape the effects of rebellion, built a city (Gen 4:17), and his descendants built a high tower as an expression of their autonomy and also of perceived insecurity (11:3–5). But even here technology is portrayed as an activity where human beings should be in charge of what is just a tool.

Because it is a human construction, as portrayed in Genesis 1—11, technology cannot but be implicated in human mismanagement of the world. Even the developments which seem to promise so much, such as the microelectronics revolution, and the development of nuclear power in previous decades, have this same double-edged nature. Both are also inextricably linked to the development of weapons systems, where a substantial proportion of research funding and human effort are currently concentrated within the scientific communities of the Western world. Why otherwise do whole communities of people find themselves redundant when peace breaks out?

This is not the place to develop a full theory of the role of technology in the modern world, but it is worth pointing out that it is an activity performed by human beings, who are both individuals and members of human communities. And it is inevitably more than just a dispassionate search for the truth about how the world works. In earlier centuries this may have been partly true: some eminent scientists of the past were men for whom scientific inquiry was a worthy hobby; nothing was at stake and therefore science was a search for truth for its own sake.

In the modern world the place of science and technology is different. It has become the work of highly skilled professionals, who earn their living as scientists, and who generally work for corporations which are mainly interested in the application of scientific knowledge. More than ever, issues of human vulnerability (or even of 'sin') surface. As David Atkinson puts it:

> Science involves commitment—to truth, to hard work, to personal discipline, to moral responsibility and social accountability. And such commitments—even the possibility of making a commitment—are often at a

high premium in a society which has lost touch with its Creator.[9]

What Atkinson means is that sin distorts human behaviour at all levels, so that even science does not proceed as it ought. It shares in the fallenness of the practitioners under whose authority it develops, who now earn their bread and butter (and that of their dependents) from it. How dangerous, therefore, it is when it becomes a god!

There is, however, another level at which science fails to be what we want it to be. This is the level at which science is no longer the dispassionate search for truth but, as it is now a part of the modern industrial machine, the search for knowledge which can be used not just for the benefit of mankind, but for profit and for advantage over competitors, or for power. Thus Thorson writes:

> Having finally understood that scientific truth is a source of power, man has made the crucial decision that from now on the will to power and the uses of power should dictate the relevance and value of that truth. Because of that decision, 'pure' science, the science of the past four hundred years, will begin to be altered in subtle ways, and will eventually disappear... the fusion of science and technology means that, increasingly, the moral decisions as to the uses of truth will be made pre-emptively, before the truth itself is even sought; we shall seek only truth which fits our purposes.[10]

Although there are other explanations (or levels of explanation) for the rise of the Green Movement, as we shall see in Chapter 8, it is certainly possible to see it as at least in part a vote of 'no confidence' in what science and technology have brought us to. Sociologist David Lyon notes that the rise of the Green Movement is one of a number of modern trends which are breaking the mould of previous generations.[11] He identifies three important factors.

There is first the new politics of a radical middle class,

giving rise to organisations concerned with issues such as the enviroment and women's rights, with memberships drawn largely from professional and public sector workers. Secondly, the rise of such modern movements is related to the decline of older movements, especially the trades unions, who are no longer able to question the very culture of the industrial society they are involved in. So, although most unions in Britain continue to support the Labour Party, most of their members vote for other parties. Moreover, the heavy industries from which their largest memberships were once drawn—coal, steel, shipbuilding, car manufacturing—are now in decline. Thirdly, the present age is one of rapid cultural change. One of the reasons for this is that society is nowadays seen to be the result of human choices rather than as the inevitable product of divine will or evolution. So instead of accepting the status quo, people are more likely to intervene in the way that society develops, through planning, politics and the economic choices they make.[12]

The Green Movement is an expression of these social changes. It reflects a radical shift in thinking among some social groupings in industrialised countries, who are willing to question the very foundations on which their national economies are based. Lyon concludes:

> The radical Green outlook is far more than a nostalgia
> for hedgerows, otters and pandas or a scaremongering
> bleat about detergents in rivers and pesticides on farms.
> It is no less than a thoroughgoing critique of
> modernity.[13]

IDOLATRY EXPRESSED IN 'GREEN' LIFESTYLES

The question of idolatry also rears its head in the question of green living. No one who stands up to give a talk on the Christian approach to environmental issues will be allowed to sit down before answering the question: 'What should we do, then?' Usually required are some hints about lead-free petrol, cars with diesel engines, recycled paper, ozone-friendly sprays, the local bottle bank and lagging the hot water tank. All these are good in themselves and highly recommended to everyone who wants to have a responsible lifestyle.[14]

We shall see more of such suggestions in later chapters, but what is important here is the expectation of the questioner. Sometimes, some gentle questioning of the questioner will reveal the attitude 'If I do these things, will the problem go away?' It betrays the idea that if we can only find a few palliatives, all will be well and no great changes will be needed of us. Neither our lifestyles, nor our attitudes to the world, its origin and its Creator need be challenged. As E.F. Schumacher pithily put it: 'a breakthrough a day keeps the crisis at bay.' In this case the speaker should gently challenge the underlying attitudes.

On the other hand, some questioners will want guidance on what sorts of practices are environmentally responsible and consistent with a conviction of the goodness of creation (see Chapter 3). Here the speaker will probably make the same practical suggestions even though the motivation behind the question is different. What will almost certainly differ are the results: the second questioner, with a much healthier approach to the whole issue and a desire to do as much as possible rather than the bare minimum, will have a far greater impact upon the world of creation (and upon his fellow humans) than the first!

POSTSCRIPT

Over-reliance on science lures us into idolatry. The main aim of this chapter has been to show why this is so. Science and technology are powerful and effective slaves but terrible gods. They are powerless to save because they are only the works of our hands. To decide to place total trust in them to solve the world's environmental problems is likely to lead to more pollution and further disasters; it is to overlook the double-edged nature of the role they have so far played in human affairs—double-edged because as servants they can only reflect the double-edged nature of the human wills that control them.

Here is a vital issue where theology is not only about academic issues but about making right or wrong choices for the future. There is an environmental crisis to be faced. The changes happening to the surface of our planet are due to our scientific knowledge and technological know-how. If we arrive at the right answers all may be well, but if the answers are wrong we may at best lurch from one crisis to another. At worst, we could destroy ourselves and everything else. Because our use of science and technology is part of the problem, these activities cannot supply the answers on their own. They are not gods who can save us, however often we treat them as if they could.

REFERENCES

1. G. Ernest Wright, *The Old Testament Against Its Environment* (London 1950), p 78.
2. Christopher J.H. Wright, *Living as the People of God* (IVP: Leicester, 1983), pp 59-60.
3. Vinay Samuel and Christopher Sugden, 'A Just and Responsible Lifestyle—An Old Testament Perspective' in Ronald J. Sider, *Lifestyle in the Eighties: An Evangelical Commitment to Simple Lifestyle* (Paternoster Press: Exeter, 1982), p 45.
4. Gunther Wittenberg, *Good News to the Poor: The Challenge of the Poor in the History of the Church* (Orbis Books: Maryknoll, 1979).
5. David Lyon, *The Silicon Society* (Lion: Berkhamsted, 1986), p 12.
6. Thomas Stonier, *The Wealth of Information* (Thames Methuen: London, 1983).
7. Bernard Ramm, *The Christian View of Science and Scripture* (Paternoster: Exeter, 1964), p 16f.
8. Alvin Weinberg, 'Raw Materials Unlimited', *Texas Quarterly*, vol 11 (1968).
9. David Atkinson, *The Values of Science* (Grove Books: Nottingham, 1980), p 15.

10. W.R. Thorson, 'The Spiritual Dimensions of Science' in Carl F.H. Henry, *Horizons of Science* (Harper and Row: New York, 1978), p 217.

11. David Lyon, 'Against the stream. 1—The current picture', *Third Way*, vol 12 no 1 (January 1989): pp 6-8.

12. *ibid* pp 7-8.

13. David Lyon, 'Against the stream. 2—Green and pleasant?', *Third Way*, vol 12 no 2 (February 1989): p 6.

14. There are plenty of books full of useful tips. See eg Hugh and Margaret Brown, *Doing our bit: a practical guide to the environment and what we can do about it* (Brown and Brown: Wigton, 1988); John Elkington and Julia Hailes, *The Green Consumer Guide* (Victor Gollancz: London, 1988).

Chapter Seven

NEW TESTAMENT CHRISTIANITY— A CREATION-DENYING FAITH?

IS THERE A FUTURE FOR CREATION?

I N THE PREVIOUS chapters we have seen how various themes to do with creation are carried throughout the Old Testament and are essential in understanding the history and calling of God's people in the land of Canaan. These include the goodness of creation, human stewardship and the all-pervading corruption of creation which flows from the Fall. But in order to demonstrate the validity of these insights for the environmental issues of the end of the twentieth century, a serious objection, first raised in Chapter 1, must be dealt with decisively.

The objection can be stated in two ways. The first goes as follows: all that has gone before is well said but the New Testament is all about a new covenant, whose blessings are spiritual (Jer 31:31–34). This covenant has nothing to do with a particular piece of Middle Eastern geography. Furthermore, the Old Testament emphasis on creation is not carried over into the New Testament, so that issues of environmental management, while important in Canaan, are now superceded by a new covenant so radically different that there is no room left for Christians to find any New Testament warrant for becoming active in Green issues.

The second way of putting the objection sounds rather different but contains many of the same ingredients. It can be stated as follows: the Fall was indeed the tragic event from which corruption of creation flowed. And corrupted it still is— irrevocably so. Why, therefore, bother with it? Given that the world of creation is now damaged beyond repair, the business of Christians is to save souls while there is still time, without diverting their energies into trendy cul-de-sacs. After all, the New Testament itself predicts the final destruction of this corrupted order of creation:

> In the beginning, O Lord, you laid the foundations of the earth, and the heavens are the work of your hands. They will perish, but you remain; they will all wear out like a garment (Heb 1:10f quoting Ps 102:25f).

> But the day of the Lord will come like a thief. The heavens will disappear with a roar; the elements will be destroyed by fire, and the earth and everything in it will be laid bare... That day will bring about the destruction of the heavens by fire, and the elements will melt in the heat (2 Pet 3:10,12).

It will take two whole chapters to deal fully with these objections. They must be examined carefully, because if they are correct, then there is no place for Christian involvement in environmental issues—all our efforts will have to be directed elsewhere. So the refutation of these views, if justified, will have to be carefully carried out. But if we can demonstrate that the theme of the goodness of creation is carried forward from Old Testament to the New after all, then this will throw a different light on the subject altogether.

Roots of Hope

Old Testament history appears to end in failure. The golden age of Israel and her empire under David and his son Solomon was long past; repeated apostasy, idolatry, immorality and injustice led to the division of the kingdom, the fall of the Northern Kingdom to the Assyrians in 721 BC and then the biggest disaster of all—the sack of Jerusalem, the inviolable city of God, by the invading Babylonian army in 587 BC. The return from exile which began in 539 BC seemed to promise a completely new start, but it was not to be. A reading of Ezra and Nehemiah, as well as some of the minor prophets such as Haggai and Malachi, shows that life in the new Judah remained hard, and the nation never regained its former greatness. It remained a small, impotent and downtrodden country, always liable to be subjugated by greater nations, firstly Persia, then Greece, then Rome.

It was through this experience that people began to see that the vision of the renewal of creation, first heralded by Isaiah and other prophets, was not about the restoration of Israel's golden age. It was to be something altogether grander; it was what God would do with the whole of creation at the end of history:

> Behold, I will create new heavens and a new earth. The former things will not be remembered, nor will they come to mind. But be glad and rejoice for ever in what I will create, for I will create Jerusalem to be a delight and its people a joy.
>
> I will rejoice over Jerusalem and take delight in my people; the sound of weeping and of crying will be heard in it no more. Never again will there be in it an infant who lives but a few days, or an old man who does not live out his years; he who fails to reach a hundred will be considered accursed.
>
> They will build houses and dwell in them; they will plant vineyards and eat their fruit. No longer will they build houses and others live in them, or plant trees and others eat. For as the days of a tree, so will be the days of my people; my chosen ones will long enjoy the works of their hands. They will not toil in vain or bear children doomed to misfortune; for they will be a people blessed by the Lord, they and their descendants with them.
>
> Before they call I will answer; while they are still speaking I will hear. The wolf and the lamb will feed together,

and the lion will eat straw like the ox, but dust will be the serpent's food. They will neither harm nor destroy on all my holy mountain (Is 65:17–25).

This passage contains a number of striking visions—new heavens and new earth (v 17; cf 66:22), reconciliation with God (vv 19,23,24; cf 59:1f), an end to pain and tragedy (vv 19,20,23; cf 11:8,9), longevity (vv 20,22), no more oppression (vv 21,22), and harmony and fruitfulness within creation (v 25; cf 11:6,7; 35:1; Ezek 36:33–35; Hos 2:18). Because of their experience of pain and suffering (which the words of Is 65:17ff clearly mirror), the Jews recognised that these conditions would not arise gradually within the present world order as a result of the best human efforts. They would be the work of God alone, decisively intervening in the history of the world to usher in a new age which could be described in these daring categories. The question which then arises is: what has the New Testament to say about the fulfilment of these promises?

Creation—The Silence of The New Testament

At first sight, the New Testament appears to say very little about creation. Admittedly, there is a clear statement about the goodness of creation in 1 Tim 4:4: 'For everything created by God is good, and nothing is to be rejected if it is received with thanksgiving.' This is only a single verse, however, and used in the specific context of refuting certain ascetic practices. So it would be wrong to place too much weight on it.

But this verse does raise the question of why Paul could so confidently reassert the goodness of creation. Then, as ever since, asceticism exerted a strong influence within Christianity. There was much in the religious and philosophical climate of the New Testament age to encourage it, and Paul might have been expected to go along with it. Instead, he clearly draws on his deep understanding of the Old Testament, even though there was much else in the understanding and practice of Judaism that he wished to reject (eg Phil 3:2–8). We have seen how important is the goodness of creation as a theme running throughout the Old Testament, and so there is a hint here that Paul saw a continuing validity to the theme.

Yet certain parts of the New Testament are noticeably creation-denying, it is sometimes claimed. Paul Santmire, for example, argues that John's Gospel and Hebrews are very 'other-worldly', negative in their assessment of the created order.[1] In aiming to show how important environmental issues are for Christians today, it will be necessary to demonstrate a rather different estimate of creation in the New Testament. However, there is an element of truth in these assertions. There are few references to creation in the New Testament, at least at first reading, and it is easy to conclude that the Old Testament doctrine was not seen to be important in the early church. It can be argued that there are reasons for this.

First, because the new covenant universalises the people of God (that is, they are from all over the world and do not live in a particular country) the benefits of that new covenant do not include a particular tract of land. Therefore many of the Old Testament themes related to creation and the stewardship of the land are bound to feature less in the New Testament.

Even so, too much can be made of this difference between old and new covenants. God's call to Abram included the promise that 'all peoples on earth will be blessed through you' (Gen 12:3). The different setting of the new covenant is therefore not as surprising as it might at first appear. But that does not, in itself, mean that issues of stewardship are no longer of any relevance whatsover. That would be true only if it could be demonstrated from the New Testament that the world of creation is of no further value in the sight of the Creator.[2]

Then, sociological factors may also help to explain the loss of creation themes in the New Testament. While the people of Israel, at least in the earlier stages of their history, were an agrarian people, for whom the relationship with the land was vital to their well-being, New Testament Christianity was largely an urban phenomenon, as a cursory reading of Acts demonstrates. Aspects of New Testament terminology may also reflect this setting.[3]

In the light of these considerations, it is important to con-

sider the defeat of the gnostic heresy which the early church
was soon to face, and which may explain some of the particular emphases in the New Testament epistles. This is not the
place for a detailed treatment of gnosticism, except to make
the point that a central tenet was the belief in a dualism
between matter and spirit. The essence of human life, it was
taught, is a divine spark which remains trapped within the
body (constituted of created matter, which is essentially evil).
Salvation, therefore, is all about freeing this divine spark from
its material prison, so that it can be freed to wing its way to its
true heavenly home. This was accomplished by access to a
secret form of knowledge (Greek *gnosis*).[4]

Textbooks of church history demonstrate how fundamentally anti-Christian gnosticism was, and it is significant that
one of the weapons used by the theologians of the sub-apos-
tolic church to defeat gnosticism was the belief in the goodness
of creation.[5] Two important questions, therefore, will occupy
our attention until the end of the next chapter: firstly, can we
find in the New Testament any affirmation of the goodness of
creation, and secondly, are these more than merely incidental
to the main subject—the redemption which God offers
humanity through his son Jesus Christ?

THE INCARNATION

We could begin by pointing to the value Jesus placed on
creation in his teaching, but the real starting point must be
elsewhere. His teaching needs listening to because of who he
is. It is the person of Jesus Christ who looms large throughout
the New Testament. It is because of who he was and is that
salvation was won; it was because of who he was and is that
his teaching carries any weight.

Christians talk easily of the Incarnation. In the person of
Jesus Christ the second member of the Trinity came to earth
to share our life. On one level the response has to be one of
worship and wonder, and that is fitting. On another important
level, it is the task of theology to state and restate this truth in

terms to which people can respond in every age. This process began almost as soon as the events of Christ's earthly life had taken place, and the pages of the New Testament show evidence of it. As already stated, one of the mortal enemies of early Christianity was the heresy of gnosticism, and it is no surprise to find that gnostic teachers had their own ways of 'explaining' Jesus that suited their philosophical presuppositions.

This is not the place to explain in detail the variations of docetism which arose at this point (Greek *dokein* 'to seem, to appear'; the docetics taught that Christ only seemed to be human). The philosophical presupposition underlining this approach was that the worlds of spirit (goodness, perfection) and matter (corruption, evil) are fundamentally incompatible. How, therefore, could God possibly come in human form? There are modern expressions of this dualistic world view dressed up in Christian clothes. It is adopted by some otherworldly evangelical groups, by others who have been influenced by New Age thinking, and by others in which biblical Christianity has to be governed and controlled by dualistic philosophy. The theologian John Knox asserts that it is 'impossible, by definition' that God should become man.[6] The argument can be stated thus:

> Since God is spirit it is difficult to see how direct
> contact can be effected with mortal beings whose only
> means of communication is through the physical
> body...if it is possible for disembodied spirit to effect
> direct communication with mortals the need for
> Incarnation disappears; the doctrine of the Incarnation
> of God in Jesus of Nazareth indicates the mediatorial
> office of Christ between man and God.[7]

This involves a radical reinterpretation of the mediatorial work of Christ, who, on this kind of world view, came as a mediator between the transcendent and the immanent—an idea that goes back to Hegel.[8] The New Testament takes an entirely different starting point. The Scriptures testify to the mediatorial work of Christ as bridging a moral gap—that between a holy God and sinful humanity. The New Testament further shows how this was only possible because Christ possessed real humanity and real divinity, a concept that dualism cannot live with. What does this tell us about the relationship between the worlds of spirit and matter?

The inescapable consequence of the New Testament evidence is that the natures of the worlds of spirit and matter are not so fundamentally different as has often been assumed. In one sense this is obvious. How, otherwise, could God be the Creator? (The answer to this question was a vexed one for the gnostics and the answer was both ingenious and sad—it was to deny that the ultimate God was the Creator; the work of creating an evil world of matter was transferred to a lesser and malevolent god, the god of the Old Testament!). But in the Bible, not only does God create everything but, as we have seen, he created everything good and rejoiced in his work.

Viewed in that light, the idea of Incarnation is not so difficult to cope with after all. Two theologians put the matter in different but equally illuminating ways:

> From all eternity Jesus had, in his very nature, been the 'image of God', reflecting perfectly the character of and life of the Father. It was thus appropriate for him to be the 'image of God' as man...Humanity was designed to be the perfect vehicle for God's self-expression within his world, so that he could himself live appropriately among his people as one of themselves, could rule in love over creation as himself a creature...The doctrine of incarnation which flows from this cannot, by definition, squeeze either 'divinity' or 'humanity' out of shape. Indeed, it is only in Jesus Christ that we understand what 'divinity' and 'humanity' really mean: without him, we lapse into sub-Christian, or even pagan, categories of thought, and then wonder why the doctrine of Incarnation causes us so much difficulty.[9]

This [Incarnation] constituted a repudiation of all

attitudes to the stuff of the world which saw it as evil, alien to its Creator, a prison from which a non-material reason, or 'soul', must seek release. God was to be seen as achieving his ends by involvement with, immanence in, expression through the very stuff of the world and its events in space and time. Moreover, the assertion that Jesus was the ultimate revelation of God's being to men in a mode they could understand and appropriate, amounted, we can now see, to an affirmation that 'nature' in its actuality, materiality and evolution, of which Jesus was indubitably a part, is both potentially at least an expression of God's being and the instrument of his action. Paradoxically, the Christian claim asserts that God fulfils man's personalness, and satisfies his most 'spiritual' aspirations, by entering the temporal process of materiality as a man, made like all men of the component units of the stuff of the world.[10]

The New Testament also insists that it is only because Jesus was fully one of us and also fully divine that his death on the cross was able to achieve salvation. In this way the themes of creation and redemption converge, and the Old Testament assertions of the goodness of creation are carried forward into the New in a way central to the gospel rather than being peripheral to it. Nor is it any accident that the Bible's emphasis on creation is not shared by other world religions. Thus William Temple wrote:

> Christianity is the most materialistic of all great religions. The others hope to achieve spiritual reality by ignoring matter—calling it illusion (maya) or saying that it does not exist...Christianity, based as it is on the Incarnation, regards matter as destined to be the vehicle and instrument of spirit, and spirit as fully actual so far as it controls and directs matter.[11]

We have already referred to Paul Santmire's estimate of the creation-denying nature of the Fourth Gospel and the Epistle to the Hebrews. Yet it is significant to note the seemingly deliberate parallels between Genesis 1 and John 1:1–14. This is indicated not only by the repetition of the phrase 'In the beginning' but by many other lexical and stylistic parallels.[12] Thus, as the German theologian Jurgen Moltmann has pointed out, the New Testament presents the new creation in a way which corresponds to the original creation of the Old Testament so that the one is a mirror image of the other.[13]

Similarly, Santmire's view is not supported by some aspects of the view of Christ in Hebrews. There is, for example, the statement that Christ is 'sustaining all things by his powerful word' (1:3), although it is possible to make too much of this: the context is the supremacy of Christ, established by a comparison of his status and ministry with those of the angels. More important is the high-priestly passage in 2:14–18 which stresses Christ's solidarity with us. Theologian Eric Mascall has stated it thus: '...so far from human nature having an inbuilt metaphysical repugnance to its assumption by God, it is precisely in such assumption that it receives its highest self-expression and fulfilment.'[14]

In Chapter 4 we considered at length the meaning of the divine image in man. One of the conclusions was that it is to do with a vital relationship between the Creator and humanity, a relationship which the New Testament reasserts. Although it is often assumed that sin removes that image, James 3:9 states that the image continues, even though we must remain sombre about the alienating effects of sin. From this, it should perhaps not be surprising to find that the Christian's body is a temple of the Holy Spirit (1 Cor 6:19). In these respects also, Christianity presents a radically different view of human life from that found in the gnostic teachings that so alarmed the early Christian theologians.

Jesus' Teaching on The Goodness of Creation

It is because of Jesus' nature as both fully God and fully man that we can acknowledge him as mediator and as teacher of divine truth. In particular, we must examine carefully the implications for environmental issues of his death, Resurrection and Ascension, and his announcement of the coming of the kingdom of God. In passing, we can note certain aspects of his teaching which underline some Old Testament themes.

One theme which is reasserted is the goodness of creation and the Father's continued care of all that he had made. It is clear to those with eyes to see that he ensures food for the birds, so we can be sure that his care extends to all of creation, especially humanity (Mt 6:26ff; 10:29; cf Acts 14:17; 17:25). It is the Creator who bestows beauty as he wills (Mt 6:29). Jesus' use of illustrations from the world of creation to demonstrate spiritual truth also shows that its value goes beyond the merely pragmatic (eg Mt 13).

The second theme of importance is his confrontation of all attitudes that smack of power, privilege and domination:

> Also a dispute arose among them as to which of them was considered to be the greatest. Jesus said to them, 'The kings of the Gentiles lord it over them; and those who exercise authority over them call themselves Benefactors. But you are not to be like that. Instead, the greatest among you should be like the youngest, and the one who rules like the one who serves. For who is the greater, the one who is at table or the one who serves? Is it not the one who is at the table? But I am among you as one who serves' (Lk 22: 24–27).

Jesus was not talking here specifically about Green issues, of course! He encountered such attitudes among all sorts of people in many different situations, even (as here) among his own disciples (cf Jn 13:1–17). The point is that such attitudes manifest themselves in many different ways, including, in a technological age, the belief that technology allows us to dominate nature in a selfish and aggressive way.

But alongside Jesus' teaching on creation there is also his enjoyment of it. It would be wrong, on the basis of Luke 9:1–6, 57–62, to conclude that he was an ascetic. What these texts show is that a simple lifestyle was a necessary part of an itinerant ministry. Asceticism is about a particular negative attitude to material things which is joyless and sombre, and is far removed from the lifestyle and teaching of Jesus.

Instead there are enjoyment and humour. The gospel narratives never refer to him laughing or smiling, but what are we to make of the story of a man with an enormous beam sticking out of his eye (Mt 7:3–5)? It is an argument from exaggeration, and there seems little doubt that his audience were meant to laugh at it as they perceived the message he was conveying. The same point can be made with the story of the Pharisee straining a gnat from his drink but managing to swallow a camel (Mt 23:24). His use of pictures from the natural world shows how keen an observer he was.[15] We also find him sitting down at meals with all kinds of people, and the first miracle which the Fourth Gospel records is the changing of water into wine—and excellent wine at that!

The Miracles of Jesus

Miracles were an integral part of the ministry of Jesus, and of the early church. Arguably they should be expected in every age of the church, although how frequently (if at all) is a matter for much divergence of opinion. What is often lacking in modern Christian thought is considered reflection on the significance of miracles.

The New Testament is clear upon the fact that they accompany the preaching of the kingdom of God (eg Mt 3:2; 4:23). This leaves open the question of how the miracles are related to the preaching. If they are not merely incidental, they must in some way confirm the content of that preaching. If we go further and think about how they confirm the preaching, two possibilities arise: either they are just magic tricks to attract attention, or else their significance lies in the way they give at least a glimpse of what that kingdom is like. This is the position taken in the gospels, and it is particularly clear in the Fourth Gospel where John deliberately refers to the miracles he has selected as 'signs' (eg 2:11). So, as we look at some particular miraculous happenings in the ministry of Jesus, what exactly do we learn about the nature of the kingdom from them?

> Then he got into the boat and his disciples followed him. Without warning, a furious storm came up on the lake, so that the waves swept over the boat. But Jesus was sleeping. The disciples went and woke him, saying, 'Lord, save us! We're going to drown!' He replied, 'You of little faith, why are you so afraid?' Then he got up and rebuked the winds and the waves, and it was completely calm. The men were amazed and asked, 'What kind of man is this? Even the winds and the waves obey him?' (Mt 8:23–27).

This, one of the 'nature miracles' of Jesus, is recorded in all three synoptic gospels. What is the truth it contains? It is often used by preachers to convey the message 'Jesus stills the storms of life', and there is some evidence that the early church did interpret it this way during times of great testing and persecution, in which they knew they truly 'followed' (v 23) their master. However, this interpretation (which is consistent with other New Testament passages) does not do justice to the full impact of the incident. The final words, found also in Mark 4:41 and Luke 8:27, surely point towards the main issue: the identity of Jesus.

As the one who controls the violent forces of nature, he is the Lord of the elements in the same way as the Creator himself, depicted in the Old Testament (eg Ps 89:8,9; 93:3,4; 106:8,9; 107:23–30; Is 59:5,6). But to assert the divinity of Jesus from this incident is to stop short of the full significance of what had taken place. In the Old Testament the sea represents the forces of chaos which are always threatening to engulf the ordered world of creation, an order always under threat also as a result of human sin (see Chapter 4). Thus, by this act Jesus not only shows who he is, but there is also a tantalising glimpse of what he came to do in the disturbed world of creation.

Most of the recorded miracles of Jesus were acts of healing. If this interpretation of the stilling of the storm is correct, then it should be possible to apply it to the healing miracles as well. Exactly why did Jesus heal people? And what was the understanding of the early church of the significance of its own healing ministry (eg Acts 3:1–10; Jas 5:14–16)? The first healing miracle Mark records is that of the paralytic who was lowered through the roof on the Sabbath day (2:1–12); Jesus made it plain that the healing was linked with the forgiveness of sins. This explanation is not given with other miracles, although it can perhaps be assumed, because forgiveness of sins (heralding the reconciliation between God and humanity which we shall refer to shortly) is central to God's solution of the human plight.

A more comprehensive view of the significance of these healing miracles can be established by linking them, as we have already suggested, with his proclamation of the kingdom of God (Mt 4:17,23; Mk 1:14,15; Lk 4:43). A consideration of all the New Testament references to the kingdom suggest that there are both present and future dimensions: the kingdom— the rule of God—has already arrived but is not yet seen in all its fullness. A useful analogy is that the kingdom is like the allied armies invading and freeing Western Europe after the Normandy landings in 1944 but before the final surrender of the enemy powers in 1945. Yet the kingdom is certainly present at least in part, and therefore miracles are bound to take place, because they declare not only that the kingdom is here but also what it is like.

What then is the nature of this kingdom, that it can be expressed in acts of healing and in the stilling of storms, accompany the forgiveness of sins, and express Jesus' compassion (Mt 9:36; 14:14; 15:32; 20:34; Mk 1:41; 6:34; 8:2)? If the kingdom is about the assertion of God's rule over a corrupted creation, then that creation is characterised by the temporary absence of the rule of God and by the painfully obvious helplessness of humanity to exercise a responsible care for creation, because of a failure to live in the image with which they were first created (Gen 1:26,28).

All the situations which are transformed by these miracles are situations which exhibit the symptoms of the absence of

God's rule—storms, disease, demon possession, hunger and spiritual lostness. These things should not be so. Disease and demon possession lead to physical conditions of the human body which are put right by the healing miracles, and underlying these is the alienation which requires repentance and forgiveness. This does not, of course, mean that there is an automatic personal connection between sin and disease. This simplistic view is demolished in Luke 13:1–3 and John 9:3. It ignores the fact that we live in community, and it is often other people who suffer the consequences of our actions. Modern forms of pollution reflect the truth of this quite clearly— radioactive clouds from the Chernobyl disaster are no respecters of national or international boundaries.

But there is clearly a general connection between sin and suffering. There is no such thing as a wrong action without consequences of some kind. In Chapter 4 we saw that Genesis 3 depicts the consequences of the Fall of men and women in terms of the disruption of all the relationships which set the parameters of human life. It is from this that disease and hunger flow, and the possiblility of demon possession as people alienated from God open their lives to other forces which, for a while, seem attractive. The rule of God cannot coexist peacefully with realities like these.

The kingdom of God is not a purely 'spiritual' entity in which the world of creation has no part. It is heralded by such miracles because, God's rule being perfectly fulfilled, it will include the renewal of creation and the destruction of all the forces which continue to corrupt it. It is, and will be, a kingdom free from disease, hunger, suffering and fear (Rev 21:1–5). It will involve the breaking down of barriers of alienation and the remaking of disrupted relationships, involving not only God and humanity, but also the whole created order.

The Death of Christ

The emphasis in the New Testament is on the death of Christ. The four gospels give apparently disproportionate space to the events of the last days of Jesus' life, and to the act of his dying.

What they are telling us, however, is not just that a man died but that his death had far-reaching consequences. The rest of the New Testament sees the early church understanding ever more richly the consequences of that salvation-winning act.

For reasons which are entirely understandable, the emphasis in the New Testament Scriptures is on the personal consequences of Jesus' death. Genesis 3 shows that the root of all our problems is the alienation that arises from the self-assertion of the human will; it is this state of alienation and hostility which must first be put right. It is no coincidence that the argument Paul uses in Romans 1:18–32 leans heavily on the language and theological concepts of Genesis 3.[16]

So terms such as reconciliation and justification are repeatedly used (eg Rom 5:1–11; 2 Cor 5:11–21; Eph 2:11–22), and the main difference between the two terms may be that justification is the legal-forensic term that Jews would understand, and reconciliation is the reality to which it refers and which Gentiles of the Roman empire would more readily understand.

The emphasis here is on reconciliation between God and human beings, because it is the most vital relationship of all, without which no other relationships can be mended. But since Genesis 3—11 went on to refer to alienation of other relationships—between a man and his wife, between two brothers, and between all humanity, it is not difficult to find references to reconciliation on these levels also. Thus Ephesians 5:22—6:4, Colossians 3:18–21 and 1 Peter 3:1–7 give a new vision of Christian family life, and other passages spell out the consequences of redemption for other human relationships (eg Eph 6:5–9; Phil 2:1–18; 4:2,3; Col 3:22—4:1; Heb 10:19–25; 1 Pet 3:8–12).

It should be obvious that we will not expect to find much in the New Testament about the consequences for the whole of creation of Christ's death. Environmental issues were not particularly important in the cities of the Roman Empire. Quite remarkable, however, are the passages which state quite clearly that there is a much wider, creation-embracing, dimension to the cross:

He is the image of the invisible God, the firstborn over all creation. For by him all things were created: things in heaven and things on earth; visible and invisible, whether thrones or powers or rulers or authorities; all things were created by him and for him. He is before all things, and in him all things hold together. And he is the head of the body, the church; he is the beginning and the firstborn from among the dead, so that in everything he might have the supremacy. For God was pleased to have all his fullness dwell in him, and through him to reconcile to himself all things, whether things on earth or things in heaven, by making peace through his blood, shed on the cross. Once you were alienated from God and were enemies in your minds because of your evil behaviour. But now he has reconciled you by Christ's physical body through death to present you holy in his sight, without blemish and free from accusation—if you continue in your faith, established and firm, not moved from the hope held out in the gospel (Col 1:15–23).

The significance of the death of Christ is described here in two separate ways. In vv 21ff it is interpreted in personal terms which are echoed in many other places in the New Testament (see above), but in v 20 the reference is to the reconciliation of 'all things' (Greek *ta panta*). Most New Testament commentators are agreed that 'all things' must refer to the whole sub-human creation—which Christ himself created in the beginning (v 16).[17] Here, as already noted in the writings of Moltmann, the passage mirrors the Old Testament:

Because humanity plays the key role in the ordering of God's world, human reconciliation will lead to the restoration of creation, just as human sin led to creation's fall...At present...the world as a whole remains unaware of the reconciliation achieved on the cross, of the fact that God will eventually remake the world and its power structures so that they reflect his glory instead of human arrogance.[18]

As Tom Wright goes on to state, this may be why Paul can go on to speak of the reconciliation of the 'powers' and of Christ's victory over them as hostile forces (Col 2:15), although this interpretation does not completely satisfy all commentators.[19]

THE GOODNESS OF CREATION REAFFIRMED

We began this chapter with the fact that there is little mention in the New Testament of the goodness of creation, in comparison to its continued reassertion throughout the Old Testament. Paul states it only once, and that in the particular context of ascetic practices. But we have now dealt with enough of the New Testament to see that it is there all the time: the Incarnation reaffirms it, and the ministry and death of Christ show that the Creator's intention is to set right the corruption introduced into the world of creation by the sinfulness of humanity. Goodness is still there, although our own experience of it is that it is not as good as it should (or can) be. Thus the intended fruitfulness of the world is in contrast to the repeated famines of the 1980s and 1990s; its beauty is marred by pollution of air, land and water, by uncontrolled urban migration and faulty planning. Its diversity is whittled away by game hunting, wanton use of synthetic chemicals, and the burning of rain forests. Few people have the ability (or the time) to experience something of the Creator by contact with it. Does it bring joy to its Creator any more?

Yet although the goodness of creation is thus reaffirmed through the person and ministry of Christ, it is still significant that Paul, whose theology of the work of Christ is so highly developed, does not say much about it. Clearly, therefore, he did not start from the goodness of creation and interpret the ministry of Christ in these categories. This is to put the cart before the horse, and is the sort of temptation that some Green writers fall into in their understandable enthusiasm to demonstrate that the Bible is 'Green'.

In fact, Paul's method was exactly the opposite. He understood the ministry of Christ in such a way that its implications for the future of creation became apparent to him. This is an aspect of the topic we have not yet begun to consider, and the next chapter will be devoted to it. Without this kind of consideration the reader may still be left with a sneaking suspicion that environmentally concerned Christians are attempting to read back twentieth-century issues into a first-century text in a wholly unwarranted way.

And what about those awkward texts from Hebrews 1 and 2 Peter 3, mentioned at the beginning of this chapter, which seem to promise the final annihiliation of creation instead of its renewal? The key to understanding these texts, and to establishing exactly how the New Testament is able to see in the ministry of Christ such far-reaching implications for creation itself, lies in the amazing fact of his Resurrection. How, then, did New Testament Christianity understand this unique event?

REFERENCES

1. H. Paul Santmire, *The Travail of Nature* (Fortress Press: Philadelphia, 1985), p 213.
2. See Christopher J.H. Wright, *Living as the People of God* (IVP: Leicester, 1983), pp 92-102 for a more detailed consideration of this issue.
3. Derek Tidball, *An Introduction to the Sociology of the New Testament* (Paternoster: Exeter, 1983), p 78.
4. E.M. Yamauchi, 'Gnosticism' in Sinclair B. Ferguson and David F. Wright, *New Dictionary of Theology* (IVP: Leicester, 1988), pp 272-274, and references therein.
5. Philip Lee, *Against the Protestant Gnostics* (Oxford University Press: London, 1987).
6. John Knox, *The Humanity and Divinity of Christ* (Cambridge University Press: Cambridge, 1967).
7. H.W. Love, *Church of Ireland Gazette* 23rd February, 1990.
8. Hans Küng, *The Incarnation of God. An Introduction to Hegel's Theologi-*

cal Thought as Prologomena to a Future Christology (T.& T. Clark: Edinburgh, 1987), and review by M. Alsford in *Themelios* vol 16 no 1, (1990): p 30.

9. N.T. Wright, *Colossians* (IVP: Leicester, 1986) p 70; cf. Eric L. Mascall, *Theology and the Gospel of Christ* (SPCK: London, 1967), pp 130-1, 149, 167, 181; J.N.D. Anderson, *The Mystery of the Incarnation* (Hodder and Stoughton: London, 1978), p 150-1.

10. A.R. Peacocke, *Science and the Christian Experiment* (Oxford University Press: London, 1971), p 157.

11. William Temple, *Readings in St John's Gospel* (McMillan: London, 1939), p 20f; see also Peter Cotterell, *Mission and Meaninglessness* (SPCK: London, 1990), pp 15-20.

12. Edwin K. Lee, *The Religious Thought of St John* (SPCK: London, 1962), pp 113ff.

13. Jurgen Moltmann, *God in Creation* (SCM: London, 1985), p 68.

14. Eric L. Mascall, op cit p 167.

15. Michael Griffiths, *The Example of Jesus* (Hodder and Stoughton, 1985), pp 112-115.

16. Marjorie D. Hooker, 'Adam in Romans 1', *New Testament Studies*, vol 6 (1959-60): pp 297-306 and 'A Further Note on Romans 1', *New Testament Studies*, vol 13 (1966-7): pp 181-183.

17. For example, Peter T. O'Brien, *Colossian, Philemon* (Word: Waco, 1982), pp 31-57; Ralph P. Martin, *Reconciliation: A Study of Paul's Theology*, (Marshall, Morgan and Scott: London, 1981), pp 111-126.

18. N.T. Wright, *op cit* p 76.

19. John R.W. Stott, *The Cross of Christ* (IVP: Leicester, 1986), p 196.

Chapter Eight

THE DESTINY OF CREATION

ANNIHILATION OF CREATION?

In Jesus Christ, God has restored the human pattern
intended at the original creation... He is the new
humanity into which man may be born, not through
biological parentage, but by his decision in response to
divine grace. Thus the Christian community, from the
standpoint of faith given by God's revelation in Christ,
looks backward and forward. It traces God's purpose to
the first creation, saying: 'In Christ all things were
created'; and it lives toward the future, saying: 'God
will sum up all things in Christ.'

IN THESE WORDS the German theologian Jurgen Moltmann shows how the New Testament presents the new
creation in a way which corresponds to the original
creation of the Old Testament so that the one is a mirror-
image of the other.[1] The 'protological' creation starts with the
creation of the world and leads on to the appearance of human
beings; the eschatological creation starts with the liberation of
human beings and ends with the redemption of nature. In the
previous chapter we saw that this is the understanding of the
New Testament, and is far removed from the gnostic idea that
matter is either intrinsically evil or so fatally flawed by human
sin that it can have no further place in the eternal purposes of

God. In this way its understanding of the goodness of creation as an expression of the mind and purpose of the Creator, is in marked continuity with the same theme in the Old Testament although expressed in a rather different manner.

What therefore are we to make of the Hebrews 1 and 2 Peter 3 texts, mentioned but not dealt with in the previous chapter, which seem to predict the annihilation of the created order? They are not often quoted in their entirety:

> But the day of the Lord will come like a thief. The heavens will disappear with a roar; the elements will be destroyed by fire, and the earth and everything in it will be laid bare...That day will bring about the destruction of the heavens by fire, and the elements will melt in the heat. But in keeping with his promise we are looking forward to a new heaven and a new earth, the home of righteousness (2 Pet 3:10,12,13).

> In the beginning, O Lord, you laid the foundations of the earth, and the heavens are the work of your hands. They will perish, but you remain; they will all wear out like a garment. You will roll them up like a robe; like a garment they will be changed. But you remain the same, and your years will never end (Heb 1:10f quoting Ps 102:25f).

In each case the verses which are taken to teach final annihilation are followed by further words which suggest the alternative goal of the transformation of creation, echoing Isaiah 65:17–25. The 2 Peter 3 reference to 'a new heaven and a new earth' will be discussed more fully later, because it appears also in Revelation 21. But what are we to make of references to creation destroyed by fire (2 Peter) or perishing and wearing out (Hebrews)?

There are detailed arguments related to the precise meanings of some of the Greek verbs in these passages and how they are to be translated, which are too minute to go into here, but which seem to suggest that the vision of annihilation is not as obvious as might first appear.[2] The best explanation and means of reconciling these expressions of destruction with the unmistakeable promises of creation transformed is to propose that they emphasise the radical discontinuity involved in the drastic purging (often portrayed in Scripture by fire imagery) which a marred creation needs to undergo as part of its transformation at the end of time. It would then follow that destruction does not necessarily imply annihiliation in this context.

THE RESURRECTION OF JESUS

In the New Testament the Resurrection is the vindication of all that Jesus came to do, the demonstration that his death on the cross has saving significance and effects. Romans 4:25 links our justification to the Resurrection. This understanding of the Resurrection links it with the preaching of the cross as the means by which God reconciles individual men and women to himself (eg Rom 5:1–11; 2 Cor 5:11–21; Eph 2:11–22, etc).

This does not exhaust its meaning, however. In particular, the New Testament statement of the cosmic significance of the cross (Col 1:20), referred to in Chapter 7, needs to be seen in the light of the Resurrection. Oliver O'Donovan writes:

> It might have been possible, we could say, before Christ rose from the dead, for someone to wonder whether creation was a lost cause. If the creature constantly acted to uncreate itself, and with itself to uncreate the rest of creation, did this not mean that God's handiwork was flawed beyond hope of repair? It might have been possible before Christ rose from the dead to answer in good faith, Yes. Before God raised Jesus from the dead, the hope that we call 'gnostic', the hope for redemption *from* creation rather than for the redemption of creation, might have appeared to be the only possible hope.[3]

The cross was not the end of the story of Christ's ministry

for human beings. In a sense it marks a new beginning, not just for human beings but for creation itself. There is a strand of Christian thinking which assumes that the Incarnation was a merely temporary episode in the history of eternity—a fleeting visit to put things right, as when the service engineer comes out to fix the broken washing machine, and then disappears again. So, it goes, Christ returned to heaven, the need for the Incarnation now finished.

A different perspective, hinted at above by the words of Oliver O'Donovan, begins to emerge when we examine the gospel accounts of the Resurrection: was Christ's resurrection body purely 'spiritual'? Certainly it was not like any mortal body. He was able to come through locked doors to reassure his frightened and sceptical disciples (Jn 20:19,26). Yet the same chapter shows that his resurrection body still exhibited the wounds of crucifixion (vv 20,27; cf Lk 24:40) and that he could symbolically breathe upon them (v 22; the allusion to Genesis 2:7 is quite unmistakeable!). He ate fish to calm their fears (Lk 24:42,43) after breaking bread with the disciples on the Emmaus road (Lk 24:30). It is a new body which Christ possesses—one which has elements of continuity and discontinuity with his incarnational body. So Francis Schaeffer writes:

> This body was not just a spirit—something to be viewed as an apparition or a 'ghost'—and this same body ascended into heaven and went into the unseen world. And the body that can eat is still in the unseen world and will one day in future history be seen in the seen world again.[4]

Here Schaeffer allows our thinking about the resurrection body of Christ to go a stage further. The gospel and Acts narratives do not allow us to think of it as the temporary dressing up of a ghost to minimise the terror of his poor followers! It was with this body—both spiritual and physical in nature—that he ascended into heaven (Acts 1:1–11). But such is the discontinuity between our bodies and his resurrection body that we cannot think of it as physical except as a physical body which has been radically transformed. It is then only a short step to see here a signpost to the renewal and transformation of creation itself.

The Testimony of 1 Corinthians 15

This wider understanding of Resurrection and its relation to creation is developed by Paul at length in 1 Corinthians 15, in a passage where, significantly, he makes it clear that his arguments are based not on new-fangled ideas of his own but on traditions which he has received from others (v 3) and on his own encounter with the risen Christ (v 8). Here there are two sections to the argument, the first to do with the Resurrection of Christ, the second to do with our own resurrection bodies.

First, following the opening section of the chapter in which Paul stresses the reality and centrality of the Resurrection (vv 1–19), Christ's ministry is portrayed as reversing the effects of Adam's sin (vv 20–28): 'As in Adam all die, even so in Christ shall all be made alive' (v 22; cf v 45). This is not to separate the Resurrection from previous events, especially the cross. Paul's intention is exactly the opposite. So the language Paul uses here is similar to that in cross-centred passages such as Romans 5:12–21; 8:1–4. While in Romans 5:1–11 the emphasis is on the reconciliation of individuals to God, the full text of 1 Corinthians 15 makes it clear that nothing short of a physical transformation is in view. Thus the risen Christ is described as 'the first fruits of those who have fallen asleep' (v 20; cf v 23). Elsewhere Paul says we will one day receive new bodies like his (Phil 3:20,21).

Secondly, the way Paul describes the resurrection bodies we await makes it clear that they will not be purely 'spiritual', entirely discontinuous with the bodies we now possess. If they are to be like Christ's, this cannot be so, as we have already established by reference to the resurrection narrative in John 20. Verses 35–49 use the analogy of the seed which has to die so that a new entity can arise from it; they describe resurrection bodies which are both continuous and discontinuous with our present bodies. Obviously there is an element of paradox here (though this should not discourage us—it is present in many other aspects of Christian truth), and the precise nature of this resurrection life is far beyond what human imagination can rise to. The same applies to the new heavens and new earth where this life will take place. But that Paul's argument and language is meant to imply transformation seems inescapable.[5]

The Book of Revelation

We have shown that the New Testament vision of the final renewal of creation is derived from the Resurrection of Christ. But it would be wrong to see this as a vision which suddenly arrived on the scene at this point. Its roots go back much further, to the Old Testament prophecies of the renewal of creation which we considered in the previous chapter (eg Is 65:17–25).

Two remarkable parallels to this passage in the New Testament declare that the renewal of creation will be centred on the person of Jesus Christ. The first is in Mark 1:12f, where, after the temptations in the wilderness were finished, 'he was with the wild animals, and angels attended him.' While some commentators interpret this statement as a reference to Christ's need for protection by his Father from the wild animals, it is not easy to see what place this idea has in the context of the passage. It is more likely that the phrase echoes the Old Testament prophecies already referred to which announce forthcoming harmony in creation—as might be fitting when the agent of creation is present.[6]

The second and more substantial parallel is Revelation 21:1–5, where the comparison with the context of Isaiah 65:17–25 is very striking indeed:

> Then I saw a new heaven and a new earth, for the first heaven and the first earth had passed away, and there was no longer any sea. I saw the Holy City, the new Jerusalem,

coming down out of heaven from God, prepared as a bride beautifully dressed for her husband. And I heard a loud voice from the throne saying, 'Now the dwelling of God is with men, and he will live with them. They will be his people, and God himself will be with them and be their God. He will wipe away every tear from their eyes. There will be no more death or mourning or crying or pain, for the old order of things has passed away.'

The parallels between the Isaiah and Revelation passages—the reference to the 'new heaven and a new earth', the end of suffering, and the presence of God with his people in the holy city—show clearly how the theme of the goodness of creation is transferred directly from the Old Testament to the New (and the comparison can be extended to Revelation 22:1–5). The promise of the renewal of creation still lies in the future, but what the New Testament adds to the Old is the way that the kingdom of God has already broken into the present world order through the Incarnation, death and Resurrection of Jesus Christ, God the Son. In the Incarnation the Father not only reaffirms the goodness of what he has created, but he also declares unacceptable the corruption that humanity has wrought upon it. But rather than writing off creation as having no future, he reaffirms its goodness also in declaring its coming renewal, and pointing towards this in the Resurrection.

Revelation 4 indirectly confirms this promise of the renewal of creation, in its vision of worship in heaven:

Whenever the living creatures give glory, honour and thanks to him who sits on the throne and who lives for ever and ever, the twenty-four elders fall down before him who sits on the throne, and worship him who lives for ever and ever. They lay their crowns before the throne and say:

You are worthy, our Lord and God, to receive glory and honour and power, for you created all things, and

> by your will they were created and have their being
> (vv 9–11).

There is, of course, no direct reference here to new heavens or a new earth, but the significant feature of this vision of the worship of God is that he is worshipped not only as Redeemer (cf 5:9f) but also as Creator. It would be difficult to see the relevance of this if creation were to be written off, its goodness now irrevocably ruined; the hymn of praise is more convincing if seen as a celebration of God's continuing authority over what he has made. Among those who worship God are the 'living creatures'—what do they represent? Various commentators give different intepretations on points of detail, but there is some convergence of opinion that they represent the world of creation. G.E Ladd sees them as either representing the praise of creation itself (cf Ps 19), or else they are angelic beings whom the Creator uses 'in executing his rule and his divine will in all the orders of his creation.'[7]

Romans 8—A Climactic Statement

The relevance of Paul's great assertion in Romans 8 that creation has a glorious future has long been recognised. In 1895 William Sanday and Arthur Headlam wrote in a famous commentary on Romans:

> There runs through his words an intense sympathy with nature in and for itself...He seems to lay his ear to the earth and the confused murmur which he hears has a meaning for him: it is creation's yearning for that happier state intended for it and of which it has been defrauded.[8]

This is the passage about which they wrote:

> I consider that our present sufferings are not worth comparing with the glory that will be revealed in us. The creation waits with eager expectation for the sons of God to be

revealed. For the creation was subjected to frustration, not of its own choice, but by the will of the one who subjected it, in hope that the creation itself will be liberated from its bondage to decay and brought into the glorious freedom of the children of God. We know that the whole creation has been groaning as in the pains of childbirth right up to the present time. Not only so, but we ourselves, who have the firstfruits of the Spirit, groan inwardly as we wait eagerly for our adoption as sons, the redemption of our bodies. For in this hope we were saved (Rom 8:18–24).

We can examine the content of this passage under four headings:

1   Creation was subjected to frustration (v 20)

The tragic situation in which creation finds itself, through no fault of its own, is characterised by 'frustration' (Greek *mataiotes*; RSV 'futility'), a concept which comes from Ecclesiastes 1:2. Verse 21 refers to creation's 'bondage to decay' and verse 22 to it 'groaning as in the pains of childbirth'. Although *mataiotes* can refer to pagan gods (eg Acts 14:15), there are no specific references to them here, and the best sense of this description of creation is that it has failed to attain its goal or fulfil its purpose. If an extension of meaning can be taken from the use of the same word in 1:21, we can go further and relate the frustration of creation to its exploitation by humanity which refuses to acknowledge its Creator.

Verse 22, through the introductory 'we know that', suggests that Paul is not introducing any new idea; his readers already know well the truth of what he is saying. Possibly he means that the contemporary Roman world had its own share of pollution problems, but it seems more likely that he is calling upon their knowledge of the Old Testament scriptures, in particular Genesis 3:17ff (it is widely recognised by commentators that Romans 1:18–32 draws heavily upon this same passage).

2   God subjected creation to frustration (v 20)

At first, this may seem surprising. Why would the Creator wish to deal with his handiwork in this way? Perhaps, it is sometimes suggested, the phrase 'by the will of the one who subjected it' refers to someone else—Adam, or humanity in general, or even the devil? But we have already noted the references to Genesis, and the reference is obviously to the Creator's curse on the ground of 3:17–19. Nor is any other identification consistent with the fact that creation was thus subjected 'in hope'.

3   Creation will be set free from corruption (v 21)

The curse on the ground of Genesis 3:17–19 was not, however, the Creator's last word. The corruption and frustration to which creation has been subjected will remain the order of the day so long as sin, and its powerful potential for alienation, continues to exist. But even in Genesis 3:15 there is a 'proto-evangelical' promise of a radical reordering, and this may well have been in Paul's mind when he wrote these words (see also Romans 16:20).

4   Creation will share our liberty (v 21)

'The redemption of our bodies' (v 23), being something 'awaited', still lies in the future. It is different from, though flowing out of, the reconciling work of Christ on the cross; the reference is to the final Resurrection at the end of time (cf 1 Cor 15:35–57; Phil 3:21), and the whole of creation will share this glorious destiny. Thus we are first-fruits of what will happen to the whole of creation (cf Jas 1:18). The liberty which creation will then enjoy is best thought of as its freedom perfectly and fully to reflect its Creator's purpose—heretofore impossible because of humanity's sin, and its alienating consequences.

Having now considered the content of this climactic statement, it remains to consider its context: by what process of thought did Paul reach this understanding of the future of creation? Another issue arises also: it is one thing to imagine that the renewal of creation is peripheral to the gospel, as if it belonged at the end of Romans 16. But because it comes in Romans 8 it clearly occupies a central position in Paul's understanding of the gospel. It is important to understand how this can be so.

Resurrection In The Old Testament

So far we have used the method of showing how the different aspects of Christ's ministry reflect the inherent goodness of creation—a goodness marred by human sin, but one day to be completely renewed after the manner of his Resurrection. Yet this is unsatisfactory as a complete theological explanation because it puts the cart before the horse again. Paul's theology, as often noted, is thoroughly Christ-centred (even though that leaves plenty of room for different interpretations). So the key question here must be: what was the significance of Christ to Paul so that he saw in him not just the reconciliation of individual sinners to God but even more, the beginning of the reconciliation of creation to its Creator and the start of its transformation? Important though it is, this question has received little attention in Christian thinking. To answer it, we must return to the Old Testament roots of Paul's belief in Christ.

We have already seen how Israel's return from exile led not to a restoration of the golden age of David and Solomon, as had been hoped, but to a continued battle for any sort of prosperity and stability in the midst of the power struggles of the contemporary Mediterranean world. It was in this context that people came to realise that the divine promises pointed forward to a radical discontinuity at the end of history, when God would intervene decisively to defeat Israel's enemies and usher in a new golden age. Different prophets saw this in different ways: national restoration (Obad), the renewal of creation (Is 65), outpourings of charismatic gifts with fearful signs (Joel 2:28–32) or eschatological conflict between God and his foes (Ezek 38,39; Joel 3; Zech 14). In Isaiah 24—27 the picture is of destructive judgement of God's (and Israel's) enemies, followed by the enthronement of God (24:23; 25:6–8), the abolition of death and the raising of the righteous dead:

> But your dead will live; their bodies will rise. You who dwell in the dust wake up and shout for joy. Your dew will be like the dew of the morning; the earth will give birth to her dead (Is 26:19).

Here is a clear Old Testament promise of Resurrection, and there are others. But it is important to note that it is national Resurrection which is in view rather than that of individuals. The same is true of other Old Testament prophecies of Resurrection, even though the details clearly link them with the raising of Christ:

> Come, let us return to the Lord. He has torn us to pieces, but he will heal us; he has injured us but he will bind up our wounds. After two days he will revive us; on the third day he will restore us, that we may live in his presence (Hos 6:1,2; cf Ezek 37:11–13; Dan 12:2).

Current speculation often linked the inauguration of this new order with the appearance of a divine figure who would play a key role in the final events. Different groups had different expectations, derived from different Old Testament texts such as the Son of Man passages in Daniel 7, and various inter-testamental scriptures, but many were looking for the one who would, in his ministry, usher in the end of history and the restoration of all things. John Bright writes of current Messianic expectations: '...even where specifically Messianic hopes are present, they are not attached to the existing order, as in old Israel, but concern a figure whom God will raise up to usher in a new order.'[9]

Paul clearly recognised in the risen Christ the Messiah-figure who featured so prominently in Jewish hopes. His own testimony was that he had encountered the risen Christ on the Damascus road, and had come to see that he was both the promised Messiah and the crucified Jesus (Acts 9:1–22; 22: 4–16; 26:9–18; Gal 1:11–24; 1 Cor 15:1–10). This recognition was not based on any expectation from Scripture that the Messiah would himself be resurrected. As Tom Wright has argued, the recognition of Jesus as Messiah is based on the fact that God had done for Jesus what the Jews expected him to do for Israel on the last day—raising from death one who was executed by pagans (a belief different from saying that the expectation was that the Messiah was put to be put to death and then raised to life). Thus all the promises of God come true in him (2 Cor 1.20).[10]

Similarly, the New Testament applied to Christ terms which described Israel in the Old Testament: eg vines (Ps 80:8,8; Is 5:1–7; Jer 2:21; cf Jn 15:1–8), stone and cornerstone (Ps 118:22–24; Mt 21:42; Mk 12:10,11; Lk 20:17; Acts 4:11; Eph 2:20; 1 Pet 2:6–8). With the Resurrection, then, the full significance of the man Jesus becomes apparent for the first time. Because of his Resurrection he represents Israel, whose national Resurrection is prefigured in the Old Testament; and with the Resurrection everything which God promised would happen at the 'Day of the Lord', including the defeat of evil and the renewal of creation, has begun.

In Romans all this is seen as an outworking of God's righteousness—his covenant faithfulness. This righteousness is not just about what God is, but even more so about what he does—he has dealt with evil, acted impartially, and rescued the helpless from their plight (chapters 1—4; especially 3:21–26). But Paul's whole experience of being a Jew, and of the plight of the Jewish people, means that he never saw the experience of this righteousness in personal terms only. Because the God who does these things is also the Creator, the redemption of his people is the means by which the whole world will be blessed; the promises which come true in the Messiah through the righteousness of God include those for the renewal of creation in Isaiah 65:17–25 and elsewhere. Thus it is a natural progression of thought from the individual's experience of God's righteousness in Romans 8:12–17 to that of creation itself in 8:18–25, and it therefore comes as no surprise to find that the two passages use very similar categories: suffering, adoption and glorification. Further, the intermingling of thoughts about the liberty of God's children and of the whole of creation within 8:18–25 also makes sense seen in this light.

THE QUESTION OF MOTIVATION

The Christian's vision of what God will do at the end of history is part of what the New Testament calls 'hope'. That word takes it out of the realms of speculation, as if all we had to do was to sit back and wait until God finally decides it is time to declare close of play on the final day. Christians who live in hope are active Christians, and joyful ones at that. This brings us to the question of why people today are so concerned about environmental issues.

Why do so many people take at least a passing interest in environmental problems? Why do organisations such as Friends of the Earth, Greenpeace and the Royal Society for the Protection of Birds flourish? The answer depends on what level we approach the problem. In Chapter 1 we examined ideas such as the desire to preserve the beauty of nature, the idea that nature has rights, and fear of the future, and found them wanting. If we take a sociological approach, we come up with an answer that appears to explain an interesting phenomenon: ecology is the preoccupation of the middle classes. Another question then arises: why should this be so? Tony Walter suggests the following explanation:

> The strength of popular ecology, like any popular movement, does not depend on the logic or truth of its ideas but on whether it meets some social, psychological, or economic need in a significant portion of the population.[11]

He argues that the demise of Christian belief in a secularised society leaves a yawning gap—where is a stable sense of order (a 'cosmology') to be found? The problem is particularly acute for middle-class people, who have had to cope with traumatic changes in recent times, such as inflation, insecurity at the prospect of large-scale unemployment (which previously afflicted the 'working classes' only), disillusionment with expectations of progress, an increasing sense of powerlessness, and the rebellion of their young. Taking up the cause of environmental protection then gives them a sense of stability through the feeling of doing something good, and pleasure at involvement in what seems radical and innovative.

If Walter's explanation is correct, then it reveals a widespread motivation for involvement in environmental issues that is inadequate. However people articulate what they are doing in this area, it is seen to be basically inward-looking, and more to do with fear and apprehension than with optimism. And this is where a biblically motivated Christian has a distinct—even unique—contribution to make. What we do should be outward-looking, not the opposite; we have an unshakeable optimism to bring to the realm of environmental care. That does not mean that we forget how sin will continue to affect our world through greed, insecurity, complacency and lack of vigilance. Rather, we insist that these things will not have the last word.

Our conviction has to do with the fundamental goodness of creation. However successful humanity has been at tarnishing this goodness, the Creator himself has promised to have the last word. His promise is that creation itself will be set free, transformed and renewed along with his people at the end of the age. If ever there was a motivation for continuing to take the best possible care of creation, this is it. It is significant that in 1 Corinthians 15, with its lengthy argument on the Resurrection of Christ and of his people, the final verse urges them not to waver in their total commitment to the work God has given them to do:

> Therefore, my dear brothers, stand firm. Let no one move you. Always give yourselves fully to the work of the Lord,

because you know that your labour in the Lord is not in
vain (1 Cor 15:58).

This verse does not, of course, apply specifically to the
realm of environmental care! But it must certainly include it.
It takes seriously the human temptation to waver, to lose hope
and to run out of patience. In his subsequent letter to the
Corinthians Paul had to encourage them to complete the
gathering of the collection for the Christians in Jerusalem.
There is a strong hint that they were wavering in their enthusiasm for this task (2 Cor 8,9). Elsewhere Paul expounds on the
fruit of the Spirit, which produces in the believer Christlike
characteristics that include patience and longsuffering (Gal
5:22). We sometimes wallow in pessimism as yet more bad
environmental news hits the headlines. How can we possibly
believe we can change anything at all?

What matters most here is not specific results but the
persistence of committed people whose eyes are firmly fixed on
the goal God has decreed for the whole of his creation. It is
persistence like this that makes a difference over a long period
of time, if not immediately. Stephen Travis writes:

> In one of my occasional nightmares, I am playing in an
> orchestra, and the composition we are playing gets
> increasingly complex and difficult as the piece
> progresses. I reach a point where I feel defeated by the
> difficulty and decide to go back to the beginning. And
> then I wake up...The fact is, the orchestral player
> cannot go back. The music is going on around him. He
> must stay with it, trusting the conductor to guide him
> through the cross-rhythms till the climax is reached and
> he is enveloped in relief and applause.[12]

When we are too conscious of still living in this world, we
lose sight of the next, to which we also belong. Thus, as
Stephen Travis says, hope is, in the Bible, a door, a helmet
and an anchor.[13] It is a door because God is always available:
he never gives up, never abandons his purposes of love, even

when his people lack faith (Hos 2:15) and obedience (Hos 11:1–4,8,9). It is a helmet because it is able to protect us from the fears, anxieties, insecurities and uncertainties of the present world where we are called to live out our discipleship (1 Thess 5:8). It is an anchor because the uncertainties of life, and the fact that so much seems to be lined up in opposition to the will of God, could otherwise cause us to lose heart and drift away from the faith (Heb 6:18,19).

We are already part of a new creation (2 Cor 5:17), already being renewed after the image of Christ himself (Col 3:10). The Holy Spirit is our foretaste and guarantee of the age to come (Eph 1:14), even in the midst of present suffering (Rom 8:23; 2 Cor 1:22). A failure to look forward, to work in the certainty of what lies ahead (Phil 3:13f), is a failure to take seriously what the Creator has decreed about the future of his good creation.

REFERENCES

1. Jurgen Moltmann, *God in Creation* (SCM: London, 1985), p 68.

2. See eg Steve Bishop, 'Green theology and deep ecology: New Age or new creation?', *Themelios*, vol 16 no 3 (April 1991): pp 8-15; Richard Bauckham, *2 Peter and Jude* (Word: Waco, 1985), p 316; Al Wolters, 'World view and textual criticism in 2 Peter 3:10', *Westminster Theological Journal*, vol 49 (1987): pp 405-413.

3. Oliver O'Donovan, *Resurrection and Moral Order. An Outline for Evangelical Ethics* (IVP: Leicester, 1986), p 14.

4. Francis Schaeffer, *Pollution and the Death of Man* (Hodder and Stoughton: London, 1970), p 45.

5. Donald Guthrie, *New Testament Theology* (IVP: Leicester, 1981), pp 828-830.

6. Dennis E. Nineham, *Saint Mark* (Penguin: Harmondsworth, 1963), p 64.

7. George Eldon Ladd, *A Commentary on the Revelation of John* (Eerdmans: Michigan, 1972), p 77.

8. William Sanday and Arthur C. Headlam, *A Critical and Exegetical*

Commentary on the Epistle to the Romans (T & T Clark: Edinburgh, 1895), p 212.

9. John Bright, *A History of Israel* (SCM: London, 1980), p 454.

10. Tom Wright, 'The New Testament and the State', *Themelios*, vol. 16 no. 1, (October 1990): pp 11-17.

11. Tony Walter, 'Home or Castle? A Christian sociological approach to the family and ecology', *Third Way* vol 2 (1978): pp 3-6. See also his book *The Human Home* (Lion: Tring, 1982).

12. Stephen H. Travis, *I Believe in the Second Coming of Jesus* (Hodder and Stoughton: London, 1982), p 213f.

13. *ibid* p 210f.

Chapter Nine

GREEN ISSUES AS GOLDEN OPPORTUNITIES

ENVIRONMENTAL ISSUES: RED HERRINGS?

IT HAS TAKEN eight chapters to cover the full scriptural testimony to the goodness of creation. This is because of the need to make a convincing Christian case for the care of creation, and because this theme is more important in the Bible than is often realised. So we started with the powerful statements about the goodness of creation in Genesis 1—11, and humanity's high calling to dominion over creation. In spite of what Christianity has been accused of, this is nothing to do with reckless exploitation, but with careful stewardship reflecting an unspoilt relationship with the Creator himself.

The fall of Adam and Eve, so tragically portrayed in Genesis 3, led not only to alienation from God, but to disruption of all the other relationships that order human life, including the relationship with the land. This sombre assessment of corrupted human understanding and capability forms part of an ethical prologue to Israel's life in Canaan. The land was eventually ruined, the result of a lethal mixture of disobedience and idolatry. All that was left was the promise of the renewal of creation at the end of time, in a series of prophecies which are either over-spiritualised, or else ignored altogether.

But the New Testament reaffirms the vision of the renewal of creation (eg Rom 8; 2 Pet 3; Rev 21) in a way that is more than incidental. It is close to the centre of God's purposes as

173

expressed in the New Testament writings. We saw how Paul restated this vision in Romans 8 because he saw in the risen Jesus the fulfilment of all that God had promised for Israel. The earthly ministry of Jesus, with its teaching about the kingdom of God, and the miracles which demonstrate total authority over a corrupted creation and the human suffering that arises out of it—shows that the kingdom is not totally other-worldly; it involves creation itself. The resurrection body of Jesus, material yet beyond-material, human yet now in heaven, shows the way forward in creation's renewal.

So does this mean that a Christian concern for the environment can stand legitimately alongside a concern for the gospel? Surprising as it may seem, the answer to this question is decidedly in the negative! The renewal of creation does not stand alongside the good news, but is an integral part of it! So Green issues cannot be red herrings. Our failure to realise this betrays some shortcomings in our understanding of the gospel itself. We have often wrongly intepreted it in exclusively spiritual categories which may owe more to the heresy of gnosticism than to a truly biblical understanding of the relationship between Creator and creation.

The Question of New Age Thinking

As in the early church, the biblical world view today has a rival which is radically different. Why has New Age thinking become so popular? The first reason is that, although the present age is generally regarded as secular, this may mean no more than that people have largely rejected institutional religion and its god(s).[1] France now has more professional fortune tellers than priests; in West Germany in 1989 there were some 30,000 Christian clergy of all denominations, but 90,000 registered witches and fortune tellers.[2] Opinion polls stubbornly insist on showing that most people believe in the existence of a god (or gods), even though this may fall far short of what Christians call faith. So, when people start to think seriously about what God is like, and about how to make sense of life and their experience of living in this world, where does their thinking lead them? Clearly, it leads some into the realm of New Age thinking.

This begs the question of why institutional religion has been so largely abandoned. The signs are that it is far more than just a rejection of institutions themselves. Philip Seddon lists a series of concerns that New Age thinking addresses.[3] They include: the dehumanising effects of scientific reductionism, including the idolatry which surrounds science; the wasting effect of secularism; the deceptions of a 'shiny and selfish materialism' which claim to offer value, meaning and freedom through increased purchasing power; the international rape of the earth, led by high-technology industry; the threat of the end of history; the search for personal significance; religious jockeying for superiority. Mainline Christianity, he argues, has become fatally enmeshed in these processes, and is therefore seen as offering no viable alternative way of thinking.

So it is no surprise to find that some New Agers have consciously rejected the Christianity they see around them. Tim Cooper quotes Donald Reeves, the rector of St. James' Church, Piccadilly, who has taken the trouble to listen carefully to what New Agers are saying:

> Many of the New Age movement are people who are disenchanted by institutional religion... It is largely the result of our decaying, life-denying institutions, where the Spirit has been firmly squashed, that the New Age movement exists.[4]

So it would be wrong to avoid environmental concerns simply because the New Agers got there first. The very influence of the movement should make Christians aware of the credibility gap that exists in the eyes of many concerning the Christian faith at the end of the twentieth century. This is in spite of loud warnings of compromise from some influential Christian writers such as Constance Cumbey.[5] We cannot contemplate ceding ground on a matter which turns out to be central to the gospel. The danger of being seduced by New Age thinking is certainly real, but this is no different in many senses to the other temptations we face every day. In this particular case the best antidote to falling into temptation is to be fully convinced of the biblical case for Christian involvement in Green issues!

We should all support moves towards a more responsible care for the world and its resources. This does not mean, however, that every Christian is called to be actively involved in the work of environmental organisations, whether secular or specifically Christian. But some certainly are, and when they enter into a world where they will rub shoulders with New Agers (and others) they are entitled to expect the constant and committed prayer support of their Christian friends and the Christian fellowships of which they are members. In this way they will be protected and able to hold their ground where they may possibly face forces of darkness (Eph 6:10ff; although this does not necessarily imply that all strands of New Age thinking are soaked in occult influence). When they are able to do that we can also look forward to the kingdom of God breaking new ground as it makes inroads into enemy territory.

GREEN ISSUES: GOLDEN OPPORTUNITIES

Green issues are not red herrings; they are golden opportunities. Since the renewal of creation is an integral part of the gospel, it must be part of the evangelistic message for the late twentieth century. If we start to wonder how this can be turned into practice, then we can happily turn again to the New Testament for guidance. This does not mean that we can lift key texts straight out of it and apply them to a world two millenia further down the road of history. The task is far more demanding than that. But there is material in the book of Acts, particularly, that will repay further study.

One of the most important features of the book of Acts is its record of early Christian preaching. These sermons (or distillations of them—as they stand they are far too short to have been delivered exactly as recorded) differ widely in their style and themes, and it is obvious that the apostolic preachers were sensitive to the world views and presuppositions of their audiences. Of particular interest here are the two recorded speeches of Paul to specifically pagan audiences. One took place in Lystra, where the healing of the lame man led the crowd to worship Paul and Barnabas as Hermes and Zeus:

> We are bringing you good news, telling you to turn from these worthless things to the living God, who made heaven and earth and sea and everything in them. In the past, he let all nations go their own way. Yet he has not left himself without testimony: he has shown kindness by giving you rain from heaven and crops in their seasons; he provides you with plenty of food and fills your hearts with joy (Acts 14:15–18).

The other was in Athens, where Paul was heard in a less charged atmosphere by Epicurean and Stoic philosophers, among others:

> Men of Athens! I see that in every way you are very religious. For as I walked around and looked carefully at your objects of worship, I even found an altar with this inscription: TO AN UNKNOWN GOD. Now what you worship as something unknown I am going to proclaim to you. The God who made the world and everything in it is the Lord of heaven and earth and does not live in temples made by hands. And he is not served by human hands, as if he needed anything, because he himself gives all men life and breath and everything else. From one man he made every nation of men, that they should inhabit the whole earth; and he determined the times set for them and the exact places where they should live. God did this so that men would seek him and perhaps reach out for him and find him, though he is not far from each one of us. 'For in him we live and move and have our being.' As some of your own poets have said, 'We are his offspring.' Therefore, since we are God's offspring, we should not think that the divine being is like gold or silver or stone—an image made by

man's design and skill. In the past God overlooked such ignorance, but now he commands all people everywhere to repent. For he has set a day when he will judge the world with justice by the man he has appointed. He has given proof of all this to all men by raising him from the dead (Acts 17:22–31).

God as Creator and the nature of creation are clearly important components in both addresses. In each case there is a determined attempt to engage the culture and thought forms of the audience, while the Athens address is also steeped in the Old Testament scriptures.[6] In both cases the theme of the goodness of creation leads to a climax in which the spotlight turns on Christ and the need to respond to the truth about him.

Unlike Acts 14 and 17, evangelism in the Western world does not always start where people are. It often answers questions no one is asking, preferring to start from the questions asked decades ago. No longer do the majority want to know 'Where can I find assurance of salvation?'; that was a good starting point when there was a large fringe of people on the edge of the church, and most had some knowledge of the content of the Christian faith. This is no longer true. There is no point of *starting* with salvation, when most people do not understand what it means in Christian terms.

British Christians were shocked by a survey in 1991 which showed how little the average person knows about Christianity. Only a minority know what Easter commemorates. Other starting points will have to be found if evangelism is to be effective, and since we all live within the world of creation, which forms the basis of our lives and experiences, where better to begin than here? So the Lystra and Athens addresses will repay careful study as we face the urgent task of examining the relationship between evangelism and Green issues in the modern world. There are a number of features which are significant in this respect.

The Creator And His Providence

Each speech emphasises aspects of the providence of the Creator. At Lystra Paul and Barnabas talked of his 'kindness by giving you rain from heaven and crops in their seasons', so that the people had food to eat and joy in their hearts (14:17). In Athens God is described as giving 'all men life and breath and everything else.' (17:25).

This statement of the divine providence goes back to the goodness of creation in Genesis 1 (see Chapter 2), which is restated by Paul against the background of false asceticism in 1 Timothy 4:1–4. It also echoes the teaching of Jesus (eg Mt 5:45; 6:25–34), and of Paul's letter to the Hebrews 1:3 ('sustaining all things by his powerful word').

It is paradoxical that belief in providence is weakest in technologically advanced societies, best able to predict and then to protect themselves from the unpredictable forces of nature. Yet here is where a first point of contact in evangelism may need to be made. Even when the Creator is left out of the picture, the other dimensions to human existence which Genesis portrays—our relationships with each other and with the natural world—form the basis of all human experience. Since all this is through the activity of a wise and loving God, evangelism must take seriously this meeting point of divine initiative and human experience, and tackle seriously the problems of belief in providence which are so evident today.

In Africa, by contrast, there is no such problem with providence. There, most people believe in the existence of a creator who orders and maintains the natural world, and one of the reasons for the rapid advance of the gospel is that such belief forms a foundation on which a Christ-centred proclamation can be built.

There are other paradoxes. One is the continuing popularity of Harvest Thanksgiving services, even where regular churchgoing is a minority pursuit. This may be folk religion, but simply to dismiss it is to miss the point. Such occasions still ring bells (in more senses than one!). Mark Silversides argues that they help to fulfil a complex set of human needs, two of which are relevant to our theme. First, they can, viewed as exercises in folk religion, help to convey 'a sense of rightness, order and safety' in an uncertain world. Secondly, they enable their adherents to come into a comfortable relationship with a sense of mystery: 'Folk religion is an exercise in distancing oneself from the numinous: not too far away, since help might be needed at odd times, but not too close to get in the way of everyday plans and activities.'[7]

A gospel presentation broad enough to take in the providence of God can make contact with the thought forms of folk religion, in which people feel 'close' to God (though not too close!) and can proceed to build on it. In the Acts speeches this was clearly done, but led on to other elements of the proclamation which demonstrated to the hearers the folly of their position, and laid out for them an altogether different picture of God, which demanded a new way of thinking, and a clearly-defined response.

An Ignorant and Idolatrous World

The background to the Lystra and Athens speeches is the ignorance and idolatry of the pagan world. In Lystra Paul and Barnabas healed a lame man and then had to convince their audience that they were not the Greek gods Zeus and Hermes (14:11–13,18). They urged their hearers to reject the 'worthless things' they believed (v 15), and to turn to the God who 'has not left himself without testimony' through the working out of his providence (v 17). At Athens Paul had had time to prepare his address and was able to speak in a more deliberate way. As reported, it fills out considerably what the Lystra speech contained.

The opening words refer to the fact that his hearers are 'very religious' (v 22). This may be a compliment—a point of contact with people he was trying to win over—but there may be an overtone of sarcasm here (the word translated 'religious' can also be translated as 'superstitious'), demonstrating to them the irony of their situation. For all their religiosity, they still had to erect a statue to an 'unknown god' (v 23), whom they ought to know but clearly did not. They were not actively seeking this God; it was an exercise in making sure that they were not leaving out any possible deity who would otherwise be offended. The atmosphere was profoundly polytheistic, as v 16 makes clear. Thus, commentators have often remarked on the link between 17:22–31 and Romans 1:18–32, where ignorance of the true God leads to futile thinking and darkened hearts (v 21; cf 2 Cor 4:4; Eph 4:17–19; Col 1:21), and thence to an idolatry which completely reverses the relationship between Creator and creation (vv 20–23,25).

It would be wrong to think that the people of Athens were happy with their lot. As we shall see shortly, Epicureanism was a religion of despair, and Stoicism was too cold and austere to appeal to anyone except an educated minority. Neither could cope with the fear that many felt, and the mystery religions proved increasingly attractive, offering as they did a relationship with the gods that would lead to cleansing, security and immortality.[8]

It was in this environment, of which Paul would have been acutely aware, that his presentation of the gospel started not with the cross, but with creation and its Creator. In many respects the current atmosphere is not greatly different. Secularisation has apparently rendered organised religion irrelevant to the great issues of the day, and science may claim to have all the answers. But, as we have already seen, even in sophisticated materialistic societies, belief in the existence of gods persists. And so does fear.

These words are being written in a week when tens of thousands were killed in the wake of a cyclone which swept across southern Bangladesh, when the public were reminded that the plight of the Kurdish people in northern Iraq had served to distract us from the impending starvation of nearly 30 million people across Africa, when Kuwaiti oilwell fires still burned out of control, and when the problem of compassion-fatigue again became evident.

People who become hardened to yet another appeal in the wake of yet another human disaster do so for all sorts of reasons. It may be selfishness, but it is just as likely to be due to despair at the sight of a world apparently out of control, and in which we seem to have no power to change anything. For some, this is compounded by the conviction that our practice of science and technology merely makes things worse. It is therefore not surprising that astrology, horoscopes and the like have become so popular. People are looking for a way of making sense of the world and of finding a meaningful place within it. Sadly, they usually look outside Christianity for the answers to questions of fear and insecurity because the churches are seen to be fatally implicated in the problems from which they are seeking to escape.

A meaningful presentation of the gospel in the modern world dares not ignore these problems. The gospel must be proclaimed in a way both faithful to God's self-revelation in Scripture and relevant to the world of the present day. Given the environmental problems of which so many people are now aware, how can this be so unless the message of the Creator and His good creation becomes an integral part of it?

> We have no liberty to edit the heart of the good news of Jesus Christ. Nor is there ever any need to do so. But we have to begin where people are, to find a point of contact with them. With secularised people today this might be what constitutes authentic humanness, the universal quest for transcendence, the hunger for love and community, the search for freedom, or the longing for personal significance. Wherever we begin, however, we shall end with Jesus Christ, who is himself the good news, and who alone can fulfil all human aspirations... Many people are rejecting our gospel today not because they conceive it to be false, but because they perceive it to be trivial. People are looking for an integrated world view which makes sense of all their experience. We learn from Paul that we cannot preach the gospel of Jesus without the doctrine of God, or the cross without the creation...[9]

The Creator Invites Fellowship

God's providence has a purpose: it is that 'men would seek him and perhaps reach out for him and find him, though he is not far from each one of us' (17:27). Paul goes on to quote in v 28 from two Greek writers, Epimenides and Aratus ('For in him we live and move and have our being'; 'We are his offspring'). At first, it may seem that he conceded too much to a pagan view of God, but Genesis 1:26 says much the same thing only in a different way (Chapter 3), and Romans 2:4 states that the kindness of God is meant to lead to repentance (and then, by implication, to fellowship).

Both to the Athenian audience and to the modern hearer, the idea of a God who seeks the fellowship of his creatures ought be good news, but it may seem strange because of deeply entrenched ideas of God that see him as far off, disinterested, eternally but remotely blissful in himself. Certainly the Epicureans thought this way, a view to which Paul refers obliquely in Acts 17.25: 'and he is not served by human hands, as if he needed anything.' But this leads straight to a religion of despair, because the peace of the gods could be enjoyed only by human beings at the cost of avoiding all possible contact with the rough and tumble of life—something clearly impossible for ordinary people.[10]

The Stoics, whose world view Paul challenged in the same address, saw the world differently. It was a pantheistic view in which impersonal reason (equated with God or Zeus) lay at the centre of the universe, whose history was governed by unbreakable chains of cause and effect. The only possible outcome was fatalism, to which the true Stoic submitted. He learned to live according to reason and accepted that, however evil things may appear, they represented the best of all possible worlds. Even evil contributed to the good of the whole, under the pervasive influence of reason. Little wonder that Stoicism never caught on with ordinary people, and that the mystery religions already referred to became so popular!

A Long-Suffering Creator

God is the Creator and sustainer of the universe. He also continues to be concerned about its future (cf Deut 11:12). But he has been long-suffering about the ignorance and idolatry that characterise human relationships with the rest of creation: 'In the past, he let all nations go their own way' (14:16); 'In the past God overlooked such ignorance' (17:30).

Attractive today, yet needing to be confronted in the name of biblical truth, is the idea that the world of creation has a life of its own. This has always been an attractive idea, expressed perhaps in the oft-used phrase 'Mother Nature', but it is now taking on a new lease of life through the Gaia hypothesis of James Lovelock. He argues that the earth:

> constitutes a single system, made and managed to their
> own convenience by living organisms. We all know that
> life here is only made possible because of the right
> balance of gases in the atmosphere. But what we do not
> realise is that this balance is maintained not by chance
> but by the very process of life in itself.[11]

This is an important strand in modern Green thinking. The strength of Lovelock's view of the world is that it recognises the inter-connectedness of all its parts, a feature of the goodness of creation that we noted in Chapter 2. But his interpretation of this is profoundly pantheistic, in a way not dissimilar to the Stoic world view of some of Paul's hearers in Acts 17. For all our scientific knowledge of how the world works, there is no less ignorance to be confronted in the name of the true God, even though it may be expressed in sophisticated ways.

But with the coming of Christ a new situation arises and repentance is demanded. This is implied in 14:15–18: 'turn from these worthless things to the living God', but is quite explicit in 17:30: 'now he commands all people everywhere to repent.' Specifically, the audience is commanded to turn from an idolatrous view of Creator and creation, and acknowledge the true God who does reveal something of his real nature in creation (cf Rom 1:20) and who can now be fully known in the person of his Son, Jesus Christ.

The speeches at Lystra and Athens are often accused of being sub-Christian, because there is little about Christ and certainly nothing about the cross. But the reports in Acts 14 and 17 cannot be verbatim because they would take only one or two minutes to deliver. What Luke has done is to give a brief account of significant features of the speeches, and since these two were delivered to Gentile audiences, it is highly likely that he concentrated on features specific to them. There is little reason to doubt that the hearers heard also about the cross of Christ and its significance.

The message which Paul would have delivered today might well have been broadly similar, given the persistence of folk religion in advanced societies and the re-emergence of false views of God. An additional note might have been that the need for repentance is made plain by the way that a wrong relationship with the Creator has led to all kinds of environmental consequences, including the slow build-up of many types of pollution, the human suffering—physical and economic—caused thereby, and the disasters caused by negligence which include Chernobyl, Bhopal and *Exxon Valdez*.

Many people are aware of these environmental problems and some are certainly deeply concerned. There is some evidence that the more people know about environmental problems, the more pessimistic they are about whether we can cope with them. There is a clear need to amend the way we handle our world and its resources, but there is more involved here than piecemeal improvements, important though those may be. A wrong relationship with creation flows from a wrong relationship with the Creator. Romans 1:18–32 describes this process in some detail, and paints a very tragic picture in which the key words are futility and darkness, as God gives people up to the consequences of the world view that they insist on embracing.

Evangelism that is wide enough to take in the goodness of creation, and its subsequent despoilation, leads directly to the question of why things have gone so badly wrong. Questions of human motivation and behaviour, often marked by greed and complacency, follow; the issue of a spoiled world leads straight to the question of how humanity in its flawed moral state can possibly do anything better, how we can ever be different, and what has happened to the relationship between creature and Creator. The world of creation, viewed sensitively, reveals all the consequences of our alienation from God. Here, for some, will be the way in to the deep human needs that only the gospel can address.

It is here that evangelism cannot be divorced from lifestyle. The idea persists that Christianity is a spiritual religion that has no real point of contact with the world of creation except to deny its value. Much of what has so far been written in this book has been intended to demolish such a view as unbiblical. There is, however, more substance to the accusation that the practical record of the church itself has been far from perfect. This must honestly be admitted, and Christians are called upon to adopt more environmentally sensitive lifestyles, as many others are already doing. Thus Francis Schaeffer wrote over twenty years ago:

> In our generation we are losing an evangelistic
> opportunity, because when modern young people have
> a real sensitivity to nature...they have seen that most
> Christians simply do not care about the beauty of
> nature or nature as such...we have largely missed an
> opportunity of reaching the twentieth century.[12]

However, it is worth pointing out that other world religions and non-Christian civilisations also have blemished records:

> Over-grazing, deforestation, and similar errors, of
> sufficient magnitude to destroy civilisations, have been
> committed by Egyptians, Assyrians, Romans, North
> Africans, Persians, Indians, Aztecs and Buddhists.
> Centuries before the Christian era Plato commented, in
> his *Critias*, on the deforestation of Attica. Since
> primitive times man has been altering his environment

dramatically, in ways that upset ecological balances.
Early hunters used fire to drive out their game.
Agricultural people everywhere clear fields and dam
streams and wipe out stock predators and kill plants
that get in the way of their chosen crops. In the modern
industrial era Western technology is widely copied
elsewhere in the world, including areas where
Christianity has had little effect. Japan has a pollution
problem worse than any in the world.[13]

To make this point is not to excuse the blemishes on the
past record of the church, but to put it in its context.

Repentance, Resurrection and Judgement

As Luke reports them, the Lystra and Athens addresses say
little that is specifically Christian. But, as has already been
stated, it would be wrong to understand what is written in
Acts 14 and 17 as verbatim reports. Luke has probably singled
out a few specific features of each address to show how the
message was adapted to the situation. In the epistles Paul's
thought is so thoroughly Christ-centred that it is difficult to
imagine how he could possibly have left Christ out of his
sermons.

Yet there are clear indications of what Paul was building up
to—both addresses take in the themes of repentance and
judgement. Thus in 14:15 he commands the Greeks to 'turn
from these worthless things to the living God' (cf 1 Thess
1:9,10); in 17:30,31 the same message is presented as follows:

> In the past God overlooked such ignorance, but now he
> commands all people everywhere to repent. For he has set a
> day when he will judge the world with justice by the man he
> has appointed. He has given proof of this to all men by
> raising him from the dead.

The argument runs approximately as follows. God has
clearly shown himself as a loving Creator in his providential

care for humanity. Yet nations have continued to cling to idolatrous world views which have refused to acknowledge him and his rightful place in the loyalties of the people he has made. He has allowed this situation to continue for a long period of time—but not indefinitely. A final date for judgement has been set, and the resurrected Jesus is the one whom he has appointed as judge.

Because the religious climate of the present age is not the same as that of the Greco-Roman world of the first century, we may not wish to use exactly the same flow of thought. But certain elements which Paul uses here are important in thinking through how the gospel is to be proclaimed against our own religious climate and the environmental issues which cause people such great concern.

The first is to do with idolatry. In Chapter 6 we described modern idolatry in terms of unrealistic expectations of the role of science and technology. They cannot alone save us from the plight we have created for ourselves by our mismanagement of the created world. There are people today, unhappy about where science and technology are taking us, for whom the first contact with the gospel will be in terms of thinking about the need for a new way of thinking about a true relationship between humanity and the world of creation—one which puts the Creator at the centre rather than leaving him out of the reckoning altogether.

The second is to do with the nature of sin. This is an old-fashioned word in the sense that everyone knew what it meant once upon a time, but nowadays few people do. We have seen how disruptions in the world of nature flow from alienation between God and his people. Many people are aware of these disruptions, and are pessimistic about the future of the planet. So we may wish to discuss with some enquirers how environmental problems flow from rebellion against the will of the Creator. In other words, by demonstrating the reality of sin through its consequences, we remove it from the realm of the purely abstract and concretise it, thereby enabling some people at least to come face to face with its real nature for the first time.

The third is to do with repentance, resurrection and judgement. It is about repentance because it is to do with the nature of sin. Fleshing out the meaning of 'sin' in terms of its consequences in the world of creation makes sin more readily identifiable for what it is. The same is then true of the idea of repentance, a term which is also open to all sorts of superficial interpretations.

Where I live in Northern Ireland, for example, to become a Christian is to become good-living ('guid-livin''), sometimes merely in the sense of becoming respectable, and having a best suit or dress and hat to wear to church on Sunday. If repentance means merely to become like this, then little wonder others see it as meaningless, even hypocritical! In fact, the concept of repentance is a much tougher, more dynamic concept. It means to turn one's back on one world view and the modes of behaviour that go with it, and to take on board without reserve the world view of the kingdom of God and the lifestyle that is appropriate to it.

Acts 17 may therefore encourage us to concretise the meaning of repentance, along with that of sin. If sin leads to creation being in bondage to decay, then repentance has to involve, amongst other things, a lifestyle which is far more environmentally responsible, irrespective of how afraid we are that our own repentance may not lead to the immediate reversal of the Greenhouse Effect!

Then there is the link between resurrection and judgement. This may seem odd at first, even though the Athens address almost certainly dealt also with the cross. Yet, there is a direct connection between them. As we saw in Chapter 8, it was Paul's encounter with the risen Christ on the Damascus road that formed the starting point for his theology and his experience of God (see also Chapter 12). Here, he saw clearly, was the beginning of the transformation of creation which the Old Testament prophets had announced and for which all sincere Jews longed, even though they had not yet acknowledged it.

The beginning of the transformation of creation is therefore the beginning of the 'last days'. It it is God's declaration that the present situation of a groaning world, subjected to futility, has only a limited time to run. It is significant that Peter, in his first recorded sermon in Acts 2, saw the coming of the Spirit not only in terms of the prophecy of the outpouring of the Spirit in Joel 2:28f, but he also linked it with the convulsions in history and the world of nature that would herald the dreadful day of the Lord (Joel 2:30,31). Another recorded sermon of Peter's, this time at Solomon's Colonnade, forms a link between Peter's understanding of Pentecost as expressed in Acts 2, and Paul's sermon at Athens:

> Now, brothers, I know that you acted in ignorance, as did your leaders. But this is how God fulfilled what he had foretold through all the prophets, saying that his Christ would suffer. Repent, then, and turn to God, so that your sins may be wiped out, that times of refreshing may come from the Lord, and that he may send the Christ, who has been appointed for you—even Jesus. He must remain in heaven until the time comes for God to restore everything, as he promised long ago through his holy prophets. (Acts 3:17–21).

The Renewal of Creation

Another significant feature of Peter's sermon is the reference to the renewal of creation which would be clearly understood by Jewish hearers in Jerusalem through the phrase 'the time...to restore everything'. We have already seen how close this concept comes to the heart of Paul's understanding of the gospel in Romans 8 (cf Eph 1:10). But twentieth century Christians may be embarrassed about making this theme a part of the evangelistic message: does it not smack too much of 'pie-in-the-sky'?

This objection would certainly be true if there were no continuity at all between this world and the next, as if we were destined to float around as disembodied spirits. That kind of view of 'the new heavens and the new earth' leads to attitudes of withdrawal that are totally unbiblical. If this world is destined for annihilation, there is no point in bothering with it (an argument with implications reaching far beyond the realm of Green issues!). Some Sicilian monks used to pass their time making wickerwork baskets—and then unravelling them again. Since the world was passing away, they argued, what else was there to be done?

But we have already seen that creation has a future, albeit involving a renewal so radical that the final product is far beyond our imagination. Creation's future is a truly glorious one. We have also seen what a powerful incentive this should be for joyful and responsible environmental care among Christians—in itself a powerful accompaniment to the evangelistic message appropriate to the end of the twentieth century.

There is, however, another link between renewal of creation and the gospel message for our age. If there is no Creator, then life is ultimately meaningless. Bertrand Russell put this view fearlessly, but tragically, as follows:

> Brief and powerless is man's life; on him and on his race
> the slow, sure doom falls, pitiless and dark. Blind to
> good and evil, reckless of destruction, omnipotent
> matter rolls on its relentless way; for man, condemned
> today to lose his dearest, tomorrow himself to pass
> through the gates of darkness, it remains only to cherish
> ere yet the blow falls, the lofty thoughts that ennoble his
> little day.[14]

But there is a Creator who, unlike the watchmaker of the deists, continues to uphold his good creation in love (Gen 9: 8–17; Deut 11:12; Heb 1:3), in spite of what we have done to it. More than this, because creation does have a glorious future in the purposes of God, life in this world has permanent significance in its own right. All its good features have real meaning; so we can enjoy its goodness without reservation and seek to share it with others. The joys which come out of it are not illusions. Consider the alternative: if the Creator has no future for his creation, then the only purpose of this life in this world is to prepare us for the next. Life by its very nature is then trial by ordeal rather than gift. And if the world of creation has no future, and is totally discontinuous with the next then in what way can this life possibly be such a preparation? This way of thinking also destroys the meaning of the Incarnation.

There are two general comments to be made at the conclusion of this section. The first is that, because the Western world is now deeply ignorant of the Christian world view and the terminology that we have used in the past to express it, new points of contact have to be made. The issue of environmental care of a polluted planet may well be one. Many people are concerned about the future of the earth; Scripture clearly relates the problems we have made for ourselves to the deeper issue of alienation from God. Here are seen in concrete form the nature of sin and the outworking of alienation, in categories which are much more clearly visible than in an abstract discussion about theological terminology.

The second general point is to do with the relationship between evangelism and intellectual argument. Our discussion in this chapter falls heavily into the latter category and the maxim 'you can't argue anyone into the kingdom!' comes to mind. Becoming a Christian involves a movement of a whole human life, not just a brain. However, it must involve the intellect which is an essential component of human life, and persuasion is part of evangelism, especially where there are deeply held intellectual reservations about the credibility of the Christian faith. The New Testament often uses the word 'truth' in connection with the gospel; it is something to be believed, obeyed, acknowledged. Evangelism involves persuasion (2 Cor 5:11) because the gospel contains a series of propositions which need to be received intellectually; persuasion is about marshalling arguments in order to convince people of the truth which is being presented. Shortly before his visit to Athens Paul was in Thessalonica, where he went into the synagogue and 'reasoned with them from the scriptures, explaining and proving that the Christ had to suffer and rise from the dead' (Acts 17:2f); the result was that some of the Jews were 'persuaded' (Acts 17:4).

GOLDEN OPPORTUNITIES TAKEN:
THE A ROCHA PROJECT[15]

The A Rocha Project is possibly unique in the Christian world as a Christian initiative which brings together in a practical way the twin tasks of evangelism and environmental steward-ship. It is based in a large converted villa on Portugal's Algarve coast, near a small village called Mexilhoeira Grande, between the tourist resorts of Lagos and Portimao. The story of the project began in 1983 when the newly-founded A Rocha Trust sent two couples, Peter and Miranda Harris and Les and Wendy Batty, to the Algarve to test the vision that they believed the Creator had given them of a centre for evangelism and conservation work.

Over a period of three years the vision was tested through many difficulties, and seen to be authentic. The Portuguese language was learned, local contacts made, and an under-standing gained not only of the religious climate of southern Portugal, but also of the bird life and ecosystems of the area, which were under severe pressure because of the rapid growth of tourist facilities along vast stretches of the Algarve coastline. In Britain the Trustees were finding a number of Christian people willing to support such work through prayer and finan-cial commitment.

In 1986 the A Rocha Trust made the decision to purchase the house which is still the centre of the project's operation. It is situated on a peninsula giving easy access to two extensive estuaries with associated saltmarshes separated from the sea by sand spits. The A Rocha staff members are making sys-tematic studies of bird, insect and plant life in a range of local ecosystems. There is a regular schedule of bird ringing, and they co-operate with national and international organisations in ornithological research projects. These are not purely aca-demic studies. The huge growth in tourism is causing pro-found changes to local environments, as new roads and bridges are built, new holiday apartments and other tourist facilities are constructed, wetlands are drained for golf courses, and dams are built inland to satisfy the increasing demand for fresh water. In addition, bird shooting is a popular pastime among local men, and EC agricultural policy means that many land owners find it financially worth their while to plant huge areas with eucalyptus at the expense of other more varied forms of vegetation. All these developments, easily apparent to an observant eye, cause profound changes to bird, insect and plant populations; these changes themselves are often indicators of more fundamental effects on the land itself.

The A Rocha team is headed by wardens Peter and Miranda Harris, with a team of assistant wardens, summer volunteers and part-time staff, mainly Portuguese and English. Surprisingly perhaps, the Harrises have been seconded to the project by BCMS Crosslinks, an evangelical Anglican mission agency. When the Harrises first applied to this agency for Christian service overseas, East Africa seemed the most likely destination for them. When the time came, however, no suitable place was available for them there. What followed was a clear demonstration of God's guidance. The Harris and Batty families, on holiday together, had shared a vision of a Christian Bird Observatory, and were so convinced by the strength of it that the Harrises no longer believed East Africa was the right destination for them. Meanwhile BCMS Crosslinks was revising its statement of faith, and believed on scriptural grounds that mission includes the care of creation. It was from these two sets of circumstances that the Harrises were seconded to the A Rocha Project.

The evangelistic impact of A Rocha is hard to quantify, but obedience is more important than numerical results. Conservation is beginning to be an issue in the Algarve region of Portugal as some people start to ask about the cost of turning the area into a huge tourist resort. At the time I am writing, there are plans to turn one of the local estuaries into a boating marina, completely changing its ecological character. The campaign to resist this is rightly led by local people, but the A Rocha Project is able to provide resources, expertise and encouragement. Apart from the value of this activity in its own right, the increasing number of local contacts which are built up through this kind of involvement in local affairs inevitably leads to opportunities to share the gospel. This could not happen unless the A Rocha team had taken time to establish themselves as authentic members of the local community.

Friendships in the local village have grown up over the years. From these has come permission from the authorities in Mexilhoeira Grande village for the A Rocha team to hold a monthly service of worship, attended by a number of local people as well as the team members. Local friendships have also led to sharing of problems, and the opportunity to pray with people and study the Bible on a one-to-one basis.

A constant stream of visitors come to the centre every year, people of all ages, some Christians, many not, from a variety of countries. The name and reputation of the centre has grown throughout Portugal due to representation at national scientific and environmental conferences, and programmes about its work on Portugese radio and television. For the non-Christians who visit, talking to A Rocha team members can bring their first insight into the fact that Christianity is about far more than personal piety. They find that it speaks powerfully about the goodness of the world we live in, and God's continuing concern for it. Because they are visitors, some of whom may be there for no more than a few hours, the outcome of these encounters will often never be known. But that this will be the start of a new spiritual journey for some is not in doubt.

Many people who hear of the A Rocha Centre for the first time are excited by a modern expression of mission wide enough to encompass two kinds of activity which Christians have often thought incompatible. One of the visions of the A Rocha Project is that it will help others to catch visions of exciting new ways of declaring the good news in all its fullness.

REFERENCES

1. David Lyon, *The Steeple's Shadow* (SPCK: London, 1985).
2. *MARC Newsletter*, no 90-2, (April 1990): p 4.

3. Philip Seddon, *The New Age—An Assessment* (Grove Books: Nottingham, 1990), p 9.

4. Tim Cooper, *Green Christianity* (Spire: London, 1990), p 115.

5. Wesley Granberg-Michaelson, *Tending the Garden* (Eerdmans: Michigan, 1987), pp 24-29.

6. Frederick F. Bruce, *Paul: Apostle of the Free Spirit* (Paternoster: Exeter, 1977), pp 238-247.

7. Mark Silversides, *Folk Religion: Friend or Foe?* (Grove Books: Nottingham, 1986), p 4.

8. Michael Green, *Evangelism in the Early Church* (Hodder and Stoughton: London, 1970), pp 20-22.

9. John R.W. Stott, *The Message of Acts* (IVP: Leicester, 1990), pp 232,290.

10. David Gooding, *True to the Faith* (Hodder and Stoughton: London, 1990), p 294.

11. James Lovelock, *Gaia, a new Look at Life on Earth* (Oxford University Press: London, 1979), p 249.

12. Francis Schaeffer, *Pollution and the Death of Man* (Hodder and Stoughton: London, 1970), p 62.

13. Thomas Sieger Derr, *Ecology and Liberation: A Theological Critique of the Use and Abuse of our Birthright* (WSCF: Geneva, 1973), p 19.

14. Bertrand Russell, *Mysticism and Logic* (Penguin: Harmondsworth, 1953), p 59.

15. Robert Pullan, *Caring for God's World: A Rocha Occasional Paper Number 2* (A Rocha Trust: Upton, 1990).

Chapter Ten

RISK, HYPOTHETICALITY AND THE FUTURE

CAN WE KNOW THE FUTURE?

HOPE IN THE return of Christ does not absolve us from responsible care for creation. Because the Christian good news includes the future renewal of creation, we have a motive for care of the earth more cogent than any other. Yet we share with many others fears over the immediate future. In a world where pollution and environmental disasters make grim headlines, and seem ever more common, what kind of future are we heading for? The Greenhouse Effect may already be modifying climatic patterns in ways we do not fully understand and cannot accurately predict. What will things look like in fifty years' time? Are we in danger of triggering environmental changes so far-reaching that we will by then have destroyed human life on the surface of the planet?

One easy response is to thumb through the Book of Revelation to see if its prophecies are at last coming true. We have already seen how Isaiah 24 and Jeremiah 4 contain visions of a land surface laid waste through the persistent sinfulness of its denizens. The temptation is to see these prophecies coming true in the present, and to opt out.

A major shift from optimism to pessimism about the future came about in 1972 when a report based on computer calculations of current trends in consumption and population growth forecast a global disaster comprising intense pollution, starvation and economic collapse.[1] Two years later, the US National Academy of Sciences Committee on Mineral Resources and the Environment produced the following statement regarding the availability and consumption of mineral resources: 'Man faces the prospect of a series of shocks of varying severity as shortages occur in one material after another...the first real shortages [are] perhaps only a few years away.'[2]

Other scientists and economists, however, remained incurably optimistic about the future. Rather than being worried about exhaustion of metal ore resources, one report stated:

> Fortunately the real situation is not all that gloomy, for a variety of reasons. First, the indicated 'lifetime' for known reserves should not be taken too seriously; accurate information on many reserves is not available and these figures are more indicators of short-term scarcities than results of exhaustive global studies. Secondly, in the mineral field, spectacular new discoveries are being made which completely change the outlook...While all wastages of mineral resources should certainly be avoided and relative shortages will be encountered for specific minerals, it appears that major difficulties can be avoided for the coming decades.[3]

How do ordinary people respond, when the experts speak with such different voices? To dismiss science as bunk will not do. What is happening is that science and technology are enabling us to make changes to our world at a rate far more rapid than ever before, and it is impossible to predict the outcome of our actions. Gone, perhaps for ever, are the certainties expressed in words such as these:

> A knowledge of the facts serves as a basis for the knowledge of the future, by which the future can be predicted and controlled with certainty. And the facts in this case teach us of the *progress* of society through

science and technique. Thus the new way of self-redemption in the nineteenth century becomes the way which science shows to the future of society.[4]

Responsible care of the earth has previously been linked with the science (or art) of prediction. Where, for example, some industrial innovation was introduced without careful investigations of its dangers and hazards, this was rightly judged to be irresponsible. Yet accurate prediction has always been easier in theory than in practice. In 1908 the British Government set up a Royal Commission to investigate the possible effects of the growth in use of the motor car. The result of their deliberations was that the major problem would be dirt thrown up by tyres passing over unsurfaced roads!

Living With Uncertainty

In the early stages of a new process we always seem to know too little of its effects, and by the time we do know enough it is difficult to make substantial changes or, if necessary, to abandon it. Take, for example, the Greenhouse Effect which we considered in Chapter 4—the heating of the earth's atmosphere due to emission of waste gases as a by-product of large-scale industrial activity. We considered this not as a universally accepted phenomenon but only as a possibility, even though a widely held one. Some scientists believe either that it is an illusion, or else that the present evidence of warming is simply the result of natural fluctuations in the earth's climate that are as old as the earth itself. Certainly there have been periods in geological history when the earth has been much warmer than it is at present, perhaps as a result of large-scale volcanic activity. Even at this stage it is difficult to be certain of the magnitude of the Greenhouse Effect; if it were to turn out that it is far more serious than at present thought, it would be extremely difficult to do anything realistic to abolish the processes causing it.

The existence (or otherwise) of the Greenhouse Effect raises other vital issues. A Channel 4 TV programme, entitled *The*

Greenhouse Conspiracy broadcast in Britain on 12th August 1990, claimed that the Greenhouse Effect has been the subject of a huge operation in media hype. It suggested four reasons for this: first, scientists need a cause like this to increase their chances of obtaining research funding (the programme featured one scientist who, some years previously, was attracting funding because of fears that the earth was heading for another ice age!). Secondly, the news media are always looking for stories that will attract public attention, and thirdly, people are always receptive to doomsday messages. Fourthly, governments are always looking for causes to espouse that will win them public support. Another TV programme broadcast in April 1991 made similar points about concern over the environmental aftermath of the Gulf War.

The programme on the Greenhouse Effect took a cynical view of the processes involved, but made one very important point which is relevant to our subject. It was that this whole process could lead to large-scale erosion of public confidence in the role of science at a time when the rapid changes through which the world is passing may demand accurate scientific judgement about the outcome of environmental practices.

Given that it is now impossible to predict the outcomes of many of our actions, there are two ways to proceed. One is to abolish all industrial and other processes which might possibly have deleterious environmental side-effects. This is impossible for several reasons, not least that such a move would lead to immediate global economic collapse. In any case, some major environmental problems are side-effects of well-intentioned actions. A good example here is the desertification of parts of equatorial Africa due to overgrazing by cattle—the increase in cattle numbers is a direct result of efforts to improve the lot of the people who live there. In a similar fashion, flooding in Bangladesh is exacerbated by deforestation in the Himalayas as people gather wood for much-needed fuel. In addition, most problems are compounded by the rapidly increasing world population—quite a separate issue—and finally, given the uncertainties involved, how could we possibly know what needed to be abolished anyway?

Effective international policing of environmental practice depends upon an equally effective body of national and international law. Yet it is difficult for legal developments to keep up with the accelerating pace and expanding scale of impacts on the well-being of our environment. To give an example from a closely related sphere of operations: our current copyright laws were drawn up for a society where the printed word in books and magazines was the principal means of communication. They are totally inadequate to deal with the micro-electronic age, with its computers, videotape and audiotape systems, and no one seems sure what to put in its place.

Hypotheticality

The other way to proceed is to acknowledge that we must learn to live with uncertainty, to accept that risk is an essential feature of life. One of the major areas where attention has been drawn to this is that of nuclear power, and it is significant that it was a nuclear engineer who coined the term 'hypotheticality':

> It is probable that 'hypotheticality' will characterise the next stages of human enterprise. The magnitude of technological enterprises will be so great that it will not be possible to proceed with the absolute certainty that there will be no negative consequences.[5]

How do we decide what is an acceptable or an unacceptable risk? How can the concept be applied to human activity, especially regarding high technology activities such as the nuclear industry, and to assessing the human and environmental consequences of catastrophic accidents? We will concentrate here on the nuclear industry, not because it is necessarily more dangerous than any other industry, but because it is there that most of the thinking has been done so far.

A CHRISTIAN VIEW OF RISK

Does God take risks? One view is that he always foresees the outcome of everything, and therefore no risk-taking is involved. But exactly how God foresees everything and ensures that history moves towards its preordained goal is something which is more open to debate. There are two separate ways of looking at the problem, using a computer analogy: one is to think of everything that happens in terms of pre-programming down to the finest detail. The other sees the computer programme as pre-programmed to cope with all eventualities, so that all that happens can be incorporated into the divine plan.[6]

Although the latter view seems at first to make inroads into what we understand by divine omniscience (God knows everything), Howard Marshall argues that it makes better sense of many scriptural texts. If this model is correct, then in it God reveals himself as a risk-taking God. Creating a world such as ours, and people with freedom to obey or disobey such as ourselves, he deliberately exposes himself to the uncertainties opened up by our free actions.

What does not follow is that there is any uncertainty about the goal towards which creation is moving. Nor was there ever any doubt about the need for a Saviour and the precise time at which he would appear (Gal 4:4). What this means is that the essence of risk is not uncertainty, though that may be a part of risk-taking, but of vulnerability—of deliberately exposing oneself to danger for the sake of some greater good.

Since God foresaw the Fall, risk-taking is an activity which pre-dates the Fall, and is part of the process of existence itself. If this is true of the Creator, it is even more true of his creatures. We have already seen that in Genesis 2:15 God put the man in the Garden to work it and care for it. If there were no uncertainties, merely an idyllic paradise in which food came from falling coconuts, there would have been no work for the man to do. A creation which needed caring for (or protecting) was one in which there were always challenges and uncertainties, and risks to be taken:

> We cannot avoid living with the unknown future and its
> risks; indeed the Christian faith endorses the acceptance
> of risks as a normal and proper part of a life directed
> towards the achievement of God's purpose...The very
> message of Jesus' own life is the willing acceptance of
> risks in the pursuit of God's loving purpose.[7]

This asserts that risks are not just to be endured; they are an integral part of human living. Since we live on the other side of the Fall, the challenge now has a sombre side to it. Sin has corrupted the relationship between humanity and the rest of creation. Into the risk equation now go all the possible repercussions of human greed, complacency, carelessness and ignorance. This still does not mean that we can opt for a quiet, risk-free life. That is impossible. But it makes the task of assessing risk a doubly urgent one.

In Chapter 6 we examined the phenomenon of idolatry, to find that it has not disappeared; it merely has new clothes. Science becomes the new religion; technology is the saviour, and the priests wear white lab coats. But this approach ignores the fact that successful stewardship depends on humble dependence upon the Creator, and on a realistic appraisal of the power of sin to reap a terrible harvest. Risk-taking has to allow for these realities. Thus all attempts to brush aside worries about the safety of nuclear power should be viewed with deep suspicion. One eminent physicist dismissed the anti-nuclear lobby as the pawns of the Russians! On a more serious note, other nuclear experts brush aside public fears in a manner totally unjustified:

> The public do not and cannot be expected to
> understand the issues of nuclear power in other than the
> very broadest terms...The public accept that planes are
> guided through cloud and at night by radio. There is no
> need for a course in radio navigation to be compulsory

before you go on your summer holiday to Spain...The public are prepared to believe that the wings are strong enough not to break and although they might be a bit apprehensive in bumpy weather they are usually more concerned about the risk of spilling their drink. Why then should the advice of the equivalent professionals in nuclear power be treated with such suspicion, particularly since their record is better than the excellent record of the aircraft industry?[8]

We will return to the issue of the public participation in decision-making later in the chapter. Suffice it to say here that such contemptuous dismissal of the fears of ordinary people betrays a complacency which itself will only breed further fears. At the 1979 WCC conference *Faith, Science and the Future* Jerome Ravetz referred to the 'ignorance and incompetence' of nuclear power scientists and engineers, and to 'the misleading and manipulated scientific information being presented to the public, and the growing suspicion of corruption in a long-standing systematic cover-up of serious hazards in that field...'[9]

It is only fair to point out that Ravetz was very heavily criticised at the conference for these remarks, but they at least point to the need for science to be conducted with total integrity; anything less plays Russian roulette with people's lives. That this is not just an abstract argument is revealed by the remarks of the first official report after the Chernobyl accident in 1986, which referred to 'a whole series of crude violations of the regulations for the operation of reactor installations' and to 'irresponsibility, negligence and lack of discipline' on the part of those concerned.[10] We can also add the fact that the Russian authorities apparently never saw the need to build reinforced concrete containment vessels around each of the four reactors at Chernobyl (this is standard practice elsewhere), and that the workers still struggling inside the entombed reactor to predict its future safety are hampered by lack of proper equipment. Nearer home, it came as a shock when an official report in 1990 revealed the 'real' cost of electricity generated from nuclear power, after the general public had been told repeatedly over many years that it was significantly the cheapest form of electricity.

The Assessment of Risk

Risks are impossible to prevent because of the sinfulness of humanity, which, as we have seen, is a far deeper condition than simply occasional misdeeds. As an attitude of rebellion that leads to a breakdown within the sphere of all human relationships, it inevitably has effects upon the world of creation.

Some pollution incidents are downright deliberate. Some are acts of environmental terrorism, as in the case of the firing of Kuwaiti oil wells during the 1991 Gulf War. Others are not deliberately harmful, but reflect callous disregard for the effects on humans and other lifeforms. This category includes oil spillages and the dumping of dangerous chemicals. More than two million tonnes of oil enter the world's seas and oceans each year. Nearly 60% of this comes from land-based activity. Individual amounts are often small and tend to be little-known in comparison with the publicity given to oil tanker disasters. But each year there are large numbers of small spillages, often far out at sea, due to ships flushing out their fuel bunkers, quite illegally, rather than pay to have the job done legally while in port.

Also deliberate is dumping of hazardous chemicals. Although in many countries there is strict legislation about the disposal of dangerous chemicals, enforcement is an entirely different matter. Illegal dumping is a highly lucrative industry in some countries; the only criterion operated in deciding where drums of chemicals are dumped is that of evading detection, irrespective of what dangers arise for human and non-human life, and chemical companies and disposal operators are equally guilty.

Sadly, this trade is also international, with some evidence that major, and supposedly reputable, companies are involved. Here the targets are Third World countries often desperate for money for development or to pay their debts to the countries from which the wastes come, and where there is minimal legislation (and even less expertise) to ensure safe operation. A catalogue of such incidents in Africa makes depressing reading. It includes 7500 litres of hazardous waste from the US armed forces, dumped in a phosphate tip in Zimbabwe, Russian radioactive waste dumped in Benin, and 4000 tonnes of Italian waste dumped at Koko, Nigeria, and returned to its host country after local workers became ill as a result of leaks. Increasingly, this practice is being abandoned as receiving countries learn bitter lessons about the effects of the materials on local people.

Other environmental disasters are 'accidents' in the sense that they are not deliberate, such as the nuclear accidents at Three Mile Island, Pennsylvania, USA (1979), and Chernobyl, Ukraine, USSR (1986), chemical incidents such as that at Bhopal, India (1984), the *Piper Alpha* oil rig disaster and the breaching of oil tankers such as the *Exxon Valdez*.

Bhopal illustrates the large-scale loss of life and long-term health problems that can come in the wake of a single incident. Water was mistakenly allowed to enter a methyl isocyanate tank, and this accident was coupled with the failure of safety equipment to operate properly, at a Union Carbide plant. In the immediate aftermath, the toxic gas cloud which enveloped the city killed 2500 people. Some 300,000 of those who survived have serious health problems, mainly with lungs, stomach, eyes, and the auto-immune system. The Piper Alpha oil rig disaster, which killed over 150 people, was the result of a communication breakdown on the rig between operational and maintenance staff, who had removed a safety valve later identified as the cause of the explosion and fire which followed.

It is possible to duck the issue of human culpability. A recent attempt to develop a theology of accident starts by assuming that, since it is impossible to imagine that Chernobyl was in any sense an act of divine judgement (a position rejected in the article due to the way judgement was caricatured therein), it must have been 'what it seemed to most people—an accident, pure and simple.'[11] Yet with few exceptions, human culpability is a major factor in environmental 'accidents'.

The human factor has always been a major one, whether through sustained environmental mismanagement or acts of carelessness. Indeed, the sombre Christian view of humanity which flows from the biblical account of the Fall makes it clear that fallen people can never be fully in control of God's world. Because of the effects of their sin on the natural world, its processes inevitably turn against them; the thorns and thistles of Genesis 3 turn out to be metaphors for the anti-radiation suits of the workers decontaminating Three Mile Island or Chernobyl, and the stranded aeroplanes unable to land relief supplies at Dacca airport whose runways were, like most of Bangladesh in the aftermath of a 1988 flood, under feet of water.

There are, of course, other disasters which appear to be entirely natural—earthquakes and volcanic eruptions. Some theologians have tried to link them all with the outworking of Genesis 3:17ff, but the explanations are sometimes so speculative as to go far beyond what Scripture actually says. Even here the human element may also be important, the dangers of simplistic blame-apportionment notwithstanding. For example, the flooding of two-thirds of Bangladesh during 1988 could be blamed simply on particularly heavy monsoon rains; but a worrying contributory factor was the deforestation of Himalayan slopes in India and Tibet, causing the transfer of large amounts of soil to the Ganges river system, which then silted up the flood plain of the river (ie most of Bangladesh). But even this is simplistic; deforestation was due to economic factors, particularly the extreme poverty of the peoples living in the upland regions.

Risk Estimation

The process of risk estimation is vital in deciding whether some new industry with environmental side-effects is to be set up anywhere. Everyone recognises that all such processes contain inherent risks. In fact, this is not as sinister as it may seem: everything we do contains such risk. The risks of travelling to and from work, or the shops, are well known and taken for granted. Even a motorway accident which kills a handful of people is taken for granted, and few people bat an eyelid. Accident figures also show that our homes are hazardous places to be in!

However, given the magnitude of the after-effects of the Bhopal and Chernobyl incidents, it is only right that risk calculation exercises should be carried out. There are two separate procedures involved.[12] The first is that of risk *estimation*, which is essentially a mathematical exercise to calculate statistical likelihoods of certain kinds of accident occurring, and their effects on public health.

In the nuclear industry, an important milestone in the development of risk calculation procedures was the *Rasmussen Report*, published in 1975. It concluded that the chance of death at a nuclear power plant in one year was 1 in 300 million; the chance of any nuclear accident killing 100 people was 1 in 1 million per year per nuclear plant, lengthening to 1 in 100 million for a 1000-death incident. Are these figures as reassuring as they sound? The answer is 'no', for a variety of reasons, although this should not be taken to imply that they are meaningless.

1   This was the first major exercise of its kind, and as with all such exercises, it has been constantly refined since, and the final figures modified, as the assumptions which inevitably go into the procedures are critically examined and re-assessed.

2   There are major problems in the way we react to figures such as these. Because the accident risk seems so infinitesimally small, they can easily give rise to the sort of complacency which could itself alter the figures themselves ('it could never happen here...'). The figures can equally well be interpreted as saying, 'The risks are certainly small, but it is just as likely that a serious accident will happen this year as any other year!'

3   Closely related to this is the fact that we can never know if enough is being done to prevent a disaster happening.

4   We are now separated from the *Rasmussen Report* by the experience of two major nuclear incidents—Three Mile Island and Chernobyl. A recent study used this hindsight-approach to predict that the mathematical probability of a reactor incident occurring in the next ten years is 86%.[13] The methodology used in this study has been criticised, and the figure of 86% rated as no more than an educated guess, but the critic concerned still concluded:

> All we can really say is that the probability of an
> accident in the next ten years is unlikely to be less than
> a quarter—a sufficiently alarming prospect not to
> detract from the main point they were making.[14]

Risk Evaluation

It is important to note that risk *estimation* is only the first stage in the process. What follows—risk *evaluation*—is at least equally important. This has been defined as the 'essentially political task of determining the significance of risk estimates, together with any effects not considered in estimation', including political, social, moral, psychological and economic effects, environmental impacts, improbable catastrophes and the differing benefits of different systems.[15]

Decisions with environmental consequences that are made by politicians and others depend as much on the risks as perceived by the local communities which are involved, as they do on the figures themselves. A study of attitudes in Cumbria to the operation of Sellafield concluded:

> There is an organic web of risk attitudes in west
> Cumbria, deriving from individual webs of experience,
> argument, agreement, reflection and resistance...there
> is a continuing need for more complete and more
> sympathetic understanding of the attitudes and

positions of communities affected by nuclear (and other) risk issues'[16].

One of the major ways forward, the study concludes, is to find ways in which the public can be enabled to share current knowledge about the operation of the facility in question—in this case a nuclear one, but the conclusion is of more general application. Here we come across a major difference between two approaches: one which goes out of its way to be as open as possible, and the other shrouded in secrecy and so structured as to be confrontational and unequal.

The former is characteristic of the approach taken in the USA. In the wake of the Three Mile Island incident already referred to, the government set up the Kemeny Commission which, as well as six nuclear experts, also contained a state governor, an environmentalist, a lawyer, an industrialist, a trade union representative, and a local housewife. As an example of open planning for the future, take the decisions taken in siting a power station in Southern California. The power utility concerned, the San Diego Gas and Electric Company

> invited to a seminar all environmental and planning
> organisations in the area where a new power plant was
> necessary. Those present were invited to elect an
> environmental advisory group to examine possible sites.
> The committee examined the requirement for additional
> generating capacity, consulted widely and
> recommended a site to the company, which was
> accepted.[17]

The same report goes on to describe the procedures used in nuclear decision-making in Great Britain:

> A contrast to this approach is the saga of the Central
> Electricity Generating Board's (CEGB) application to
> build a Pressurised Water Reactor (PWR) nuclear
> power station at Sizewell, on a stretch of Suffolk
> coastline of special value to environmentalists because

of its unspoiled remoteness and wildlife. A confrontational Public Inquiry lasted 340 days and the CEGB poured public money into establishing their case to the extent that their Chairman announced that he would resign if they did not win. The opposition was argued on grounds of safety, nuclear waste disposal problems, and environmental objections by a number of organisations... for this large sums of money had to be raised.[18]

What is described here is a confrontational approach which, by its structure, ensures that people of strongly held but differing views shout at each other but fail to listen. The major issues had all been settled before the inquiry began; there was no scope for discussing alternatives in a rational manner. The financial, scientific and legal resources available to the CEGB far outweighed those of the opponents. Yet within the nuclear industry there are far-sighted people who believe that this will not do. Wolfgang Häfele, whose work on the 'pathfinder role' of nuclear energy has already been quoted, is one such, and he describes the 'pathfinder role' as one in which dialogue and concensus in nuclear decision-making can point the way forward in other confrontational spheres of activity, including arms negotiations.

This raises another important issue: that of how much the general public can understand of such highly complex issues as nuclear power. The USA approach assumes that people can understand something at least, and can therefore be trusted to be involved in decision-making processes. The British approach, fostered by the nuclear industry and the government, is 'leave it to the experts!' This is not to say, of course, that the experts will not continue to play a major role in the decision-making process. The point is that the issues are too great to be left to the experts alone, especially when the issues involved are not purely scientific ('trans-scientific', to quote Dr Alvin Weinberg) and when the decisions to be made affect the lives of millions of ordinary people.

Comparing Risks

Also involved in the assessment of the risks involved in nuclear power operation is the comparison between nuclear and non-nuclear futures. Briefly, the particular problems to be considered are as follows: first, the expansion of the nuclear power industry is the most obvious single means of making inroads into the problems of atmospheric carbon dioxide and the Greenhouse Effect. Is this sufficient reason for going down the nuclear road? Secondly, to fail to expand the nuclear option is to risk a huge energy shortfall in twenty or thirty years' time as supplies of fossil fuels start to dwindle. Can the world risk this? Can we be sure of having enough available energy from alternative sources (such as windpower, solar power, geothermal sources, and greater use of energy conservation methods)? Many environmentalists would like to believe this, but given the size of possible energy shortfalls by AD 2020, it seems by no means certain that the gap could be bridged in this way.

What casts such a dark cloud over an energy future based on 'clean' supply sources is the systematic underfunding of research and development over the years, in stark contrast to the vast amounts of money channelled into the nuclear option. In answer to a question on this subject in the British House of Commons in 1990, the following figures were produced:

Department of Energy R & D Expenditure on Energy Sources[19]
(Figures as percentages)

	Nuclear	Coal Technology	Renewable Sources	Efficiency Measures
1979-80	84.2	1.0	5.5	0.6
1980-1	85.1	1.2	6.5	0.9
1981-2	81.5	1.8	6.4	1.0
1982-3	85.2	1.2	5.2	1.8
1983-4	85.7	1.3	5.0	2.9
1984-5	84.6	0.3	6.4	2.7

1985-6	85.4	0.3	6.1	1.5
1986-7	83.0	1.0	7.0	2.0
1987-8	79.9	0.8	9.1	2.3
1988-9	81.3	0.7	8.9	1.7

What these figures reflect is a process which could be called 'self-blackmail'. What this means is that, once so much money is committed to the development of nuclear power, two things happen. The first is that it becomes very difficult even to contemplate the possibility that it might become necessary to abandon nuclear power; a similar process operated during the development of the supersonic aircraft *Concorde*. So much money had been spent that it became necessary to complete the project, irrespective of its usefulness. The second is that competing projects—in this case, renewable energy sources—are systematically underfunded. In this way alternative energy policies that might lead to a more environmentally viable future are closed off.

How Are Disasters To Be Prevented?

Major environmental disasters such as Chernobyl and Bhopal are followed by inquiries which seek to find the cause(s) and make recommendations about how to avoid future potential incidents. Significant in this respect was the Three Mile Island nuclear accident in Pennsylvania, USA, in 1979. The Kemeny Commission, already referred to, found that there were three major human factors involved in the accident: operator error, deficient emergency procedures in place at the plant, and shortcomings in the layout of the control room.

Put another way, the Kemeny Commission found that the operators who were in the control room during the shift when the emergency occurred did not know what to do. This was not a matter of incompetence on their part. The nature of the emergency was such that they had not been trained to cope with those particular circumstances—it was not in the rule-book. The result was that their first attempts to cope with the situation were not the right ones; these came only after some delay, by which time the damage to the reactor plant was far worse than it might otherwise have been, and the risk to the general public (whose main illnesses were due to stress, not to radiation) correspondingly greater.

This, then, raises the question of the philosophy behind training for operatives in high-technology industries. The previous philosophy was a 'rule-book' one, based on learning instructions for all possible eventualities, and rested on the assumption, proved false at Three Mile Island, that all eventualities could be foreseen.

An alternative approach—that of problem-solving—is gaining ground. The philosophy behind it is that, given the impossibility of predicting all eventualities and setting up rules for dealing with them, it offers a better chance of the problem being quickly solved.[20]

Of even greater significance are the findings of Electricité de France, presented at a 1987 conference on human reliability and nuclear power, that particular innovations (new 'rules', in other words) in safety techniques are only effective for about one year, after which staff become desensitised to the reasons why the innovation was introduced in the first place. More important, they believed, is the creation of a 'human dynamic' activated by the staff themselves, in which motivation, responsibility and honesty are vital.[21]

The reason why this is such an important development is that it takes more seriously than before the human element in the operation of high-technology processes such as nuclear power stations. It may not be a specifically Christian way of looking at how things operate, but because it attempts to integrate the scientific and moral aspects of stewardship, it may well indicate the way forward in the responsible management of risk.

REFERENCES

1. Donella H. Meadows, D.L. Meadows, J. Randers and W.W. Behrens III, *The Limits to Growth* (Universe Books: Washington DC,

1972).

2. C. Norman, 'Material Shortage Shocks Ahead?', *Nature* vol 253 (1974): p 674.

3. M. Batisse, 'Global Prospects for Natural Resources', *Nature and Resources*, vol 10 (1974): pp 2-7.

4. H. van Reissen, *The Society of the Future* (Presbyterian and Reformed Publishing Company: Philadelphia, no date given).

5. Wolf Häfele, 'Hypotheticality and the new challenges: the path-finder role of nuclear energy', in John Francis and Paul Abrecht, *Facing up to Nuclear Power* (Saint Andrew Press: Edinburgh, 1976), p 62.

6. I. Howard Marshall, 'Aspects of the Biblical View of History', *Faith and Thought*, vol 110 (1983): pp 54-68. See especially pp 61-63.

7. *Shaping Tomorrow* (Home Mission Division of the Methodist Church: London, 1981), p 17.

8. Sir John Hill, 'The quest for public acceptance of nuclear power', *Atom* no 273 (July 1979): pp 166-172.

9. Jerome R. Ravetz, 'The Scale and Complexity of the Problem' in Roger L. Shinn, *Faith and Science in an Unjust World* (WCC: Geneva, 1980), p 90.

10. See eg Malcolm Grimston, 'The Chernobyl accident reviewed', *Atom*, no 413 (May 1991): pp 12-20; Vera Rich, 'Lax standards confirmed', *Nature*, vol 342 (2nd November 1989): p 10.

11. Michael Tucker, 'Accident and creation', *Crucible*, (1987): pp 153-160.

12. For a good introductory review of what is involved, see R.A.D. Ferguson, 'Risk estimation and evaluation', *Science and Public Policy*, vol 9 (October 1982): pp 251-254.

13. S. Islam and K. Lindgren, 'How many reactor accidents will there be?', *Nature*, no 322 (21st August 1986): pp 691-692.

14. A.W.F. Edwards, 'How many reactor accidents?', *Nature*, no 324 (4th December 1986): pp 417-418.

15. R.A.D. Ferguson, *op cit* p 251.

16. S.M. Macgill, 'Sellafield: what the locals say', *Atom*, no 372 (October 1987): pp 20-23.

17. General Synod Board for Social Responsibility, *Our Responsibility for the Living Environment* (Church House: London, 1986), p 27.

18. *ibid* p 28.

19. Source: *Atom* no 400 (February 1990): p 47.

20. Nigel Holloway, 'The significance of human actions for plant safety', *Atom* no 379 (May 1988): pp 2-7.
21. Wendy Peters, 'Human reliability in nuclear power', *Atom* no 377 (March 1988): pp 19-20.

Chapter Eleven

JUSTICE, PEACE AND THE INTEGRITY OF CREATION

POLLUTION AND POVERTY

Dodong Balayon is a typical Filipino farmer... In 1989 Dodong is in his mid-forties, though he looks much older. He is a *kainginero*, a slash-and-burn farmer. Each planting season Dodong burns down a further half-hectare of the dwindling rain forest in order to grow rootcrops and corn. This is how he feeds his wife and six children and earns a few pesos with which to buy the necessities of life. On a few occasions I have shared with him my concern at watching him burn this... forest. I point to soil erosion and the heritage of a wasteland for his children and grandchildren unless the forest is protected. He is not unaware of this, but he insists that his scramble to meet today's needs is his primary concern. Tomorrow will have to take care of itself.[1]

PUT IN ITS baldest terms, the problem is this: the relationship between environmental issues and the plight of millions of the world's poor people is so direct that the two problems cannot be tackled in isolation. Given the poor international record in facing world poverty, it is going to be extremely difficult to solve the problems of poisoned environments. Nor is it any use blaming governments and international organisations. Free elections in Western countries are fought on a wide variety of issues, but one which seldom comes to the top of the list is that of the poor, either at home or abroad. How many hopeful politicians, knocking at doors and asking for votes, expect the first question to be: what will your government do for global redistribution of wealth? The most effective way to capture people's votes is to appeal to their pockets.

The general preoccupation in First World countries is with personal affluence, and many governments have encouraged this in the name of freedom of choice. The middle-class members of environmental organisations are seriously concerned about a clean environment, and are willing to recycle plastic, paper and glass, use lead-free petrol and insulate their lofts, but they can afford to do this, and feel rightly that they are doing something responsible by deciding to spend their money this way. But this does nothing towards the redistribution of resources and power within the wider world. And it ignores the fact that the majority do not have the luxury of being able to make such generous choices.

Try knocking on doors in a deprived area of a Western city, and telling the people there that they need to be more environmentally responsible. The reply is likely to be that they have other more urgent problems to cope with—debt, unemployment, illness, rising damp and the like. Or imagine trying to convince the authorities in a desperately poor African, Asian or Latin American country that they should expel a certain multi-national corporation because of its poor environmental record. Here the reply is likely to be that the country is in urgent need of that company's goods to provide an export market, foreign exchange, and employment for at least some people, even if the wages are not terribly high and there is some pollution. Green issues are a luxury for the rich, they are likely to say. The poor know better than the well-off what are the links between justice, peace and the integrity of creation.

JUSTICE, PEACE AND THE INTEGRITY OF CREATION

Justice, Peace and the Integrity of Creation is the theological title of ecumenical programmes designed to awaken churches around the world to these coupled threats to the quality (and even the future viability) of human life. It is sad that the debate within the World Council of Churches has been obscured by dubious theology, some of it owing more to New Age influences than to Scripture (see Chapter 1), and the failure of its Secretariat to be properly answerable to its member churches.

An altogether more sober attempt to face the problems squarely has been made by the churches of Europe. The process began with the 1986 General Assembly of the Conference of European Churches (CEC), which decided upon a European Assembly entitled *Peace with Justice*, eventually held in May 1989. The first draft of a statement on the subject was published in October 1988, and a version revised after input from working groups from all over Europe formed the basis of the 1989 Assembly. The final Assembly document, *Peace with Justice for the Whole Creation (The Basel Declaration)*, was adopted by an overwhelming majority of the 504 delegates—481 in favour and 12 against, with 11 abstentions.

Poverty is a massive tragedy in a world which has the technological resources to abolish it. Nearly one billion people lack the basic necessities of life—food and water, education and basic health care. Millions die each year from a range of causes related to poverty—hunger, thirst and disease. Many of the world's poorer countries are unable to raise the level of care for their subjects because of falling prices for their exports and rising prices for imports, and because of crippling levels of debt repayment. Because their poverty is related to the wider international economic order, they cannot on their own bring justice to those who have never known it.

Poverty is not relative to an absolute standard of living; rather, it is about relationships between the rich and the poor, and the lack of power the poor have to change their situation.

It is alive and well in almost every city in the developed world, whether in Europe, the USA, or Hong Kong and Singapore. Here, as elsewhere, poverty is not dwindling as general living standards rise. The number of poor people is rising, and with it the gap is widening between them and the better-off.

At the same time, vast amounts of money, manpower and effort are directed towards development of weapons systems, ostensibly for 'defence', but in fact used to wage the 100 wars that have taken place in the so-called post-war period since 1945. The *Brundtland Report* sums up the position:

> Global military spending in 1985 was well in excess of $900 billion. This was more than the total income of the poorest half of humanity. It represented the equivalent of almost $1,000 for every one of the world's 1 billion poorest. Three-quarters of this expenditure is in the industrialised world.
>
> The distorting effects of the 'arms culture' are most striking in the deployment of scientific personnel. Half a million scientists are employed in weapons research worldwide, and they account for around half of all research and development expenditure. This exceeds the total combined spending on developing new energy sources, improving human health, raising agricultural productivity, and controlling pollution. Military research and development—$70-80 billion world-wide in 1984—is growing at twice the rate of military spending as a whole.[2]

Ethiopia, one of the poorest countries in the world, was spending 60% of its Gross National Product on arms until the collapse of the Mengistu regime in May 1991; this is one reason why its people are so poor. One of the ironies of this situation is that when international peace threatens to break out, as when the superpowers sign arms limitation treaties, an immediate effect is large-scale redundancy in the weapons industry.

Such is the technological effort that has gone into the

development of modern armaments research, that the cost of each individual weapon can be a major item, diverting money from better causes. One bomb dropped by a USAF B52 bomber costs $11,000 (1991 prices); the same money would pay the salaries of 180 staff in a Bangladeshi clinic serving 4,000 people. British daily operating costs in the 1991 Gulf war were £3.6 million, equal to Save the Children's entire 1990-1 budget for work in Ethiopia. The five Tornado aircraft lost by the RAF cost £105 million; the same sum could have bought enough grain to feed for one month the 20 million people likely to die of starvation in Africa in 1991. In the same war the US forces had fired 216 Tomahawk cruise missiles by January 19, costing a total of $280 million, equal to the cost of 6 months' food aid for Ethiopia.[3]

One of the main strengths of the document *Peace with Justice for the Whole Creation* is that it refuses to think of environmental problems except in relation to global poverty, and vice versa. Examples cited include the problems of the Amazonian rain forests (Paragraph 14), the refugee crisis (Paragraph 15), and the population explosion (Paragraph 16).

Deforestation

In Brazil, as elsewhere in the tropics, the rain forests are being cut back at an enormous rate, a process itself made possible through the power of modern high-technology machinery. There are many reasons for this: the demand for grazing land for cattle (a by-product of the high demand for cheap meat in the northern hemisphere), the economic potential of wood for paper-making and furniture, and geological exploration for minerals, oil and gas. All these factors are exacerbated by the chronic debts incurred by many Two-Thirds World countries and the need to generate fast money for repayments. The tragedy is that the side-effects of deforestation include not only environmental degradation but also human disasters:

> The most infamous World Bank project is the
> Palonoreste project which is to open up the Brazilian

state of Rondonia in the Amazon region. The World Bank is financing road construction in virgin tropical forests, which in 1980 still covered virtually all of the state. The roads open up Rondonia to extremely poor, landless farmers from South Brazil, to adventurers and to land speculators. The Indians and rubber tappers, now living in harmony with the forest without harming it, are being expelled from their home grounds—they are often in fact chased away at gunpoint—and the farmers move in...What remains is a ghostly landscape, with half-burnt trees and stagnant pools, which are major sources of malaria. The farmers soon have no other option but to move on. In a few years' time the entire state of Rondonia, an area as big as West Germany, will be bare. Already, not enough land is available for the continuing inflow of immigrants. For this reason, the Inter-American Development Bank, a regional sister of the World Bank, recently undertook to finance roads that are to open up the neighbouring state of Acre even deeper in the Amazon region.[4]

Elsewhere in the world other rain forests, not so well known as those of Amazonia are similarly threatened. In 1985 some 270,000 hectares of forest were felled in Sarawak; unless this rate is cut back, the whole of this forest resource will be destroyed by the end of the millenium. The local climate is changing as a result. There have been several severe droughts, and flooding after heavy rainfall has also taken place, because the vegetation cover which helps the soil retain the rainwater had been stripped away. Loss of life and massive soil erosion are just two of the side-effects of this process.

Much of the Sarawak timber is hardwood of a type suitable for making doorposts and window frames. Japan and the European Community are the major importers of this wood. Japan's role in particular has been heavily criticised by the Worldwide Fund for Nature. According to the WWF, Japan's overseas development assistance programme has provided funds for projects which have helped in the destruction of

South-east Asia's rainforests, and damaged the health and economic welfare of its indigeneous peoples.

Columban missionary Sean McDonagh writes from first-hand experience of what is happening to the rainforests of the Philippines. Dodong Balayon, with whose plight the chapter began, was the victim of circumstances over which he had no control. In the 1960s he had owned a two-hectare farm in a fertile valley as part of a government agricultural development programme. He cleared the land and planted a variety of crops. In the early 1970s he was advised by government agri-cultural advisers to abandon this mixed farming for a money-spinning alternative—a new high-yield variety of rice. For a few years things went well, but then he lost two successive crops through drought and pests. Meanwhile the cost of fertil-iser was rising steadily, and the straw which broke the camel's back was the increase in interest rates to 22% in the early 1980s. Eventually he was forced to sell the farm to pay his debts, after which there was so little money left that he was forced into the rain forest as a *kainginero*.[5] His story is not unique.

But it comes as a shock to find that there is also a direct link with our own lifestyle:

> It is hard to visualise that a meal in one's favourite fast-food restaurant damages the tropical forest. The conversion of tropical rain forest to cattle ranches to supply the fast-food hamburger industry of First World countries is the most wasteful and destructive use of the tropical rainforest. The land is normally cleared through burning the cover. The soil is quickly degraded as erosion is speeded up by the constant pressure of cattle hooves on the fragile soil. When the land becomes exhausted, the ranches move on to repeat the cycle of destruction. The beef thus produced is cheaper, less than half or one-third the cost of beef produced in the US, so it is readily snapped up by the fast-food industries. In this way the cycle of destruction

irreversibly destroying the tropical forest can begin with that cheap hamburger.[6]

Environmental Refugees

The refugee crisis in the 1990s is greater than ever before, as wars fought with devastating high-technology weapons and merciless efficiency drive people from their homelands. Early in 1991 the world was profoundly shocked by television pictures of Kurdish refugees shivering and dying in the bitter cold, snow and mud of the mountains on the Iraq-Turkey border. Difficult though it was to understand from the comfort of a European armchair, the Kurds chose this rather than face the uncertain future of their cities under the control of Saddam Hussein's troops, systematically armed over many years by a range of countries eager to benefit from the Iraqi ruler's oil money.

This is by no means unique. Millions of refugees from the Russian military adventure in Afghanistan still live in camps across the Pakistani border. The Palestinians, dispossessed by the creation of the state of Israel over forty years ago, still live in makeshift towns and refugee camps in a variety of Middle Eastern countries; the problem of Arab-Israeli relations remains insurmountable. Refugees from the civil war in Mozambique flee to Malawi, from Ethiopia to Sudan. Starvation seems the most likely prospect, because the wars simply compound the effects of drought and poverty. In Peru the population of Lima swells daily as rural families, often bereft of menfolk, flee the cruelty of the Marxist guerillas of the 'Shining Path'.

The term 'refugee' is usually applied to peoples displaced by the results of war, but the United Nations also recognises the existence of *environmental refugees*, forced to leave their homelands, mainly in rural areas, because of a variety of environmental problems. Their destination is usually the world's cities, which continue to grow at a seemingly unstoppable rate, and it is often the largest cities, set in the poorest countries, which grow fastest. The following table gives examples from different continents.

City Population Growth

City	Population in 1950	Population 2000 (UN prediction)
Mexico City	3,050,000	26,300,000
Sao Paulo	2,700,000	24,000,000
Bombay	3,000,000	16,000,000
Djakarta	1,450,000	12,800,000
Cairo	2,500,000	13,200,000
Lagos	270,000	8,300,000

The explanation of this huge growth is found in what can be called the 'push-pull' phenomenon. There is the 'pull' of the cities and the 'push' of rural living conditions. Thijs de la Court writes:

> The cities have also gained a certain attractiveness, with their neon advertisements and luxury products, and with their government offices, factories and universities. If one ever wants to become 'upwardly mobile', one must live in the city. In rural areas one remains 'backward' and grows isolated. That those daring enough to make the move to the city often have to live there in the most horrendous conditions does little to detract from this attraction.
>
> Farmers receive very low prices for their products, and in many cases most of the land, and the best land at that, is owned by big agricultural companies, operating on a commercial basis. For simple peasant families, forced to move to less productive soil, it is hardly possible to earn a living. The result is often erosion, water shortage, deforestation and other environmental problems, forcing the poorest to flee the rural areas altogether.[7]

This gives some insight into the reasons why so many people continue to flood into the world's major cities, believing that they can find better prospects there than in the rural areas they are deserting. Vast areas of land in Africa and elsewhere are being turned into desert through combinations of drought, war and inappropriate agricultural methods. The result is desertification. Each year some 60,000 square kilometres of land are turned into desert. During the past fifty years 650,000 square kilometres of productive land have been lost in the southern Sahara; in southern Sudan the desert advanced by 100 km from 1958 to 1975. This also helps to explain why people remain in cities in abject poverty and suffering, rather than return whence they came. Again, Thijs de la Court describes the situation graphically:

> Hardboard, plastic, cardboard, corrugated iron, clothes and wood are the main 'building' materials of the shanty towns in many Third World cities. At night there are thousands of small fires, around which women crouch to cook their food. Large numbers of children, chickens, goats and pigs roam the 'streets'. The poor hygiene defies description. There are usually no sewers, no water, no toilets, no electricity, and when it rains the 'streets' turn into pools of mud. Infant mortality is very high, and almost everyone suffers from worms and infectious diseases. Although most of the people living in shanty towns do have work, it is not a registered, formal job. These are hardly to be found.[8]

The 1990s have seen the outbreak of a pandemic of cholera in South America. Health experts believe the organism was introduced in sewage discharged from a ship off the coast of Peru, and found its way into the human food chain through fish which form an important part of the Peruvian diet. Many of the shanty-town dwellers of Lima and other coastal cities are at continued risk because they eat the fish raw. Cooking it would destroy the cholera germs, but in the shanty towns fuel is a luxury which cannot usually be afforded. The cholera then spreads further through human excrement in large city areas where there is no proper sanitation or clean water for washing, cooking and drinking.

The outbreak has now spread throughout large areas within other South American countries, where urban poverty and squalid living conditions remain an intractable barrier to its eradication. This is just one example of the suffering that can befall millions of helplessly poor people, often as a result of them becoming environmental refugees.

Population Growth

A further cause of global poverty is the growth of the world's population, which passed 5 billion in 1987. It is the poorer countries of the world where population growth is fastest. In Kenya, for example, 50% of the population is under fourteen years of age; the population is rising by over 4% per year. In the future such growth may put severe strain on the ability of traditional agriculture to provide enough food, and social pressures will result from families of increasing size being forced to divide their land holdings into smaller and smaller portions for the different family members.

But to imagine that birth control education programmes are all that is needed is to misunderstand the nature of the problem completely. It is in countries with limited resources that the problems of teaching birth control methods, and making them available, are most severe: they include lack of qualified teachers and the educational infrastructure to support them, the money to fund them and the birth control techniques that might otherwise work.

And there is stubborn resistance to be faced from people themselves. A way of looking at old age is argued with irresistible logic. When I am old and too weak to work, I will need a family to support me; the more sons I have, the easier this will be for them and for me. Vincent Cable, advisor to the Brundtland Commission, put it like this:

In many cases the major priority is to slow population

growth. Where population is growing at over 3%, it is difficult to see how a disastrous cycle of declining living standards and a deteriorating environment can be averted. There is no short cut to lower birth rates. Until poor families see that family planning will bring higher living standards, and that health services are good enough to reduce child mortality, they will have a strong incentive to have a large number of children. In many countries, little can be done until the status of women is raised, their economic contribution recognised, and their literacy increased; sometimes this has to be done in the face of centuries of tradition.[9]

The faster a country's population grows, then, the poorer they are likely to become unless the country itself is growing richer. Often this is not happening, or else the new riches are being concentrated in the hands of a few, if not being exported to pay off foreign debts and interest payments. This increases pressure on fragile environments, which often contain poor soils forced to support more and more crops.

The major fuel available for cooking is wood; woods and forests are cleared, people have to go further each day to gather wood, the soil is eroded. At Mvumi, in Tanzania, is a hospital where a missionary doctor once wrote his *Jungle Doctor* stories; there is now no forest to be seen from the hilltop on which the hospital stands, and local women walk miles with bundles of firewood balanced on their heads. The twin spectres of malnutrition and desertification raise their evil heads.

In some areas animal dung could be dug back into the soil to help maintain its fertility. But where acute poverty gnaws at the stomach, surviving until tomorrow takes precedence over planning for next year. Dung can be burned as cooking fuel, or else sold to other people for the same purpose. Thus a small amount of money can be had for buying food when there might otherwise be none. The vicious cycle of poverty and environmental degradation remains unbroken.

POLLUTION AND POVERTY IN THE RICH WORLD

Even in the world's rich countries pollution and poverty go together. James Plunkett's book *Strumpet City*, set in Dublin at the beginning of the century, introduces one of its main characters in this way:

> The morning air had a sulphur smell about it, a compound of mist from the river, smoke from the ships, slow-drifting yellow fumes from the gas works. It was like the look on Rashers' face. Hungry, dirty, and because so many things conspired to kill him, tenacious. His beard straggled. His gait was uncertain. He dragged his fifty years in each step forward through the streets of the city. She had not denied him her unique weapons. Almost from birth she had shaped his mind to regard life as a trivial moment which had slipped by mistake through the sieve of eternity, a scrap of absurdity which would glow for a little while, before it was snatched back into eternity again...His city had never offered him anything else. Except her ashbins.[10]

Something of that lack of air quality still perists in Dublin, and in many other major cities today. It happens particularly during winter months when high-pressure air systems give rise to clear skies, intense cold and slack air. These conditions cause what is known as an 'inversion', in which the city is blanketed by a layer of heavy air in which pollutants gradually build up to very high levels. Health problems arise for the old, the very young, and people with chest and heart complaints.

In the case of Dublin, the main offender is tens of thousands of domestic fires burning high-sulphur coal; the sulphur dioxide emitted into the air in massive quantities can be easily tasted until you get used to it. In one recent winter day, the EC directive on smoke pollution, which specifies a daily upper limit of 250 microgrammes per cubic metre, was exceeded by almost an order of magnitude—a figure of 1429 micro-grammes per cubic metre was recorded in one western suburb, with very high figures registered throughout the city day after day during such clear, still spells of winter weather.

The answer to this problem is easy to state but much more difficult to implement. The answer lies in the use of high-grade low-sulphur coal such as anthracite. It is in the implementation of this solution that two particular problems arise. The first problem is that anthracite is substantially more expensive than the high-sulphur domestic coal it is supposed to replace. This is not an obstacle for people with plenty of spare money, but the suburbs where the chimneys were contributing the greatest amounts of pollutant into the winter air were often the poorest, and where unemployment rates were particularly high.

The second is that, for technical reasons, people who wanted to burn the high-grade coal needed to have their domestic burners modified to take the new fuel. The cost of modification was sometimes to cost hundreds of pounds. Again, people in a poverty situation found themselves trapped. Burn the new fuel or break clean air regulations, was the threat; burn the new fuel and fall deeper into debt was the reality.

THE ULTIMATE CHALLENGE

Because the problems of poverty and environmental degradation are so closely related, realistic solutions have to tackle both simultaneously. This takes us far beyond paper recycling, bottle banks and lead-free petrol. Public opinion surveys of public attitudes show that most people are willing to take action to reduce pollution, but the questions which are asked usually fail to recognise how many of the main causes of environmental problems are extremely deep-seated and related to the endemic poverty of whole nations.

The solutions to both sets of problems will be radical, and therefore painful for the rich, because they must inevitably involve a major shift in the balance of economic power between the rich and poor nations. Built into Israel's laws were regulations to do with the care of creation (Chapter Five). There were also laws governing the way the rich were to treat the poor. At the heart of this area of Israel's life is the law of Jubilee (Lev 25:8–17) which, as we have seen, was designed to restrain the gap between rich and poor by the requirement to return land to its original owner every fifty years. Many of the world's poorest nations are crippled with debt. They are completely unable to repay the capital they have borrowed; it is all they can do to keep up with the interest payments. As a result, instead of money flowing into the countries which most need help, there is a net outflow into the rich nations because debt repayments are greater than the amount of aid currently being given.

So long as the present rules apply, they will never be able to improve the quality of life of millions of their people, and creation itself will inevitably share their suffering. One radical solution would be to cancel all these debts, at least for those nations with the worst plights. *This would be to put into practice the biblical principle of the Jubilee year.* The CEC declaration *Peace with Justice for the Whole Creation* grasps the nettle fearlessly:

> For the debt crisis we recommend that the poorest developing countries be released from their debts, while effective measures are taken towards the alleviation of the debt of all indebted countries including those of Eastern Europe. Governments are in a position to cancel or reschedule debts and to assist commercial banks and international institutions undertaking similar actions. Conditions should be created to prevent these countries from getting indebted again to the current extent (prevention of capital flight, revision of the international monetary system, changing the policies of the IMF, revision of the terms of trade, etc) and to make sure that the funds released are being used for the benefit of the victims of poverty.[11]

This, the CEC declaration also sees, is only part of the wider new order of things which needs to be instituted:

> There is an urgent need for a new international economic world order for the entire humanity, with special priority for the poor, the oppressed and the powerless. Every economic development has to be submitted to the criteria of social sustainability, international sustainability, sustainability for the environment and sustainability through generations. Such action should include the regulation of international trade relations, the lightening of the debt burden of the poor countries, development co-operation through organisations which enable people to invest for justice...as well as the restructuring of production and consumption which are increasingly being based upon the new technologies and introducing a dual society for the rich and the poor.[12]

It is beyond the scope of this book to deal with the details of what might be involved, and how such a new order can be instituted.[13] What is really important, for Christians who may have been lulled into a sense of false security with hints about how to 'do their bit for the environment' is that any realistic moves to tackle the problems at the root will involve sacrifices on the part of members of rich nations. While political parties continue to score points off their opponents by claiming that their own policies cost the voter less, some Christian leaders are challenging the rest of us to be willing to pay higher taxes for the sake of others.

This is the kind of challenge which goes to the heart of the matter—the ultimate challenge. The word 'ultimate' is appropriate here for two reasons. First, because it is the only kind of response that is likely to produce more than cosmetic changes or relieve the suffering of more than a few. Secondly, it is about our attitudes to poverty, about whether we are sufficiently moved by the plight of others, whose poverty is inextricably linked to our affluence. As so often the Bible challenges us here: at the level of the motivation which is needed to make any new practices work successfully:

> If there is a poor man among your brothers in any of the towns of the land that the Lord your God is giving you, do not be hard-hearted or tight-fisted towards your poor brother. Rather be open-handed and freely lend him whatever he needs. Be careful not to harbour this wicked thought: 'The seventh year, the year for cancelling debts, is near,' so that you do not show ill will towards your needy brother and give him nothing. He may then appeal to the Lord against you, and you will be found guilty of sin. Give generously to him and do so without a grudging heart...I command you to be open-handed towards your brothers and towards the poor and needy in your land (Deut 15: 7–11).

REFERENCES

1. Sean McDonagh, *The Greening of the Church* (Geoffrey Chapman: London, 1990), pp 9-10.

2. Thijs de la Court, *Beyond Brundtland* (Zed Books: London, 1990), p 105.

3. *The Guardian* 26th January 1991.

4. Thijs de la Court, *op cit* p 120.

5. Sean McDonagh, *ibid*.

6. Sean McDonagh, *To Care for the Earth* (Geoffrey Chapman: London, 1986), p 35.

7. Thijs de la Court, *op cit* p 80.

8. *ibid* pp 80-81.

9. *ibid* p 32.

10. James Plunkett, *Strumpet City* (Panther Books: St Albans, 1971), p 21.

11. *Peace with Justice for the Whole Creation*, para 84 (b).

12. *ibid*, para 84 (a).

13. See eg *North-South: a programme for survival* (Pan Books: London, 1980); Ronald J. Sider, *Rich Christians in an Age of Hunger* (Hodder and

Stoughton: London 1991); Donald A. Hay, *Economics Today: A Christian Critique* (Apollos: Leicester, 1989).

Chapter Twelve

KNOWING THE CREATOR

WHAT IS SPIRITUALITY?

MUCH OF THIS book has been about bringing the light of Christian faith onto the issues of responsible management of the created world. In that sense the purpose has been pragmatic. But we have seen that the goodness of creation is about much more than simply its ability to supply our physical needs and wants. It is to do with how God makes himself known to us through the works of his hands. There is therefore a direct link between the goodness of creation and spirituality.

Similarly, it is wrong to think of the divine image in human beings as dealing only with our role as stewards of creation. Fundamental to our ability (or lack of ability) to fulfil this demanding task is the fact that the divine image is about a living relationship with the Creator. It is about the Creator's generous love, power and wisdom on the one hand, and about the invitation to trust and obedience on the other. Again, this is to do with spirituality. In these two ways, it becomes clear that any consideration of the goodness of creation, and our place in it, is incomplete without exploring the world of spirituality.

Spirituality is about our relationship with God on a day-to-day basis. It is about knowing him, experiencing fellowship with him. The New Testament speaks powerfully about the death of Christ as an act of reconciliation, in which enmity is abolished so that the believer may enter freely and confidently into the presence of God (eg Rom 5:1–11; 2 Cor 5:17–21; Eph 2:11–22; 3:12; Col 1:21,22; Heb 10:19–22). Christian spirituality is therefore about a relationship with the God who has revealed himself to us in the person of his Son, and through his revelation of his character in the pages of Scripture.

One introduction to the subject defines it in this way: 'The test of Christian spirituality is conformity of heart and life to the confession and character of Jesus as Lord (1 Cor 12:3). The guarantee of Christian spirituality is the presence and power of the Holy Spirit in the life of the believer...'[1] Yet, although the same article stresses the fact that the nature of the relationship is closely controlled by the nature of God's self-revelation, it contains no reference to the fact that God the Father is also the Creator. We have already seen something of the exuberance of Old Testament worship containing as it does so many references in the psalms to the wonder of creation and the glory of the one whose handiwork it all is.[2]

Faulty Creation-based Spirituality

Christian spirituality in the Western churches may be so Christ-centred or Spirit-centred that it fails to express the creation aspect which is so important in Scripture. However, this serves to keep the Christian well clear of the kind of pantheistic New Age spirituality which seems to accord creation a life of its own, and to which some supposedly Christian spiritualities owe too much. Thus Lawrence Osborn has helpfully analysed the creation-centred spirituality of the American Dominican Matthew Fox, whose work comes under this heading even though he retains much standard Christian terminology (unlike Teilhard de Chardin).[3] Fox's work is widely accepted, and has been uncritically presented by some Christian ecology writers.[4]

Fox relies heavily upon the mysticism of his own Dominican order, a mysticism steeped in Augustinian influence even though he rejects Augustine's influence on Western theology, introducing as he did a 'Fall/redemption' ideology. His key idea is that of Original Blessing, which is variously explained as the power of fertility and the desire behind creation. This is equated with Eros which, in Hellenism, caused the diversity of creation to yearn for divine unity. Fox is able to link this with the important New Age principle of the inter-connectedness of all things physical and spiritual; all things, including God, are then ultimately one. Dualism is then equated with original sin, of which the worst kind is the notion of divine transcendence.

What then emerges is thoroughly pantheistic. Overcoming dualism involves the uniting of the divine and demonic qualities we recognise within ourselves. Even God's work of redemption is interpreted as the union of good and evil rather than the defeat of evil. It is then a very small step to incorporate into this spirituality not only a radically-reinterpreted Christianity but also all other religions including witchcraft.

Liturgical Resources

There is, however, a great deal of help to be had within the liturgical traditions of mainstream churches. Given this wealth of material, it might seem that there is no problem with a truly biblical spirituality broad enough to encompass creation and its Creator as well as Christ and the Holy Spirit. Every church has liturgical resources which remind its worshippers that God is Creator, and is to be worshipped as such. Similarly, he is to be thanked for the good creation we enjoy. Several of the Psalms (eg 8, 19, 104, 147, 148) are particularly appropriate. Hymn titles come to mind immediately: 'For the beauty of the earth', 'All creatures of our God and King', 'All people that on earth do dwell' and 'O worship the King, all glorious above'. For those who prefer modern offerings to golden oldies there are: 'King of the universe, Lord of the ages', 'For the fruits of his creation', 'This is the day' and 'Jesus is Lord, creation's voice proclaims it' as well as modern versions of psalms and canticles that concentrate on God's creatorship.

The lectionaries which many churches worldwide are now

using set aside a number of Sundays and special occasions for themes which are directly related to creation. For example, in the *Alternative Prayer Book* of the Church of Ireland these include the following:

> 9th Sunday before Christmas—theme: The Creation. Readings include Psalms 29 and 104, Genesis 1:1–2:3, 2:4–25, Colossians 1:15–20, Revelation 4:1–11, John 1:1–14 and 3:1–8.[5]

> 8th Sunday before Christmas—theme: The Fall. Readings include Psalms 10:13–20 and 130, Genesis 3:1–15 and 4:1–10, Romans 7:7–13, 1 John 3:9–18, Mark 7:14–23 and John 3:13–21.[6]

> Harvest Thanksgiving. Readings include Psalms 65, 67, 104:21–30, 145, 147, 148, 150, Genesis 1:1–2.4, Deut 8: 1–10, 26:1–11, 28:1–14, Acts 10:10–16, 14:13–17, 2 Corinthians 9:6–15, 1 Timothy 6:6–10, Revelation 14:14–18, Matthew 6:24–34, 13:18–20, Luke 12:16–31, John 4:31–38, 6:27–35.[7]

There also exist many collections of prayers, some of which contain excellent material for leading public prayer on various aspects of creation and human responsibility for its well-being. Many liturgical prayer books also contain such material, in three separate forms. First, there are individual prayers, both as collects for Sundays and other special days, and in a separate section of occasional prayers; secondly, there is the Litany which, in some prayer books, is extensively revised from that of the 1662 Prayer Book and may contain a petition such as:

> Teach us to use the resources of the earth to your glory
> that all may share in your goodness
> and praise you for your loving kindness.[8]

Thirdly, some prayer books contain sets of weekday intercessions, designed for public and personal use. The Church of Ireland *Alternative Prayer Book*, for example, uses a framework

with an opening affirmation, a series of intercessions which
can be elaborated, a thanksgiving and a closing prayer. On
Mondays the theme is 'Creation in Christ: Creation and Providence'. The opening prayer is:

> Almighty God,
> maker of all good things and Father of all men;
> you have shown us in Christ the purpose of your
> creation
> and call us to be responsible in the world.

After intercessions for the nations, world peace and racial
harmony the thanksgiving and closing prayer are as follows:

> Almighty God, we give you thanks
> for the order of created things
> the resources of the earth
> and the gift of human life...
> for the continuing work of creation,
> man's share in it,
> and for creative vision and inventive skill...
> for your faithfulness to man in patience and in love,
> and for every human response of obedience
> and humble achievement...
> May we delight in your purpose
> and work to bring all things to their true end;
> through Jesus Christ our Lord. Amen.[9]

Having such liturgical resources is one thing: using them to
the full, and absorbing the biblical truths they seek to reflect,
is another. Many Christians who use them every Sunday (and
during the week) still need convincing that they should be
concerned about the care of creation (see Chapter 1). Two
reasons for this are related to the question of spirituality: first,
the use of creation-centred resources may not have been fully
integrated into a Trinitarian understanding of God, and secondly, our own experience of God may not have been fully
thought out in this same Trinitarian framework.

THE CHURCH OF GOD THE FATHER

Because the revelation of God-in-Trinity is so difficult to grasp, it is easy to find ourselves in the position of emphasising one Person of the Godhead at the expense of the other two. Peter Adam has painted a picture of a church whose spirituality majors on God the Father, and is thus creation-centred.[10]

In a church like this, the conduct and content of worship emphasises the order and stability that are in keeping with the Creator's character, and favourite hymns, such as 'O God, our help in ages past', 'Immortal, invisible, God only wise' and 'O worship the king, all glorious above', reflect this understanding of God. Adam continues:

> Belief in the Fatherhood of God leads to a positive affirmation of the value of all men, and so to a belief in the brotherhood of man. So this church will be reluctant to be precise about its boundaries, and will rather be anxious to include all men of good-will in its own life, and it will be happy to support charitable causes without applying any test save that of genuine care for humanity. This church functions well as the church for the local social community, and will probably have annual services for education, local government, rotary, doctors and nurses. In these services the God-given abilities and callings of all will be affirmed. Intercession will be addressed to God the preserver of society and giver of peace and justice, and there will be prayer for stability, harmony and justice. The rule of God is extended through the co-operation of all men of good-will. Concern for the brotherhood of man throughout the world will be expressed in collections for famine relief and occasionally in political action.[11]

The church's understanding of the sacraments will reflect this emphasis on God the Father and Creator. They will be seen as sacraments of creation rather than of salvation. Baptism becomes a thanksgiving for the birth of a child, and a reminder of the child-like quality of trust in a heavenly Father. The Eucharist, or Holy Communion, becomes a thanksgiving for the gifts of creation and, in response, an offering of all life to God. Adam continues: 'Thus the sacraments develop a kind of Harvest Festival theology, and the Harvest Festival itself may take on an almost sacramental significance.'[12]

Is This Trinitarian?

Adam's short treatment of the subject inevitably leads to over-generalisation and a sense of caricature, but that does not detract from his overall argument. He goes on to show how this church, because of its emphasis on the Fatherhood of God, underplays the work of Christ and the Spirit. Therefore, although we might at first expect it to take environmental issues seriously, this is by no means likely to be the case. This is because it is not likely to understand fully the significance of the work of Christ or of the Holy Spirit within the context of the relationship between God-in-Trinity and his creation.

To understand this more fully, consider firstly the work of God the Son. Adam suggests that:

> This church will tend to underplay the seriousness of man's predicament as sinner, and so on the one hand it will be guilty of accepting the easy standards of the world, and on the other hand it will not offer any real hope to those who know themselves to be sinners, for a church which does not preach salvation is unlikely to preach judgement or grace. It will be embarrassed by a sermon on the sinfulness of man, and annoyed at a gospel which lets prostitutes into the kingdom before respectable people.[13]

As we have seen, the problems of environmental care are deeply rooted in an alienation between man and God which spills over into every aspect of human existence. Our relationship with the world of creation then degenerates from one of care and genuine thanksgiving to another characterised by domination, greed and insecurity. To take as sufficient the understanding of God as Father as described by Peter Adam, ideas of order and stability will dominate over those of the consequences of sin. Environmental problems are likely to be seen as merely temporary aberrations which science can take care of: God in his providence will ensure that it is so.

Nor is such a church likely to place much emphasis on the work of the Spirit. An understanding of God which concentrates on the order and stability seen as essential to the Creator's character cannot easily make room for his dynamic dealings with a deeply corrupted world. The coming of the Holy Spirit at Pentecost, as recorded in Acts 2, was a deeply disturbing event, which forcefully thrust the early disciples into a new spiritual realm where they had to learn very rapidly a totally new understanding of God and his dealings with humanity. In Acts 10 Peter was faced with Cornelius and his friends and had to un-learn within the space of a few minutes all the anti-Gentile prejudices which had accreted to the Old Testament understanding of the special place of the Jews in the economy of God.

As Acts 2 also makes clear, the coming of the Spirit fulfils the prophecies of Joel 2:28–32. While the emphasis is often on the beginning of this prophecy ('I will pour out my spirit on all people...'), Peter's first sermon also incorporates the verses which follow, in which God promises:

> ...wonders in the heavens and on the earth, blood and fire and billows of smoke. The sun will be turned to darkness and the moon to blood before the coming of the great and dreadful day of the Lord (Joel 2:30,31).

Prophecies like this, whose themes reappear often in the New Testament, suggest that the age of the Spirit in which we live (the final age—the 'last days'—which began not recently but on the day of Pentecost) is not to be thought of purely in terms of order and stability. In fact, the opposite has generally been the case, not least in the twentieth century. The Creator's dealings with his creation, and with those to whom its care was entrusted, are not such that we can assume that things will continue indefinitely. Rather, this present age will come to an end (Rom 8:18–25; 2 Pet 3:10–12, etc) with final judgement and the radical transformation of creation; only then will it fully fulfil the Creator's purpose and reflect his glory in an untarnished fashion.

THE PRACTICE OF THANKSGIVING

The church of God the Father has much to teach us, however. Why are so many evangelical prayer meetings such grim affairs? There is much fervent intercession, much outpouring of concern and even anguish for the plight of a sin-stained world. This is right and proper, but the notes which are often missing at meetings like these are those of thanksgiving and hope. Gatherings of a more charismatic nature can put less exuberant evangelicals to shame in the ease with which praise and worship form the context in which intercession takes place.

In both cases, however, the element most likely to be miss-ing is that of thanksgiving for the gifts of creation, in spite of Paul's testimony in Philippians 4:4–20 and 1 Timothy 4:4, and the oft-used words of the General Thanksgiving from the 1662 *Prayer Book*: 'We bless thee for our creation, preservation, and all the blessings of this life...' My experience of innumer-able discussion groups and workshops on Green issues con-vinces me that many Christians have a real problem here: how do we allow thanksgiving for the goodness of creation to regain its biblical place as a vital element in Christian spirituality?

If this is an area of real failure in Christian spirituality, then it may be necessary to begin with an act of repentance, which may also need to be repeated on a regular basis. There are wrong attitudes to be rejected: to God himself, who has revealed himself to us as Creator as well as Saviour and life-giver; the attitude which takes everything for granted, out of sheer thoughtlessness; and the deep-rooted gnostic tendency that finds it difficult to accept wholeheartedly that everything God created was (and still is) good.

Then we need to understand the problem of perspective: an increasing proportion of the world's population are city-dwellers. Most readers of this book will live in cities, and they will be relatively well-off urban dwellers at that, surrounded by the technological trappings that support the lifestyles to which we have become accustomed. So we live one step removed from the immediacy of creation. Bishop Michael Baughen tells the story of a party of young people from a Manchester church being taken into the Peak District of Derbyshire:

> We climbed to the top of Mam Tor and gazed across the marvellous panorama of hills and valleys. In the far distance there was a cement factory and a chimney belching smoke. 'Ah, reality!' said one of the lads.[14]

To be able to give thanks for the Creator's gifts presupposes being aware of them, and having time to stop and appreciate them for what they are. Holiday times offer such opportunities, although even a few minutes in a busy day will suffice. How about stepping out into a park or garden, taking a few deep breaths and then reflecting on how we take for granted the very air we breathe? Then think about the other necessities of life which the Creator provides, and give thanks for them, praising God the Creator.

If you can then find a quiet place out of doors, look around you. Take note of the enormous range of colours, shapes and textures of everything you see. Then listen. What at first may seem to be complete silence may well reveal itself to be a veritable kaleidoscope of sounds—insects, birds and animals, the breeze blowing through grass and trees. In the same way an orchestral conductor summons up more instruments as the music builds towards a crescendo, add your sense of touch. Become conscious of the warmth of the sun and the wafting of the breeze on your skin. Sense the touch of clothing upon your skin, the texture of wood, leaves, grass and stones. Add to the symphony your senses of smell and of taste.

Lawrence Osborn, whose suggestions these are, makes the very important point that an exercise like this seldom goes far before we become aware of the deleterious impact we often make upon the world of creation, so that what starts as an exercise in praise and thanksgiving can also become one of sorrow and repentance.[15]

Another ideal context for thanksgiving over the gifts of creation is to consider the way we use our Sundays. It does not matter that the Christian's weekly day of celebration is not the same as the Old Testament Sabbath; what is important is that we celebrate creation, Resurrection and the coming of the Spirit (thus the modern chorus, based on Ps 118:24: 'This is the day that the Lord has made/when he rose again/when the Spirit came'). Because of the embargo on work on the Sabbath day in the Old Testament, the desire to protect its special character has led to all manner of rules and regulations, some of which have nothing to do with celebration. The lessons of Jesus' controversies with the Pharisees have not always been learned. I once attended a clergy conference where I sat in on a group whose members were discussing how they encouraged their parishioners to observe the Sabbath. 'I don't allow my people to play football on the Lord's Day,' said one. Others chipped in with what they forbade their flocks from doing. I asked them, 'What *do* you allow them to do on Sunday?' There was a shocked silence, but no reply!

If the Israelites celebrated creation on their Sabbath (Exod 31:16), then Christians should celebrate three times over. But to assume that the church morning service is the end of the matter would be wrong. Exodus 31 is about corporate celebration, and there are all sorts of ways in which we can celebrate together. Some churches have a family breakfast before morning worship, or lunch together afterwards; another possibility is a family outing and picnic tea in the afternoon. Sunday is an ideal day to exercise the ministry of hospitality (1 Pet 4:9), especially for those in need (Rom 12:13) and for visitors (Heb 13:1,2). This is a particular way of sharing with others the goodness of all that the Creator has given us, and should also be seen in the scriptural context of meals as occasions of fellowship not only with each other but with the risen Lord (Lk 24:28–31; Rev 3:20).

CHRIST-CENTRED SPIRITUALITY

Enough has been said to show that a truly biblical spirituality should be a Trinitarian spirituality; in other words, it should be broad enough to encompass our experience of God as Creator as well as Saviour and life-giving Spirit. But there is more to be said, because a Trinitarian understanding of God is not about three 'gods' but about God-in-Trinity, within whom the three Persons—Father, Son and Holy Spirit—are eternally bound to each other in relationships of mutual love (the technical term for this is 'co-inherence').

Does Christian spirituality commonly reflect this, as it ought to? More specifically, when Paul talks of knowing 'Christ and the power of his Resurrection' (Phil 3:10), how is our experiential knowledge of the risen Lord related to his Incarnation which, as we saw in Chapter 7, is the supreme demonstration of the goodness of creation? As Richard Baukham says:

> Belief in the Incarnation may therefore be expected to give Christian spirituality its distinctively *Christian* features... the human figure of Jesus stands at the centre of the spiritual life, as the focus and channel of all Christian experience and service of God.[16]

One of the major points Bauckham is making is that the kind of Christian experience we look for is not always sufficiently grounded in the person of the incarnate Jesus. Take, for example, the popular and powerful idea of Jesus as our 'friend', based as it is on texts such as John 15:15: 'I have called you friends, for everything that I learned from my Father I have made known to you.' A typical evangelical way of describing this will be in terms of a 'personal relationship with Jesus'. However, unless this is carefully understood and described, there are a number of dangers in thinking of our relationship with him in this way.

First, there are some clear differences between knowing Jesus and knowing a human friend. There is no physical contact, even if the human relationship has to be by means of letter, telephone or computer link. Does this mean that our relationship with Jesus has to be thought of telepathically, or that the idea of friendship is analogical rather than literal? Secondly, such a friendship could be thought of as fantasy. Most children have imaginary 'friends'; is our friendship with Jesus then merely a hangover from childhood? Thirdly (and more substantially), what has friendship with Jesus to do with fellowship with *God*? After all, Jesus taught clearly that he was the way to the Father (Jn 14:7).

Here is where it is vital to grasp the full implications of the Incarnation. In the person of Jesus of Nazareth, God the Son lived a genuinely human life amongst us, receiving the full spectrum of human experience from intense joy to the excruciating pains of hostility, rejection and crucifixion. The incarnation was not a temporary episode in the history of eternity, as if God had decided upon a fleeting visit to see how we were getting on. The gospel accounts and the Pauline epistles make it quite clear that the one whom we now worship as risen and ascended is the man Jesus. He did not return to heaven as disembodied spirit, but as resurrected man; he has brought our humanity into the heavenly places, where he now lives for ever. As Bauckham states:

> ...the risen Jesus remained permanently a human individual, the model of what our risen humanity will be. Of course, Resurrection, for him and for us, involves a transformation of human individuality which we cannot hope to be able to describe this side of our experience of it, but it cannot involve the loss of individuality as such, without which we would no longer be human persons. It is clear from the New

Testament that the risen Jesus, though unique in his relationship to God and to the rest of the human race, remains a human individual.[17]

Our knowledge of the living Christ, then, has two aspects which cannot be separated. The first is that his dealings with us are the same as with the disciples with whom he shared three years of his life during his public ministry. The second flows from it: our present experience of him must be 'informed and interpreted' by the gospel accounts of his life.[18] These become more than mere history (although few scholars believe that the intention of the gospel writers was as neutral as this); they become the way of interpreting his dealings with us in the course of our Christian lives.

This is why it is so tragically sad to find so many church-goers' understanding of the Christian life as a matter of 'doing my best'. The biblical understanding of Christian experience goes far beyond this. Because he is the unique way into the Father's presence (Jn 14:7), Jesus enables us to come into the same close relationship of trust and love which he himself enjoyed (Rom 5:1,2). Not only did he call the Father 'Abba'; the Holy Spirit enables us to use the same address (Rom 8:15; Gal 4:6). This address expresses a relationship of utter peace and security, which can be known in no other way, and in which nothing can separate us from the love of the Father (Rom 8:28–39).

The same Spirit transforms and conforms us to Jesus who is the model of human life. It has often been noted that the fruits of the Spirit in Galatians 5:22,23 (love, joy, peace, patience, kindness, goodness, meekness, gentleness and self-control) are the very characteristics of the human life of Jesus, and certainly many of these qualities are predicated of God elsewhere in the New Testament. Similarly, the work of the Spirit as described in 2 Corinthians 3:18 is one in which we are transformed into the likeness of Christ himself.

These considerations are also important when we reflect upon the severe trials and sufferings that Christians suffer as keenly today as at any other period in the history of the church. The Epistle to the Hebrews was written to encourage such Christians, who were in danger of discouragement, falling away and even apostasy. One of the major arguments the writer of that letter uses is that Christ himself, as the man Jesus, went through the same ordeals (2:14–17; 4:15; 5:7–9). It is these experiences that have made him who he is, and have qualified him for his office as High Priest on our behalf in heaven. Thus hard-pressed Christians can find not just inspiration *from the memory* of his sufferings; far more important is that, because of his experiences, he is well able to provide active help now for others in such situations.

It is important to re-emphasise that all this is possible only because God the Son became incarnate in the person of Jesus of Nazareth. Other explanations of the relationship between Jesus and God the Son are less than fully adequate and can only emphasise the distance between humanity and Godhead, so that Christian experience is attenuated into a vague mysticism. The Incarnation is the ground of the relationship we enjoy with the Father, Son and Holy Spirit as the normal experience of the Christian life.

REFERENCES

1. T.R. Albin, 'Spirituality' in S.B. Ferguson and D.F. Wright, *New Dictionary of Theology* (IVP: Leicester, 1988), p 657.
2. Robert Faricy, *Wind and Sea Obey Him: Approaches to a Theology of Nature* (SCM: London, 1982), Chapter 5; Sean McDonagh, *The Greening of the Church* (Geoffrey Chapman: London, 1990), pp 147-150.
3. Lawrence Osborn, *Meeting God in Creation* (Grove Books: Nottingham, 1990), p 21f.
4. Tim Cooper, *Green Christianity* (Spire: London, 1990), p 266; Sean McDonagh, *op cit* p 196-7.
5. Reproduced with permission from *Alternative Prayer Book 1984*, copyright 1984, The General Synod of the Church of Ireland (Collins: London, 1984), pp 323-7.
6. *ibid* pp 327-31.
7. *ibid* p 747.

9. *ibid* p 97.

10. Peter Adam, *Living the Trinity* (Grove Books: Nottingham, 1982), pp 7-12.

11. *ibid*.

12. *ibid*.

13. *ibid*.

14. Michael Baughen, *The Prayer Principle* (Mowbray: London, 1983), p 62.

15. Lawrence Osborn, *Meeting God in Creation* (Grove Books: Nottingham, 1990), p 19f.

16. Richard Bauckham, *Knowing God Incarnate* (Grove Books: Nottingham, 1983), p 3.

17. *ibid* p 11.

18. *ibid* p 12.

Index

A Brief History Of Eternity

by Roy E. Peacock

How should we perceive the universe?

Does it conform to mechanical rules? How does it work? Why is it there? It is expanding: does that imply a beginning, or has the universe always existed?

Stephen Hawking's bestseller A BRIEF HISTORY OF TIME tried to answer some of these questions, arriving at a model of the cosmos without beginning or end.

Roy Peacock, a Professor in Aerospace Sciences at the University of Pisa and an authority on thermodynamics, regards the popular concept of Hawking's work as flawed. He builds an alternative picture of the universe which deals with not only the *how,* but the *why.* His highly readable quest for a satisfactory understanding of the cosmos takes the reader into the realms of black holes, big bangs and entropy: a *tour de force* of research, logic and imagination.

ISBN 1 85424 062 5   £6.99

Monarch
Publications

Reason & Faith

by Roger Forster and Paul Marston

- Can there be adequate historical evidence for the central claims of Christianity—especially that Jesus rose from the dead?

- Does the Bible contradict the teaching of modern science about the formation and evolution of living things?

- Has the church always tended to suppress free thinking?

These three questions raise issues that are central to the current debate about the relationship between modern science and the Christian faith. Carefully and clearly, the authors examine the biblical, historical and scientific evidence. Their conclusions are at times startling—both for believers and for those enquiring yet unconvinced about the central teachings of orthodox Christianity.

ROGER FORSTER has studied Theology and Mathematics at Cambridge University, gaining an MA degree. He is the founder leader of the Ichthus Christian Fellowship based in south-east London, which is involved in training and world mission.

PAUL MARSTON has studied economics, politics and scientific and statistical methodology at the LSE, London University.

ISBN 1 85424 054 4   Price £9.99

Monarch
Publications

Monarch Publications

Books of Substance

All Monarch books can be purchased from your local general or Christian bookshop. In case of difficulty they may be ordered from the publisher:

> Monarch Publications
> Owl Lodge
> Langton Road
> Speldhurst
> Kent
> TN3 0NP

Please enclose a cheque payable to Monarch Publications for the cover price plus: 60 pence for the first book plus 40 pence per copy for each additional book ordered to a maximum charge of £3.00 to cover postage and packing (UK and Republic of Ireland only).

Overseas customers please order from:

Christian Marketing PTY Ltd
PO Box 154
Victoria 3215
Australia

Omega Distributors Ltd
69 Great South Road
Remuera
Auckland
New Zealand

Struik Christian Books
PO Box 193
Maitland 7405
Cape Town
South Africa